A CAGE OF SHADOWS

ARCHIE HILL

A CAGE OF SHADOWS

Tangerine Press • London • 2017

Publisher's Note & Acknowledgements

When it was first published in 1973, Archie Hill's *A Cage of Shadows* received enthusiastic reviews from *The Times, Times Literary Supplement, Sunday Telegraph, New Statesman* amongst others and was universally hailed as a classic. Renowned oral historian and sociologist Tony Parker said 'there is not the slightest doubt in my mind that here is an author who can write not only well but at many times brilliantly ...' But the brutal honesty of Mr Hill's depictions of Black Country life, his ongoing struggles with alcoholism, the degradations he encountered in prisons, mental institutions and on London's skid row proved to be ahead of its time. Libel action in 1975 meant copies of *A Cage of Shadows* were pulped, with an edited version being published two years later. This Tangerine Press edition reinstates the original 1973 text, thereby making it readily available for the first time in over forty years. The publisher is grateful to Melanie Dresti for drawing attention to this extraordinary book; also Georgia Glover of David Higham Associates for her friendly efficiency. Extra special respect and thanks are due to Robin Hill, for his support of the project, granting access to his father's archive and expanding on the story of the life and career of an unjustly neglected author.

ISBN 978-1-910691-11-3 (paperback)
      978-1-910691-10-6 (hardback)

A CAGE OF SHADOWS. COPYRIGHT © 1973, 1977 ROBIN HILL
PHOTOGRAPHY. COPYRIGHT © 2017 ROBIN HILL
THIS EDITION FIRST PUBLISHED 2017 BY TANGERINE PRESS
18 RIVERSIDE ROAD
GARRATT BUSINESS PARK
LONDON
SW17 0BA
ENGLAND
eatmytangerine.com
PRINTED IN ENGLAND
ALL RIGHTS RESERVED

Printed on acid-free paper

For my Son, Robin.

Out of the dark brown earth he came,
my father, whom I did not know,
and carried a seed which bore my name
and sowed it, in the long ago.

Now I in turn have sown a seed
before all soil should blow away,
and soon shall see a flower or weed
spring up around my father's clay.

A.H.

A CAGE OF SHADOWS

Chapter One

I was the eldest but one, with nine brothers and sisters and mom and dad to make us into a dozen. It should have been a Baker's dozen, because I was a twin, but the other half died at birth.

Evenings and nights at home are the worst things I remember; I'd sit to the banked-up fire as late evening closed in and the others would troop off to bed, pulling coats over them to supplement lack of blankets. I had to sit up till the dad came home in case the police had to be fetched, if he came home fighting drunk.

I used to make pictures in the fire, painting them with my imagination, until my ears – sharp as a weasel's – tuned in to his footsteps coming down the entry. If they were straight and quick and firm I'd relax a bit, knowing at least his bad temper would be sober. But if they hesitated, if they came in gusts and rushes, I'd tremble inside and ask God only the favour my dad would be so drunk he'd go to sleep straight away and there wouldn't be a row. Heaven was the snoring regularity of a drunken dad too drunk to move, Paradise was the tip-toed hush about the house to keep the Heaven safe. But like as not, the row would start anyroad; and I'd lock myself up in private armour as mam started to curse and rave and the dad towered mightily. They used words I shouldn't understand, but did. Then the bits of furniture would get smashed, the table tipped over, and there'd be a herd of brothers and sisters wailing at the head of the stairs. And I'd look at my gargoyle parents, at the nappies spilled over the hearth, at the broken furniture and the cardboard stuck in broken window panes to keep the draught out, the dirty floor-quarries, and think to myself quite simply and cleanly 'Fuck everything and everybody'.

After, I'd lie in bed sharing it with two of my brothers while the street lamp outside spattered through the uncurtained windows. Downstairs, mam and dad fought our world. Dad's voice a rumble, a power, a dynamo of building rage. Mam's voice shrill, plaintive, jangling. The crash of my dad's fist against wood, the last warning. Welsh-witch mam keeping her mouth shut for half a dozen heartbeats. The late silence broken as dad clears his throat and spits into the grate; the back door creaking open, water splashing in the yard as he pisses against the wall. His tobacco smoke fills the house, his near presence is as close as fear itself.

Then after a bit the house silence would lull me into false sleep and I'd drop my guard. Then wake up with fear-sickness to find my mam miouwing over me. I looked at her with loathing as she plucked at the bed coverings, and I hoped God was waiting in the entry to crash the doors down and take me to safety. But He was never around when He was wanted.

'Wake up, you 'un,' my mam said, 'Goo and sleep in t'other room with him. Ah'll stop here with Pete and Al, you sleep with your dad. Ah can't stand it, it's a driving me mad.'

I went shivering to the bare landing, listening to the sounds of my dad below stairs. I went into his bedroom and sat on the edge of the dirty bed till he came up.

'What'n yoh doing here?' he asked, with drunken quietness; I could see a swim of rage at the back of his green eyes, and the bastard didn't even let me explain. He caught me a lowking with the flat of his hand and I lay on the floor trying to switch my mind off. I let my hate blaze up at him, hoping that it would burn him from existence, hoping that it would wash him away forever and ever. I promised my soul that when a man's years had weighted my arms I would crush my dad into pulp. I would destroy him and kick the remnants about until they disappeared....

Dad lurched off into the other room and Pete and Al came sleepily in – it was ever like that, playing a sort of musical chairs with the beds and bedrooms, so you might change round three or four times in the course of a night. I reckoned if it was all set to music it would've drawn box-office as a comic opera.

Dad had hardly settled into the other room when he bungled out again, and I thought he was coming for another sort out. But all he wanted was to piss in the stinking bucket stuck out on the landing, but he missed with most of it and I could hear the pool spreading and following itself down the stair-treads. It would dry out by morning, and only the stink would remain.

I slept till morning and the clear sunlight mocked through the dirt and poverty. It was school holiday for some, but not for me. I was off to the foundry to earn some money, half of which would be slashed up the wall by the old man. My Uncle Tom worked in the foundry, he was a moulder there, but he didn't have a lot to do with us lot. He was a respectable sort of bloke, my dad's brother. If I put a full week in the foundry I'd pick up good money come the weekend. Not as much as a man would, although I'd have to work as much as a man. But the foundry gaffers liked it that way – there were unemployed men all over the place, but it still suited the gaffers to pay a lad's wages for a man's work. I didn't complain any. I wanted the money. Witch-mam would grab a lump of it for groceries, the dad would take some beer money out of it, but if I was sharp I could fiddle a bob or two for myself. I climbed over my brothers without waking them, scrabbled into my work clothes. Then I knocked on the door where dad was, he and mam locked in each others arms and still sweating from a quick jump. Nine months by the clock and there'd be a few more nappies in front of the fire.

'Seven o'clock, dad,' I called, 'if you'm going bird-catching.' I called him twice before he heard me. His voice came back thick and irritable.

'Don' stand theer, then. Go and put the kettle on.' I could hear him fumbling for the oxo tin in which he kept his tobacco, rolling the first cough-making cigarette of the day. I pushed on down stairs into the kitchen, shoved the piled up dirty crockery to one side so's I could get the kettle under the tap. I struck a match to the gas jet and a cloud of grease fumes rose up against the other smells. When the kettle was boiled I mashed tea, and my dad came down. I watched him from the corner of my eye.

'One day,' I thought, 'I'll kill you, you bastard.' I felt the hate in me so big he must see it.

He saw sod all.

I looked at him and saw a big man. Not tall, but tight-muscled and strong. When he worked, which was seldom these days, he was a coal miner. But now he didn't work very often in these pre-war days because most of the pits were shut down, and men hung round the street corners waiting for them to open up again. And the gaffers still rolled round in their big cars, polished shiny as ice, and their bellies warm from well-filled pantries.

Dad trapped birds – singing birds – down in the Osier beds near the River Stour, and sold them in the markets at Brierley Hill or Dudley, or in the pubs. Mostly in the pubs. Linnets he caught, for the most part; with sometimes a goldfinch or bullfinch. Goldfinches were called 'seven-coloured-linnets' by the Black Country men; a bullfinch was called a 'nope'. A nope fetched about five shillings from them as had got the money to buy with, and a seven-coloured-linnet fetched about seven and six. But a good singing linnet, young and sleek and cock, was worth anything up to a pound. My old man was a good bird-catcher, he'd got the way for it. I'd sat with him in the Dingle woods as a nipper, the strange mist-shrouded autumn woods, with the clapper-nets set up and baited. Set in a tiny cage disguised with grass and twigs would be a hen bird, imprisoned fast with only her song free to call the other birds down. Dad was different, somehow. Quiet and patient and intent, natural and movement-perfect as a Red Indian. He'd almost talk the birds down into the nets, chirruping with his tongue and whistling a low sad mating song. They were the only really happy days I remember having with my dad. There in the woods with tendrils of mist licking and lapping at the trees, and with bird-song like shards of silver staining the air. The smell of the woods was almost a taste, a nose-tingling mixture of spices and herbs, a curry-pot of deliciousness. Dad would stiffen, lift a warning hand of silence, himself poised netwards like a pointer dog. A flash and a ruffle of feathers down at the nets, a lance of colour from an air-treading wing, and dad would glide his hand backwards with the draw-string and the nets would spring shut like a giant oyster's jaws, and the bird would be a fluff and bundle of agitation trying to escape. Its mate would hover overhead, plaintive and crying to the quiet woods. Then dad would untangle the captured bird with fingers more gentle than any woman's, and all the time he'd talk and croon to his future beer-ration like it were his best friend in the world. And off the bird would go to pub or market to be imprisoned till death in a little cage hanging in somebody's parlour; and like as not it would sing its tiny heart out in a cancer of distress and listeners would think it was singing from contentment....

I watched my dad now as he sat in a rickety chair. One of his socks needed darning or chucking in the ash-grid. A blackness of unwashed skin showed through the holes. He drank his tea in gulps and slurps, then went across the yard to the brewhouse for his bird nets. He planked them on the kitchen floor and sorted them, unravelling creases and knots, more fussy than any girl trying to get her seams straight. When he'd finished he had a go at me for not getting up earlier and lighting the fire to give mam a bit of a break. Always like that, the sod was. He beat her up first, knocked her up second by ringing the bell for another kid, then worried about her welfare till next time round. My old man should have been a politician or a church leader – he knew more about hypocrisy – instinctively – than they ever had to learn. He nodded for me to fill his tea mug, slushed it down, then took his collection of nets away to the Osier beds. I hope a bloody big hawk gouges your eyes out, I thought. The last of the Mohicans. I hope a herd of vultures chew your balls off.

I unearthed the marmalade pot and spread some on a chunk of bread for breakfast. In the pantry I came across a wafer of brown bread, a bit of Hovis, and I put it between two slices of white bread. I could chew on this at snap time, and anybody round me would mayhap see the colour and think I was eating a meat sandwich. Pride was a currency. Out I went into the cold sunlight of still early morning. The sun was weak, giving way to cloud.

The iron foundry was at the end of the long street, and I was a bit self-conscious as I stamped my new card in the time clock. Not that I wasn't used to foundry work, I'd been around them ever since I was old enough to remember. But now I'd got a full six weeks to put in while school was broken up for the holiday, the gaffer made me clock time like a regular worker. I stood looking at the huge foundry-shop, a vast barn of a place with high windows that had no glass to them, all smashed out by the men to get a gasp of ventilation, and over all was a thick carpet of grey dust suffocating the floor. I felt the faintest whisper of depression talk to my mind as I breathed in the dead dryness of the place, as I saw the many work-benches among the piles of black moulding sand, and the mounds of scrap-iron waiting for the labourers' barrows. Over everything was a high monotonous rumbling, a sound that mixed with the very air itself.

'Them's the barrels yoh can hear,' my Uncle Tom shouted as he came up, 'that's wheer the castings go to get cleaned up.'

'I've been here before,' I shouted back sulkily, 'I know me way around.'

'The gaffer's put yoh with me,' Uncle Tom said doubtfully. 'Yoh'll be helping me on my stall.' He moved away and left me standing there.

At the far end of the foundry shop was the furnace, a great turgid cylinder which thrust through the roof like a space rocket waiting for Flash Gordon on its launching pad. Two men in duffle coats worked on it, wrenching and heaving with iron bars, tearing the green and yellow slag away. A third man wielded a sledge-hammer at the frozen green sea of glass-like slag which had erupted from the furnace jaws the day before, now congealed into solid waves and ripples. Now the furnace had to be cleaned and toileted for the work to come. Cold and silent it stood, a monster having a manicure, waiting for fire to be lit in its belly. It stood in the bleak grey dust and an atmosphere of men's tiredness and spent sweat.

My Uncle Tom came back through the greyness with another man. 'Hello Archie, me lover,' said the foreman, 'Going to werk wi' your Uncle Tom for a bit, then. Get the full hang on it, like. He's not very big, is he?' he said to Uncle Tom, 'but mayhap he'll fill out a bit when he's pushed a barrer for a couple a weeks.'

'Don't stand looking at it,' my Uncle Tom said, a bit on the snotty side because he liked to keep well in with the gaffers. 'Get a wheel barrer and clean my work bed up for starters.' I fetched the barrow, hefted it, hated the sight of it and went over to Uncle Tom's work stall. He produced a sieve, shovelled grey sand into it from the floor.

'Riddle it like this, see,' he showed me, just like he was imparting the secrets of rare craftsmanship, 'over the barrer. Save the bits of metal and put 'em in the scrap pan over there. When the pan's full, tek it to the furnace. When the barrer's full, tek it to the tip and empty it. Right, lad – get started.' I slogged away at it. Dust powdered my face and hair, clogged my nose up. After a bit, when I spat, the spit was black. 'Bit o' dust won't hurt,' encouraged Uncle Tom. 'You has to be at the job at least five years afore it starts rotting your lungs.'

I carried pan after pan to the furnace, until my muscles were sore and my hands blistered.

'Yoh'll never get tough,' jeered me dad's brother. 'Yoh'll be wearing silk gloves next.' I plodded on.

'Here, me lover,' one of the furnace men called to me, 'tell you what – get some o' that black sand and piss on it. Just a drop of piss, then slap it on your hands like a poultice. Good for you, that is.' Piss off, I thought back.

All round me in the foundry shop the lean men worked at their benches making the moulds which earned their livings. Strange, individual men, the iron moulders. Deliberate, independent, solid in their strength. They looked a bit like cowboys with their chequered work-shirts, short waistcoats, felt trilby hats, and sweat rags tied round their throats like bandanas. They each wore a thick leather belt with heavy buckles low on their hips, the buckles pushed to one side or fastened at the back so's not to intrude against the work operations. The belts were to keep their belly muscles firm, to keep ruptures away when they strained to the castings and carrying pots.

They seemed to work from the waists only, swaying from the waist up, their legs solidly splayed and anchored to the floor. There was a neat compactness about their movements, an economy, bending from the waist to shovel black sand into the moulding flasks, an above-waist movement and swaying as they sieved and rammed, a flexing of shoulder muscles as they pulled the bench levers to force compression, then a quick sure flurry of full movement as each finished mould was carried to the increasing rows laid out neatly on the floor. The men whistled at their work, called to each other in rough language.

The sun struggled from behind cloud and made searchlight pathways through the dust infested air. When the lunch-time hooter blew I was ready for it, even if it only meant a sit-down. I didn't fancy my brown-bread sandwich. But my guts were rumbling away, my belly thinking its throat had been cut. Uncle Tom caught the drift of things as he saw me hesitating there.

'Get the snap out'n my bag,' he said, a bit on the reluctant side, 'there's some streaky bacon in it. We can cook it down at the annealing ovens.'

I got his bag and followed him down to the ovens. He opened the straps and fished his fittle out. Bread and bacon, half a pork pie, a gob of margarine and a russet apple. He looked at the apple and stuck it in his pocket, glancing at me sideways with a bit of a miser look.

'Have to have the apple meself,' he said, 'for me health, yoh knows.'

'You can leave me the core,' I told him back, 'it's time I started looking after my health as well.'

The ovens were huge. A double row, each eight feet wide, nine high, twenty long. Running the full inside length of them were the fire chutes. When the moulders finished making their moulds they were brought here – the wares, I mean – not the moulders. They were packed into iron barrels with red-lead gravel and placed in tiers inside the ovens. The entrances were then bricked up, clay-skimmed over, and the coal-chutes fired. The heat building up inside was something unbelievable, it was kept going for two or three days for the annealing to take place.

Uncle Tom picked one of the ovens which had been broken open and left to cool; he raked the glowing coals apart to put his tea can on. Then he slapped the blob of margarine onto the blade of his shovel, laid the strips of bacon across, and sizzled them over the heat. When it was crisp and golden cooked he made a couple of thick wedged sandwiches, gave me one. Then he put tea into the boiling water. I dragged a couple of wheelbarrows close to the warmth so's we could tip the handles against the floor and use them as armchairs. We got stuck into the snap.

'Wheer's your dad, then?' Uncle Tom asked suddenly, his voice coming from the back of wet chewed bread and bacon fat.

'Went bird-catching,' I said. 'Down the Dingles or the Osiers.'

Uncle Tom sniffed, muttered something about regular work and wasters.

'The pit's on quarter time,' I told him, 'it's nigh on closed down. Me dad even tried the clay pits in Stourbridge, but they'm turning over slow as well.'

Uncle Tom chewed noisily at his food. I could hear his false teeth clicking on the bacon rind.

'My nipper's about as old as yoh,' he said, for no reason at all that I could think of. 'He'd mek two of you, though. Got brains, our chap has. And he's a dresser – I don't keep him short of anything, if I can help it. Work in an office, he will, when he leaves school.'

'He's a bloody fairy, if you ask me,' I answered from behind a chew of crust. 'He'll grow up funny.'

'Do what?' Uncle Tom said, not hearing me. 'You shouldn't talk with your mouth full. Not manners, that isn't.' He dropped off to sleep, his belly rumbling like a couple of locomotives meeting in a tunnel. I must have dozed off as well because the work-hooter was suddenly playing merry hell, and before it shut off Uncle Tom was already half-way up the yard. I followed him, dispirited as a whippet dog who's just had his tail docked.

* * *

I knew already that I hated the iron works, the rough hard work and the dry marrow-sucking dust. My mind raced ahead and faced the future by freezing the present out with better images. Here lay only the withering of private freedom and personal ambition. My spirit rebelled against the dryness and dust, the dead iron, the creaking machinery and strange men who methodically accepted the crushing monotony.

'Put a bloody move on,' my Uncle Tom called. 'Get this sand out'n my way. I'm behind as it is.'

I shovelled spilling sand into the barrow, wheeled it to the tip and hefted the load upwards so that it flowed onto the ever-increasing pile. Then back to the foundry shop for another load, and another, and another. My hands were sore, muscles tired, but there were work beds to clear, scrap iron to take to the furnace, barrows to push and the bulk of the day's work yet to come. And at the end of it all was a pigsty home to go back to and a wail of rubbish which was supposed to be human.

The furnace itself was changing. The green scabs of slag were all prised away, the scarred mouth no longer oozed with frozen dribble. Its grin had sharpened out now that its jaws and lips were lined with fresh clay. Its bowels rumbled quietly and contentedly as it digested a giant's feast of coke and limestone; high on its platformed side two furnacemen stacked charges of pig-iron ready for feeding into its raw hungry throat. The moulders too had changed. They had tightened up. They no longer called to each other or whistled at their work; they tightened up inside themselves and put on more pressure. The rows of black moulded boxes increased on the foundry floor, like square droppings of a strange monster. The men were time conscious now, quickening to make their day's allocation before the furnace decree that they put their shovels down and wait on it. Each moulder had clay-lined his pouring pot during the lunch break, and these were stacked round the furnace to dry out.

Without the clay linings, the metal from the furnace would melt the pots when they were filled. To the rear of the furnace a long deep trench had been scooped to accept the first waste pourings – against every factory regulation in the book; but these were indifferent times. No one would complain while for every man in work three stood outside waiting for his job.

I was grateful for the few minutes' rest.

A furnaceman peered at his gauges then went to the cupola mouth with an iron spear. He pushed it deep in, withdrew it with white-hot metal adhering. His mate stepped forwards with another iron pole, blocked the weeping mouth with a clay plug. The furnacemen seemed satisfied. One of them called down the foundry shop.

'Harold. Tom. Yoh, Johnny – Fred and Ernie. Yoh tek the slag off, right?' The moulders nodded, blurs of motion at their benches, racing the clock for an extra mould apiece. A bell pealed out, and the men tapered to a halt. Now it became the time of the furnace.

Its rumbling could be heard like a moan of sea wind, beating waves of heat across the air. The men came trooping down to it, took their long-handled ladles and clustered round the mouth. They all wore leather spats round their ankles in case of spill or splash-back; they rolled their left shirt sleeves down to protect skin from pitiless heat, rolled the right ones up to grab every kiss of coolness. They looked somehow brave and romantic in the fire-red shadows, hats pushed back of heads, standing nonchalant with unconscious grace and ease. A furnaceman reached out with a probe and picked the button plug of clay from the mouth, and the opening glowed white and angry like a great eye in the contrasting shadows. Then the molten river flowed down the clay-lined chute.

A moulder placed his pot under the stream, bracing the long steel handle across his left knee, bearing down on the weight of it against pressure from his right arm. Another man put his pot under the first, took over as the other pulled out and away. Ladle after ladle was poured into the trench to spit and bubble like a sun gone mad. Then the good iron came through and the men collected it in their pots and scuttled to their moulds with it, like strange bees bearing strange honey to the hive. Sparks jumped and hissed the length and breadth of the foundry, the air was thick with heat and sweat, pungent iron and sickliness of sulphur. I was dazed by it all, stunned. These were aspects I was not over-familiar with since my after-school work mostly consisted of clearing up after the workmen had gone home. I watched red shadows burn against the walls, saw blue flames leap from moulds as gas formed and exploded through the escape holes. Sometimes a mould burst open to spill its glowing contents and a man would curse frantically while trying to stem the escaping metal by slapping moulding sand against the fracture. The foundry was a nightmare of steam and smoke with men running to and from the terrible chuckling furnace, men dashing and scurrying with sweat bursting from their brows and breath gasping and fluttering inside their lungs.

'Gis a hand,' my Uncle Tom shouted, 'I'm all behind. Here, do it like this.' He raced to a row of poured moulds, picked one up by its base-board, rushed back to his workbench and tipped it into the pile of sand. The casting inside glowed red and angry, savage at being disturbed.

'Chuck 'em up like that, see,' said Uncle Tom. 'Ah can pour six off'n one ladle. There's fifty to pour altogether. Give the iron two or three minutes to settle then chuck 'em up like ah've showed you. When yoh've chucked a dozen up, do it like this.' He grabbed a long pair of pincers and a rapping bar, dug the pincers into the sand and dragged a hot casting out. Black dirt stuck to the iron's redness and Uncle Tom rapped it away with the bar, then placed the article gently to one side.

'Do it like that,' he repeated, 'only don' be too rough on 'em. They'm still on the soft side and yoh'll knock 'em out of shape, else.' He rushed away through the smoke and steam, a sweating demon caught up in work-frenzy. Suddenly he came bursting back.

'Tek it easy when yoh picks 'em up,' he warned. 'Make sure you gets them by the base-boards. Yoh'll burn your fingers off, else.' His throw-away line came back over his shoulder, taking the compliment of personal concern away.

'Don't want any accidents happening,' he said. 'Ah'm all behind as it is.' The steam and smoke swallowed him again and he left me to it. I struggled away with the poured moulds. They were heavy and awkward. The heat from them sucked at me as I staggered to throw them up, then I took pincers and rapping bar and rescued the finished products from the black mess. When I rapped the bar against them I felt nausea tearing my guts into pieces as dust and sulphur ate into my lungs. My scalp burned with prickly heat, my thighs ran rivers of sweat.

'Put yoh're back into it,' Uncle Tom yelled, lunging with spark-spitting ladle through the turmoil, and I pulled and tugged at the castings. Run to the moulds one at a time, pick up, run to the work bench, throw up, run back for another. On and on and on so's legs and arms and brain and lungs cried out for sanity and order. Take pincers and rapping bar, fish into hot sand, rap and clean and drown in sulphur shit and dust.

Adolph Hitler, for fuck's sake come and save us. Come and put us into concentration camps so's we can all be safe.

Uncle Tom came back with another full ladle, arguing backwards over his shoulder with one of the other moulders.

'You went out of turn,' the man complained, 'it wasn't your turn to go under.'

'Sod you,' said Uncle Tom with family eloquence. 'You'm always moaning about something or t'other.'

'You'm not the only one as wants to get finished,' the man flared back. 'You stand from under next time and wait your turn.' They both went back to the furnace, still arguing, and I cursed my mind and limbs to come awake. I longed for the knocking off whistle, longed to shut my mind, longed for bed and sleep. My old man was somewhere down in the Osier beds lying out with a bottle of beer, or stuck in some market pub flogging his linnets, and here was me trying to earn the Sunday dinner.

Bugger them all, I thought; I'm damned if all my years will he tied to this, I'm buggered if my boyhood and manhood will be imprisoned forever in black smoke and crippling heat of furnaces. I could feel tears of self-pity dry on my cheeks as heat drank the moisture away.

Then down at the furnace someone screamed. A long-drawn-out scream of terror and pain. Then there was shouting and bellowing of men and flurry of movement as the furnaceman reached forward and halted the work by plugging the furnace mouth. I went towards the furnace, stood a little way back, trying to see. 'He fell in,' one of the moulders was saying, hysteria bubbling under his words. 'He just lost his balance and fell into the slag trench. It's still molten, look.' The men bunched together, frightened and serious, while a terrible smell hung everywhere. Something that wasn't quite a man moaned and threshed beyond the circle of light, covered with donkey-jackets and cradled by two or three moulders.

'His legs am burned off,' somebody said, a gobble of helplessness in his throat, 'went in knee deep, he did. He seemed to stond theer, half-way up his legs in it. O my Christ.'

I could see my Uncle Tom being sick near the sand-mill; I could see lumps of undigested apple sticking in the vomit. I went up to him, he waved me away.

'Goo on whum, me lover,' he said. 'Go home. There's nothing for you here.' I left them to it, felt the late afternoon air greet me outside.

'Tell the doorkeeper to keep the gates open for the ambulance,' the foreman shouted after me. 'Tell 'em to keep the entrance clear.' I nodded and sped up the foundry yard to the lobby. A cluster of office girls whispered there, looking towards the furnace. The Gaffer came rushing out with a bottle of ointment and a bag of bandages.... I didn't see what use that lot 'ud be. I was almost home when the ambulance came by, its bell clanging and tyres screaming on the tarmac.

My mam was out with the youngest baby at a neighbour's some place, and my dad was out on the piss. I did my homework for school and when it was time for bed I packed my brothers and sisters off upstairs, banked the fire with slack and gleads, and went off upstairs myself. Before I got into bed I pulled the loose foot-long section of floor-board up and got my money tin out. Inside, I'd got twenty-eight shillings and some coppers – all won by fiddling my mom and dad with the wages I earned. The money was mine by rights if not by consent; when I'd got enough I intended to buy myself a complete rigout – a suit from the Fifty-shillings tailor, shoes, socks, the lot. Even underwear. I'd never worn underwear in my life.

Chapter Two

I was one of those who started to hate the world from the first moment of standing on two legs and taking a look at it. I didn't end up on the scrap-heap, I started life on the scrap-heap. I only knew that rare happiness was a mom and dad laughing together, or a clean hearth and a welcome fireside, or new shoes which fitted me.

Happiness was a mingling with other boys as one-of-them, and not as the lad whose father was ever in prison or drunk; the boy whose mother never kept her house clean and tidy and whose mouth was mostly packed with screaming hysteria and her belly packed with litter.

Happiness was in not being different....

... the school-teacher looked at me and I dropped my eyes to hide the defiance in them, and I didn't want the acid of his words to eat me away. He beckoned, and I went slowly to the front of the class, feeling twenty pairs of eyes burning my going, aware that the patch on the arse-end of my trousers stood out like soot on a white-washed ceiling. He took my arithmetic book and scalded me with sarcasm. The class tittered and mutilated me, and then the bastard turned his attention to my scuffed boots and foundry-grimed hands. I'd got loyalty of sorts, a stubborn sort of loyalty or shame not letting me explain that there was no boot polish in our house, nor cleaning brushes. I mumbled that I'd forgotten to clean them, willing the kids and teacher not to know that our house lacked such refinements. The teacher told me to go to the wash-room and clean myself up. I wouldn't tell him that our house had got no soap more often than not, and that our house used odds and sods for towels, like dirty shirts waiting for the dolly-tub.

I left the class-room and went along to the ablutions, hid my face in shame-cooling water, lingered over the cleanliness of sink and soap, the crispness of roller-towel. I built muscles for my emotions to face the class again. My mind lingered with the teacher, hated him. I made up my mind if he started on me again I'd chuck books or ink-wells at him, and then make a run for it. Why should the bastard pick on me all the time.

Then I remembered how my mam had come to the school last time that dad got lifted by the police. I remembered mam crying and belly-swollen, standing in front of teacher, telling him there was no money in the house to buy food. Teacher gave her money from his own pocket and from the shadows of the Assembly Hall I watched my mam try to embrace him, almost greedily. Like a greed, she was, and teacher backed away from her wild hair and tear-stained face.

Suddenly I knew that teacher didn't pick on me for the hell of it; he only picked on me to keep my mam away. I went back to the class-room without hating him. He opened his mouth for another dose of sarcasm; then somehow he read me. He clamped his words off before they were said, and nodded me back to my seat. Once, when I looked up, his eyes were on me. Strange, thoughtful, almost yearning. He looked away almost immediately, but I felt warm in my belly towards him. I felt good and warm, and swore to myself that I'd do better with my arithmetic.

I never let my mates call for me at home. I asked them to shout for me, outside. I didn't want them to come in. Didn't want them to see how we lived.

See, I wanted to dress myself in my own identity when I stepped out – wanted to be measured for what I'd learned in books and thoughts, wanted to be measured for what I was and not what I came from. So I had to build barriers to keep the spies out. I didn't want them – my mates – to see the stained walls with the patches of damp plaster and peeling paper; their eyes mustn't see the gloomy staircase with bare wooden treads and risers climbing up to the poverty of bedrooms. I didn't want them to see the downstairs places where I lived and grew, the empty front room which was empty because we'd got nothing to put into it. I didn't want them to see the living-room with its bits and pieces of other people's throw-outs – the best pieces always being sold by dad so's the man in the pub could live. Old rag rugs, rickety chairs, an old horse-hair sofa with its back broken, an old table made from unvarnished planks and plywood – doors swaying drunkenly on strained hinges, the fire-place with broken bars and filled over-spilling with dead ashes and gleads. Windows, dirty, and some of the panes broken and stopped up with cardboard to keep the cold out. And the kitchen all cluttered up and smelly with stained sink, the room itself as slim as a coffin housing childhood misery.

I didn't want any of my mates to see this. I didn't want them to come inside and see the greasy stove, the chipped cups, the lack of things in general. Because we had filth as well as poverty.

I didn't want them to know that our house didn't even own a tin-opener, that we used old scissors to open cans. I didn't want them to know that we, my brothers and sisters and self, had to stand at the table because only mam and dad had chairs, and we had to take turns to use the only couple of knives we had.

Why should they know that outside, in the backyard, the thin-ribbed dog, chained to its wind-leaking kennel, waited for what was left over but like as not would end up with a chunk of bread dunked in cold tea.

I didn't want any of my mates to see any of this; they could guess at it, they could speculate, but as long as they didn't actually see it could be denied. The secrets of poverty, in an era of poverty, had to be kept from open knowledge. Otherwise all my strength would be gone and the world would kick me in the teeth with mockery and contempt, just because my mam and dad went to bed too often and produced a litter of inadequacy. Most of all I didn't want my mates to learn that I wasn't young with them, that I stood outside the windows of their world, looking in. If they knew, they wouldn't understand. If one of them ever got through my guard, through the barriers I'd built, I'd fight him. Fight with desperation and hopelessness. I'd swing my fists hard and fast, pendulumned to hatred, and I'd rely on the return punches to give me motive to carry the fight forwards. I'd hammer forbidden knowledge from the other boy's mind with fists or boots; I've fought lads and seen fear come into their faces, fear of what they could not understand. I'd make the bastards run no matter what the size of them. I'd hammer the grinning mockery from any lad's face and I didn't give a damn how big the other side was. Then, as sometimes happened, the police would be brought into it. So I'd switch myself off. Away from all responsibility, regret or remorse; I came to learn that people didn't really matter.

I'd hear my dad talking to the policeman.

'Ah don't understand what the kids am coming to these days. Yoh does yoh're best by 'em, but they still runs wild. Yoh mark my words, ah'll gie him a lowking. He's up the stairs with his trousers off and the belt's on him.'

Each time I'd say to myself – this time, if my bloody dad kills me, I'll not cry out. Not ever again will I cry for this Thing called dad. So I'd switch my mind off and send it to far places so's I couldn't be hurt by a man's arm and waist belt. Then, after the man had gone downstairs, I'd lay on the bed face down. Inside, deep in the gloom of self, I cursed my mam and dad and brothers and sisters and God and Christ. The anger was deep, my essential self, but I knew even then that my mind wasn't really old enough to have such darkness.

I knew. It was all a prison. Every bit of it a prison, every rotten God-forsaken minute. All you could do was fight, and know in the fighting that you'd lose in the end.

I don't reckon I ever did have a childhood. It was an experience upon a battlefield. The battlefield was life. Life in the Black Country among the reek and heat of iron foundries and the thunder of rolling-mills where sheets of steel were pressed and hammered out, and the sulky glower of pitheads stripped the countryside of all except smoke and dust. An area from which Hogarth and Dickens drew grim inspiration, and still could were they still on the scene. The Black Country, spewing its filth, lacerated with sluggish canals ('cuts', we called them) all sombre and dark and brooding. A place where men worked hard with the might of their muscles, drank hard, made love like rabbits and bred almost as much. Strange rough men whose everyday speech is still rich in pure Anglo-Saxon, who use words and expressions which were in vogue in the days of Chaucer. Men who delight in racing their pigeons on a Sunday morning, or their whippet dogs, or catching linnets and bullfinches for their bird-cages. Gypsy-like men who invariably scorn the redresses offered by Civil courts but settle their own arguments toe-to-toe, fist for fist, with a time-keeper in each corner and a herd of watchers to see fair play. Fight in the Wallows or the Dingle Woods, with boys posted as look-outs against the police. And the place-names for miles around echo of different days, of days before the Industrial Revolution, when a mad poet must have stumbled half-blind, spilling his thoughts like confetti. Places named Bumble Hole, Mouse Sweet, Tippity Green, Gornal Wood, Delph Coppice, Brierley Hill, Swinsford, Amblecote – names, clean names, which in the imagination carry the pollen of catkins and blossoms, a swarming of honey bees; but in reality they carry concrete, pylons, earth-scars, heat sweat and dirt.

I was born in a garden shed at a place called Pensnett, at the back of Brierley Hill. Pensnett was a slum left over from the 1840s. A grim slum. Mention of the place for miles around would cause Priests to cross the road as well as themselves. Winson Green prison, over in Birmingham, was a sort of satellite to Pensnett.

I can't remember the garden shed; I learned later that I was born there because my mom had had a rough with dad, and wouldn't sleep in the same house as him. That was my Grandma's house, my dad's mother's. It was a collier cottage, one of a long joined-up row, with one room down and two up, none of them big enough for even pigmies to stretch themselves. The thing I mostly remember about my early days, days old enough to keep hold of memories, was a slow and monotonous parade of policemen at the door. Dad in prison, dad out of prison; dad drunk and seldom sober – and a new baby on the way every time he took his trousers off. There were ten of us alive by the time he put his trousers back on for the last time. My mam turned to physical ugliness as child after child dropped from her body. Days of two penn'orth of breast-of-mutton bones to make a boney stew. Sometimes dad came home by starlight with somebody's chicken under his jacket; sometimes I kept guard for him while he pinched coal from the wharves, or potatoes from Wordsley farmers 'buries'.

One night, me about six years old, I was with him in the dark at one of the coal wharves. He heaved a massive solid lump onto his shoulder – it must have weighed all of two hundredweight – and we started to walk home with it along the cut-side bridle path. And then I saw the policeman up ahead, coming towards us. I felt frightened, and pulled at dad's jacket. 'Whass up?' he asked, eyes and head turned a bit downwards under the weight he was carrying.

'The copper,' I whispered, 'there's a copper coming.' Dad's stride didn't falter.

'He's not bloody well frightened of us,' he said.

We came abreast of the policeman, and passed him.

'Goo'night, Bill,' said the policeman.

'Goo'night, Bert,' dad answered. And then the policeman stopped.

'Hey, Bill,' he called, and dad turned round to face him, still holding the great coal-lump on his shoulder, fixed there at the point of balance. He waited on the policeman's words.

'Bist yoh going out on another coal visit tonight, Bill?'

'Ar,' dad answered. 'Ah reckon ah might, at that.'

'Well,' said the policeman, 'doh forget my back door-step, will you. We'm a bit low on coal back whum.'

Dad eased his burden into a better position, cleared his throat and spat phlegm onto the tow-path.

'Aw' right, Bert,' he said, 'ah'll drop a lump off for you.'

The policeman was swallowed up into the darkness, and then we turned a bend on the tow-path. Dad eased his lump of coal onto the grass verge, and told me to wait for him. He slipped away into the density of the hawthorn bushes and willow trees that flanked the River Stour. I thought he'd gone for a piddle, but wondered why he should go into the 'jungle' to do it when there was nobody to see all along the tow-path. I heard a 'nope' – a bullfinch, sprinkle the sky with a sudden burst of song. It sang out loud and strong, ruffling the woods in a mixture of half plaintive sadness and half happiness.

After a bit dad came back, grunted as he swung the coal up, and I had to trot to keep up with him, so quickly he walked.

'I heard a nope,' I told him, 'it sounded a real beauty.' Dad grunted. We carried on in silence for a bit, and then a bit of surprise crossed my mind.

'I heard a nope,' I repeated, 'but they don't usually sing at night, do they?'

'It weren't a bloody nope yoh heard, you silly bugger,' he said, 'it was me. Ask yourself. What's Bert the copper doing along the tow-path this time o' night? He's after Pope Tolley and Old Konk, they'm a poaching game together. They'd hear me whistling like a nope, catch on to how the wind was blowing, and get the bloody hell out of things before Bert catches up with 'em. Bert the copper's too noggin'-yeaded to know that a nope never sings at night.

'Yoh must be learning a load of saftness at school if it teks you that long to catch on that a nope only sings in the day time,' he grumbled, as we strode along. 'Now yoh're grandfeyther – my dad that was. He taught me to copy any singing bird with my lips. By the time I was yoh're age ah could whistle the same tune as any bird yoh'd care to name.' He stumbled, staggered, corrected himself.

'Yoh'll learn nothing at school,' he said, 'except a load of fanciful rubbish that'll stand yoh in no stead.'

After school I'd go home and stand on the back-step listening to the voices of my mam and dad. If they were shouting and rowing I'd creep away and sit on somebody else's doorstep, some place where human peace dwelt as hearthstones, and Trust lay behind the door. Once, sitting so, I got invited inside; and I couldn't understand or realise that *they* belonged to the real world, and I did not. I couldn't understand why the other boy's mother was clean and pretty, while my own mam had wild-blown hair and a potato sack wrapped round her waist, and none of a woman's softness. I couldn't understand why the other boy's father was young and wholesome, with laughter lines in his face and kindliness in the heaviness of his hands. I couldn't understand the tablecloth set for tea, with buttered toast laid on and more plates and cutlery I'd ever seen at one time. I couldn't understand how man and wife should talk to one another with such affection and respect, pure clean respect. I couldn't understand their acceptance of contentment; as if such things and home-peace were a right, and not a rare reward....

I didn't understand. I started to show off to hide my own bewilderment, and sensed the dislike I was earning for myself. Things grew from worse to worse. I showed off more, boasted about my own mam and dad and the comforts of *our* house. I tried to salvage and to share, but I ended up knocking what *they'd* got. Dislike of me increased and spread. The toast was eaten in silence, and my New World crumbled, and I did not understand. I went home slowly, and I *did* understand. Our kitchen floor had no covering, except a sprinkling of sand on the rough quarried floors. Our tea-pot had no handle, you could pour from it only by wrapping a piece of cloth round it and gripping it with two hands. The fire was banked with slack and coal dust and in front of it were squares of rag and cloth ripped into nappies for babies bottoms; our mam would have the youngest on her lap, the front of her dress open to let her red swollen breast squirt life and energy into the bundle of inadequacy she was holding. I'd look at my brothers and sisters and hate them; and they'd look straight back at me and hate in turn.

I learned in infancy that any bloody fool can beget kids; but it takes a real man and woman to raise them. Some people shouldn't have kids, shouldn't be allowed to, and my mam and dad were of these. They had no healthy terms of reference by which to rear them.

Most things relating to childhood were steeped in hypocrisy and deception. If I lied to *them*, mam and dad, I got worked over with a belt-lowking. If I stole for them, it was alright – but if I stole *from* them, like a halfpenny from the shelf, I was for the high-jump.

When the baker's step came up the entry mam would hide on the stairs and send me to face him.

'Tell him ah'm not in,' she'd whisper. 'Tell him ah've had to go out – but get a loaf off him.'

So I'd face the baker, the rent-man, the bob-a-week-and-misses man, commonly known as 'the Tally-man', and say that she was out but she'd pay next time.

The lies, the deceits, the dressing up of nonchalance. Lie to the milkman, the grocer, the coalman; after a while lying became natural even when it wasn't necessary.

Yet sod me – there was always money for booze, always money for bottle beer and jugs of ale and sometimes a cheap bottle of strong wine. Mam often cried to the world's ears that she didn't touch a drop, that it was her misfortune to be married to a wastrel and a scoundrel; but she tippled secretly, a drop here, a drop there. Never drunk like dad, but often topped up with orange blossoms of colour in her cheeks, a wisp of smell to her breath, and glass in her eyes.

I never felt comfortable when neighbours dropped in at our house. I didn't like outside eyes peering in at our poverty. But sometimes some of them called, bringing food left-overs and bits of clothing their own kids had grown out of or didn't want. In the rough and tumble of Black Country living none of the houses in our street were absolute palaces. But our house was more disgusting than most. To anybody who called, our mam had something to say about it, about the state of the place – as if drawing attention to it would absolve her from all responsibility for the neglect.

'Just look at my house,' she'd whine, 'ah'm that ashamed of it. Just look at it. Ah just don't have the heart these days.'

I'd wriggle inside myself at the sugar-sweet hypocrisies of my mam. But she was shrewd with it. She'd lay it on in such a way that the neighbour usually parted with a couple of coppers without being directly asked, but embarrassed into the giving.

'Bastard old sow,' I'd fume inwardly, 'whyn't you get stuck into the bloody pigsty and get it cleaned up?'

But I reckon if pigs *had* lived at our house, the Health People would have taken them away as in need of care and protection.

When your dad puts his boot into your ribs there's no law says you have to love him for it. And when you find your mam lying on the bed knocking it off with the Tally-man, her skirts dragged up to her arm-pits, you don't have to honour her for it. And when you've got nine snotty-nosed arse-bare brothers and sisters mixing in your life like wood-rot, you don't go down on your knees and give thanks for the blessing of family unity.

What you do is look at yourself in a cracked mirror one day and say to yourself, 'Bugger the lot of them. A few more years and I'll get out from under this lot.'

You never do, of course. Get from under, I mean. You take a bit of it with you forever and always, only sometimes you dress it up a bit and it feels different.

But men like me are liars if they won't admit to being sad at times; sad because the hearth of home knew only miserable inhospitality, apathy, ambivalence and sourness of soul to last a normal life span. I don't think I ever reached full manhood; emotionally, I mean. I didn't find maturity other than in outward appearance as my body grew and strengthened and my chronological years passed away and divided me from the valleys of childhood – I don't think I was ever equipped to leave those valleys, no matter how dark they were, simply because I had never experienced their potential richness other than in small glimpses here and there. I was mostly an onlooker to childhood, seldom a participant. But I did learn to hate. When the worms of fear burrowed deep into the structure of the place we called home. I reckon my hate was the cleanest thing there. But, to be fair, there were areas of something approaching happiness, marred only by the nag at the back of the mind that the magic moment would slip away and be lost forever beneath debris and rubble. And, I think, once I stepped from our house there were good influences abroad; and in the sombre stark ugliness of the Black Country tracts, I often saw beauty which plucked and quivered at permanent memory.

The Black Country is no part of Birmingham, never has been. Draw a line from Stourbridge to West Bromwich, over to Walsall and Bloxwich, on to Wolverhampton and back into Stourbridge – then all the land enclosed inside that boundary is the Black Country. An area filled with deep cultures and rare craftsmanship, and above all a pride in that craftsmanship, especially noticeable among the older men. Crystal tableware glass, hand-made pottery, leathercrafts, iron and steel – and it is an area where men always regard themselves as self-employed, despite the fact they take wages from a Gaffer. When a man has put in a good stint to please himself, its on with his hat and jacket, and off down the road.

Coal, iron, limestone, clay, quarry-stone are the foundations of the Black Country. Minerals which the area contains in good supply, minerals which started the Industrial Revolution from 1750 onwards, and which were to become famous throughout the world and set the pace of commercial progress. A cruel and merciless area whose traditions are steeped in jumbled mixtures of pride of craft and strength, in exploitation by Gaffers, and poverty to follow. In the hungry thirties these men felt bruised to the quick of their pride because their hands, or most of them, were forced to remain idle. They were forced to humble themselves to Labour Exchange labour clerks, or Means Test officers to get vouchers to obtain shoes for their kids. Their pride of belly, watches and waistcoat chains handed down from grandfather to son, and yet again to son, were 'popped' at Uncles, the pawn shops.

And men there were who remembered the Tommy Shops, the Tommy Shops where an employer paid part of a man's wages in token coins to be spent in the Gaffer's private shop where goods were sold at an invariably inflated price. The Tommy Shop system was supposed to have ended half-way through the 1860s, but it never did. It carried on, and then when the issuing of private token coins was stopped altogether, the Gaffers merely started using tally-books. Which meant that when a man shopped he signed the tally-book to the tune of what he'd spent, and the total was deducted from his wages at the end of the week. Sometimes men would find that they'd 'subbed' to the hilt, with no money to come, and they had to start straight back on the tally-book and get goods against wages yet to be earned. Too, women built like Amazons pumping the great bellows in the drop-forge and chain-striking sheds. Other women working barebreasted in the heat of brick-yards, with skin like leather, hair cropped close as a boy's against the heat of the kilns. Sexless women with weight-lifter's bodies.

The Black Country had iron in its soul. Hard, cruel, inflexible. Those who leave it hate it forever; and forever afterwards want to go back to it – whether to make terms with it or challenge it, I've never quite decided.

Anyroad, if I ever do go back now I'll only go back to 'mont' it; to swank down the High Street of Stourbridge or Brierley Hill, to buy drinks all round in the Blue Brick Pub at Round Oak, or park my Jag outside the Stewpony Hotel on the road to Kinver.

... I don't know, though. I might be content to lie in the stillness of Wordsley Common listening to the creaking of slimmer grasshoppers or the distant drone of field-swept tractors, or walk along the cut-side at night when work is done and the gaunt glass-works hunch in a mass of coal, like tired old men, on the dark opposite banks; whilst the remaining canal barges fret at their moorings. I hate the Black Country, and yet I love it. And that's the trouble with most things and places, I've been thinking.

We had Him at school. God, I mean. Every morning and dinner time, in the Assembly Hall, with a couple of sugarcoated hymns to soften Him up. And the crates of free milk for the Means Test Poor stacked like white sacrifices, the better-off kids edging away from it like it was bottled poison. I never got the hang of it, all the bowing and scraping and chanting of hymns – I always reckoned we were praying and singing to old Bingley the Headmaster, worshipping him up there on the platform. I always reckoned old Bingley was God and that the other feller, the one we never saw, was a sort of caretaker hiding it out in the school boiler house. I know old Bingley himself reckoned he was God, the way he walked round with his cane swishing round his legs. When he used the cane on a boy, he'd make the boy push his head inside his – Bingley's – legs. High up, inside the groin. Then he'd close his thighs on the lad and wallop his back-end with the stick. I thought it was one way of giving a hiding, until one time, I saw Bingley's face while he was doing it. A funny look he'd got and his mouth was all loose and wet ... his face looked like my mam's when the man had his hand up her skirt.

Once, old Bingley called me to the front of assembly so's the other kids could measure me with their eyes and ask their mothers if they had clothing to spare for me. Old Bingley talked of charity and compassion; I thought of red murder and how delicious it would be to blind the bastard and slowly twist his tongue out by the roots. Old Bingley never knew how much I hated him for that exposure, not until I was older and helping to fight the world with the Royal Air Force. I gave Bingley a hiding then, with his own cane, in front of all the kids in Assembly Hall. I got Bingley over the rostrum desk and I belted the dust from his backside, and the kids whooped and cheered, and a couple of the male teachers came at me to stop me, but they wouldn't close in on me. They kept a distance. I only lathered Bingley because he'd left weals half an inch thick on one of my brother's backside, and the kid couldn't sit down what with the pain. I was sorry I lathered into Bingley, after; because he was almost an old man ... and I knew I wasn't hitting him for my brother, but for myself.

But I almost did escape from the prison. Find a way out from the mess, I mean. When I was thirteen and due to leave school, the next year, I came up from the foundry where I did my spare-time work one Saturday lunch time and there was my witch-mam waving an opened letter.

'You didn't say,' she trilled. 'Whyn't you tell us?'

It was a letter from the Art School Governors saying I'd passed the entrance exam and there was a place waiting for me. In the whirl of excitement nobody thought to mention I'd forged my dad's signature on the papers – perhaps if they had a thought of it, they'd have accepted it as proof that I'd got artistic ability.

Mam called dad in a golden sober moment.

'He passed his exams,' she said, overlooking that I'd only passed one.

The days followed in a scrounging whirl. There was some charity or other which gave me vouchers for school uniform and shoes – the first shoes I'd ever worn, always boots. I stood on the threshold of a world of paint and colour, I'd got pencils and brushes to sip at the heart of the world's rainbow before It disappeared forever.

I listened to my dad.

'Ah didn't say anything,' he said. 'Ah said nothing – but ah knew he'd got it in him. Teks after my brother Benny, he does. Give Benny a photo and he'd copy it perfect.'

I don't want to copy, you saft bastard, I thought; I want to invent. There's a bit of difference.

'He should be werkin' soon, though,' my dad said. 'Should he pulling his weight.'

I slipped away with the frog of fear in my throat, went down to the foundry and saw the Gaffer, poured my soul on the doorstep of his understanding. And he nodded his head like a magician's wand and agreed to pay me twenty shillings a week for more work in the foundry. Work from five in the morning till eight, then after school work from six till eight, all day Saturday and Sunday.

I could pay my own way. Pay board and keep, and buy my own books and clothes and bus fares. The world started to slot into near perfection. The world of linnets and bird-nests, of ferret twitching pockets and oxo-tinned tobacco, of sack-skirted mam and drink-stained dad went away between nine in the morning and four-thirty in the afternoons. I walked a different scene, a different world, a world of tolerance and understanding, of colour and dimension, of perspective and harmony. Only at night did I have to return to the crumbling house and crowded bed. But in a way, for a little while, home conditions didn't seem to matter so much. I started to strip the canvas of my mind of the years' stains; I suppose I started to get ready for Tomorrow. I absorbed atmosphere, sat with charcoal and pencil and dreamed my ideas onto paper. Covered my defects and concealed my distortions. Then one day the Art Master called me to one side.

'Your father uses the Bird in Hand public house, doesn't he?'

I nodded, wondering what was coming.

'Well, look – I gave your father a Hunter watch to mend for me. Ask him about it, will you. Probably slipped his mind.'

I was curdled inside.

'When?' I asked.

'Some weeks back,' he said.

I knew that hatred of my dad was burning holes in my eyes.

'You shouldn't have done,' I blurted. 'He sold it. I saw him sell it to a bloke who came to our house.' The master laid a quiet hand on my shoulder and never mentioned the matter again.

I went home sobbing inside, but not with my eyes.

'What bloody watch?' my dad denied hotly. 'Ah don't know anything about it, you silly bugger. He's got me mixed up with somebody else.'

'It was you,' I insisted. 'He knows you. It was you.'

Dad laughed it off.

'He's got more'n we'n got,' he said. 'Ah don't reckon as he'll miss an old watch like that.'

I was sick with betrayal, sick of the world.

… but even the Devil, I suppose, has qualities of goodness; like me, my dad was shaped and fashioned by *his* father.

My dad's hands, when sober, were the hands of a craftsman. He could make things from nothing, beautiful things, to delight childhood. Toys he made, dolls' houses and cradles, forts, trucks, wheelbarrows, trains with cotton reel funnels, and a boy's dream of scooters. They were wonderful, rare, made from a bewilderment of sawdust. When he was sober and felt like making things – although the results seldom came to *us*, they were sold in pubs – I'd help him willingly. Help to smooth the shapes, the splendid shapes, from planks of wood and imagination. Among the sawdust and shavings, the paint and the glue pot the world was my heritage, the promise of boyhood lay in the creative hands and the mind's planning.

It was the scooter I wanted. A little wooden scooter which was worth a few shillings from somebody's pocket, and I'd worked hard at it, fetching and carrying for its construction. I sanded it down with fine emery, cleaned it to wood-white purity, and how my bloody heart wanted it. When the dad came to paint it he'd only got enough for the job, and none to spare. I passed him the tin, and dropped it, and spilled it. Dad's face sneered at me and I was trapped in my own shell of impotency; the magic of pride and accomplishment soured to ashes.

I shuffled the empty paint tins together, pots of different colours and emptied the dregs into one can until enough came together to paint the scooter. It was green, a lovely green of springs and summers, and the laurel leaves of salvaged happiness. I looked on as my dad painted the scooter, and he said it was mine, and the world sang in my ears because of the scooter's colour, the colour I had made, the mistake I had rectified, the displeasure I had cancelled.

Then dad sold the scooter to a bloke down the road for his son, and dad went to the pub with the money, and I hated the boy who had my scooter with the coldness of stone for a long memories' worth....

Chapter Three

There was a poem …

> 'Oft in the stilly night
> Ere slumber's chain hath bound me
> I see in a misty light
> Other days around me …'

That's the one. The book had no covers on it and the pages were faded and yellowed, but I kept it for myself from a collection of oddments a man was burning in his garden. I read the words and they plucked at my mind and I couldn't fully understand them; but I read them and hugged them into me like a deep rich secret that was touched with sadness….

The man burning the rubbish was Old Billy – he wasn't really old, I suppose. He just seemed old because I was young. I suppose he was about fifty. My dad took me to see him the first time, but after that I used to go on my own.

Billy was God. He made things from nothing, and the tools he used were mere extensions of his mind.

I knocked gently on his shed door, letting my fingers smooth at the rough unpainted woodwork. My friend Billy answered from inside, his voice a growl and a protest at being interrupted.

'Who's it, then? Who's theer?'

I pushed my way inside, my eyes stunned by the rush of darkness.

'It's yoh then, is it,' Old Billy muttered. 'Don't stand theer with the door open, chap – yoh'll break me glass, else. Shut it, quick – put the wood in the hole.'

I shut the door and stood watching my friend.

'Ah'd forgotten yoh was a comin',' he said, 'ah promised ah'd make something for you, didn't I, me lover?'

I nodded. My mind and eyes were intent upon the work and beauty bursting in blooms of colour from the old man's fingers.

The shed was small and dark except for the glow of a single candle and the needle-flamed blow-lamp which Billy used for his work. The shed was filled with shadows ... but the work-bench itself was alive with living shapes.... I swear the air moved with tiny living breaths. Green and blue Birds of Paradise paraded in plumage of coloured glass, squirrels sat frozen for eternity on glass boughs, litters of black-eyed pigs wrinkled glass snouts as if someone were banging a swill-bucket inside their memories; glass dogs and ferrets, penguins, cows, horses, a crystal sliver of fish darting upwards for a glass fly suspended on a gossamer thread; a glass spider sat in a glass web, a glass stag grazed bark from a glass tree, a ruby-eyed crocodile curved back on its own tail, a cobra shone in its own coils, and a glass butterfly waited for a glass flower....

Billy, Billy ... how I loved Billy and the magic of his fingers which shaped the smiles which came tumbling from his mind....

Neatly stacked against one wall were rows of coloured glass canes, half-inch thick pencils of raw materials. Billy selected a cane of crimson and put one end into the needle-flame. The glass started to melt and Billy plucked it with tweezers, teasing it towards the secrets of Creation until suddenly a two-inch-high exotic bird came out of the mystery of the fire.

He fused other colours into it; a deckle of green into the fragile wing-span, a breath of blue into the head crest, a froth of white onto the breast so that the crimson lost ground and became pink. White into the eyes, just a tiny touch to be flattened out in the heat, then an iris-point of black – and the bird was ready to flyaway into far tropics and burst into song to charm the silence.

'Make me a peacock,' I cried, and the old man smiled at me.

'Another time, me lover,' he said, 'it teks a lot of werk to make a peacock. Here, though – watch. Ah'll make something you'll be proud on.'

I pressed closer to him as he took up a stick of white glass. A pull here, a tug there, bathing the heat of the flame against the metal, nursing life and shape and colour until a mother sow and five little piglets stood bright-eyed in the candlelight.

'Mine,' I breathed, all I could say.

'Ar, they'm your'n,' he said, 'just let 'em cool off a bit. Have to cool gradually, see, otherwise they'd bost to pieces when you got 'em outside. They has to go into that little paraffin oven to get annealed. Look at 'em, chap. If you'm careful, you can stand all six of 'em on a tanner piece.'

When the pigs were annealed Billy packed them inside a matchbox lined with cotton wool. I put the box in my pocket and worshipped it with my hand. I thought I felt the piglets stirring inside, and my mind leaned in on tip-toe to hear them squealing. When I got home I would put them in my secret place under the floorboard.

I kept my little piglets for a long time, for many years, to lose them eventually on the bomb-sites of London....

I now watched the old man, thickset and square, hunched over his work-bench, his sausage-like fingers twirling the glass canes into blue hissing flame. Gently at first, Billy would bring the glass to the fringe of heat, let the flame whisper against shining colour, then play it persistently and firmly to the hottest point. The glass would dull suddenly, grow black with startled reaction, then blend in with the common purpose and grow red and flexible, like soft wax. Billy knew the exact moment that it could be manipulated, the exact molten second that his tweezers could snip and pluck full creation from the heart of things. A touch and a twirl, a pat and a probe, and a white cat poised itself with lifted paw and erected tail, waiting for a grey mouse which joined it moments later. Then he took a cane of crimson glass and kissed life into it with the flame, pulled and coaxed it away from the monotony of being a coloured cylinder, transformed and freed it from its prison so that it burst forth and became a rose. Large as my fist, soft as satin to look at, with the petals nestling and throbbing with beautiful secrets.

Billy nursed other colours into it, traced delicate marble-like veins into the petals, trickled a tear of clear glass against it so that it hung there like a pearl of dew. He fashioned leaves and thorns, joined them on. Then he made a honey bee, tawny gold and black with smoky wings, and he mated it deep to the heart of the rose. The flower and the bee haunted the light with perfection, haunted the edges of my entire soul, and then Old Billy blended unclean yellow against the rim of a petal and the flower became imperfect. I was distressed because of the mutilation, I cried out against it; and Billy knew. He put his heavy kind hand on mine. 'Nothing's perfect, me lover,' he said, 'not in this world, anyroad. The mouse poisons the pantry, the cat kills the mouse, the dog kills the cat. It goes on forever. There's nothing perfect, me lover … and it's for the best, really. If everything in the world was beautiful there 'ouldn't *be* any beauty, see? There has to be t'other, to balance out. You'll find out as yoh grows older. It can be a cruel world out theer.'

He made Birds of Paradise in the flame. Twelve of them, made to perfection, all the same size but different in expression. Here were two male birds preparing to fight, their plumage anger-bright, one with neck and beak stabbing out like an unsheathed sword, and toes turned to talons; the other, fixed in a backwards flow of escape, wings almost a-flutter, eyes glittering an alert watchfulness. Three other birds sat on a green-leafed bough, singing their hearts out against an unknown sky. Another sat her eggs, beak outstretched and touching the beak of her mate in kiss of unity. One bird sat with head beneath wing, sleeping a bird's sleep, dreaming a bird's dream. Three others promenaded themselves in wealths of colour, vain and proud as living peacocks and living men. But the twelfth lay crumpled, limp and lifeless and dead forever in its glass world.

I mourned for it.

'Why?' I asked Billy.

'It's life, me lover,' he said, and I watched him take up a thick tube of green glass. His fingers fascinated me. Heavy, short, splayed; with broken finger-nails and ridgy knuckles, they were the hands of man-brute and not the hands of a Creator. I looked at my own hands; young, supple, white – holding a thousand promises, holding a hundred dreams. But I knew in a vague troubled sort of way that my hands would never have anything to give. Mine were Taking hands. Billy's were Giving hands, their goodness was inexhaustible.

Years before – me about six or seven, mayhap – I'd watched Billy down at the market. He'd taken two firm apples from a stall, balanced and weighed them in his hands.

'Bet yoh can't do it, Billy,' the stall-owner shouted. 'You'm past it now, lad. Yoh've had your day.' Men jostled round, eager as boys watching a playground fighting challenge. Billy juggled the apples, let his fingers whisper over them, a little smile tugging the corners of his mouth to be let out.

'How much am yoh a-betting me?' he asked.

'Pick o' the stall against half a dollar,' the stall-owner answered. 'If yoh wins, yoh can tek a week's vegetables.'

Billy closed his hands and fingers on the apples; and all of a sudden the juice and pulp squirted between them, and when he opened his hands two blobs of mess fell to the rough flagstones of the market-place.

Plop, plop. And the apples were no more....

Billy took his vegetables home to the roars of delight of the iron moulders and chain-strikers, the strong Black Country men who respected only superior strength.

Billy's strength was as legendary as his gentleness.

It's shallow hollow men the world stocks these days; but not then, not when such men as Billy walked.

I watched the sure fingers talk to the green glass. The shadows blurred up at Billy's face, masking him in mystery. Years later I was to see a picture of Beethoven in his later years ... and I recognised my friend Billy.

The fingers talked and crooned and in the circle of light the cat and the mouse and the Birds of Paradise seemed to be watching and waiting. Somewhere in the green glass a pulse throbbed, and the glass writhed in an ecstasy of heat, and I watched in awe and delight as a face laughed out at me. Eyes and nose and bearded chin, high cheek bones and widow-peaked forehead; pointed cars and crinkly hair, slanted eyebrows. The green flowed into even contours, the face grew perfect in head-tilted arrogance; and in the eyes were knowledge and humour, strange cynicism and the faintest hint of cruelty behind overall kindness. Small perfect horns grew out above the temples, and the sensual mouth above the beard was creased at the corners with secret laughter.

'It's the Devil,' I cried out, explosive with surprise.

'Mephistopheles,' replied Old Billy, with satisfaction both at the object and the word. 'It's Mephistopheles. He's a sort of Devil, me lover. Only yoh listen to me – them's some as reckons that God isn't all good, what with wars and hunger and things. Then there's them as reckons the Devil isn't all bad, otherwise he 'ouldn't have so many satisfied customers. There's a bit of God in all on us, and a bit of the Devil. Yoh needs to take the best bits of both on 'em, ah've been thinking.'

He annealed the strange wonder in the small oven, then after a while he gave it to me.

'It's for you, me lover,' he said.

I took the green head home with me, wrapped in cotton wool, and I put it with my piglets, money and other treasures under the bedroom floorboard. And I came to love it in a way I couldn't understand, and have pretend talks with it which weren't really pretend, but boyhood real and serious. I never let my dad see it. I felt if he did, he might think it worth something and sell it.

Time went by, weeks and months and a year or two; and I kept calling on my friend Billy as he worked in his shed. Then came a time when I didn't call on Billy for several weeks because a fine hot summer came in and in between pocket-money work there were kites to fly and balls to kick; there was fishing and poaching and walks in woods and dingles, and dusty lanes to roam over at Kinver. There were boys pastures to roam and sunlight to drink, and sometimes whooping fights and laughter....

But even so, daily or nightly without exception, I spent a few minutes with my green Mephistopheles; took it from its hiding place and puzzled at it, looked into the wise eyes and cruel-kind mouth, and a strange haunting quality would sit on the back-step of my boyhood understanding and grope towards manhood knowledge. The green face seemed to live, as if all the world's knowledge existed in the green skull, as if no secrets of life or death fermented beyond the green brain.

And then I dropped the Mephistopheles and it shattered into fragments on the uncarpeted floor. I stood looking at the pieces, numb and lonely inside as if I'd destroyed a friend. After a while I bent down to the pieces and saw with shock that the head had been hollow after all. I picked the pieces up carefully and put them in my handkerchief, seeing a broken eye winking up at me, a broken smile nursing the cruel tenderness. I ran to Old Billy, longing for the strong fingers and healing flame to mend the shattered face. I knocked on the shed door, but no one answered.

I knocked again and was afraid of the silence.

'Billy,' I called, 'Billy – it's me. It's Archie. Please, can I come in?'

There was no answer. I leaned my head against the rough wood, waiting.

'Who is it?' a sudden voice shouted; but it was not Billy's voice. I saw a slut of a woman standing in the yard, her hair in paper curlers, a potato sack round her thick waist. She was one of Billy's neighbours.

'What'n yoh want?' she asked.

'I want to see Billy,' I answered, dismayed by her ugliness.

'Yoh can't see him,' the woman said, 'nor can erra body else for that matter. He's dead and buried – they buried him last week.'

I couldn't comprehend. I tried to kill her with my mind, with my thoughts, tried to kill her to take her words away.

'Was workin' in his shed,' she said, sniffing ugliness, 'was workin' in theer and had a heart attack or someat. Anyroad, he's dead, and that's all there is to it.' She tightened the potato sack round her waist.

'Can't stop here canting all day,' she sniffed, going back inside her pigsty house. I let my hands trouble against the shed door.

'Billy,' I whispered, 'Billy. It's me. It's Archie.'

I opened the door quietly, expecting to see him hunched over the hissing flame. But the shed was dark inside, and silent. I let the door swing back so that a blaze of sunlight came to the bench and stroked against the canes of glass and coloured creatures sleeping in the darkness. I half expected the rough growl to come – 'Put the wood in the hole. Shut it, quick' – but no voice existed in the quiet place. I stood for a little while in the still and the calm and the sadness, then I took the pieces of green glass from my handkerchief and placed them on the work-bench. I stood quietly, listening.

In the quiet and the hush I thought I heard the bee droning in the crimson petals, heard the cat purring and the mouse scampering on glass pit-a-pat feet to its sanctuary. I thought I heard a butterfly's wing beating the air, and the pearl of dew splash from the rose.

I crept from the shed and dropped the latch, and swear I could hear the Birds of Paradise singing....

Home I went and tried to tell my mam and dad that Billy was dead; I wanted them to tell me that he wasn't really dead, that he'd only gone away for a little while. But the dad was out using a boozer someplace, and mam was talking to a neighbour who had dropped by with a pan of unwanted stew. I stood in the passage way listening to our mam.

'Like on Monday,' she was saying, 'like on Monday, our Pam comes home with a note from the teacher saying she had nits in her hair. That's their fault, that is. Ah keeps my kids clean even if ah can't buy 'em new clothes and all that. The house isn't bad now, only wants a bit of dusting and tidying.'

Nits in the hair, nits in the mind, nits in the whole bloody rotten stinking world. I went into the kitchen and stood looking at the filth, at the layers of newspapers serving as tablecloths; when one layer got soiled, another one was placed on top, so that tea slops and jam stains welded the lot together like plywood. Two herrings were suspended over the grate, hanging from trivets over the fire. The fat from them hissed and spluttered, smoke from the fire blackening their skins. They smelled good and I wondered where the luxury of bloaters had come from, whose teeth would sink into them. I tried to clean the kitchen up a bit, just to take my mind off things, but it was no use. The whole lot wanted taking outside and shaking, or a match put to it....

I crept upstairs, quiet and sad. The bedroom was empty of brothers or sisters. I sat on the bed and cried for Billy....

Chapter Four

The piano came to live at our house when I was ten years old. I don't know where it came from, I only know that dad and his mate Pope Tolley turned up with it one night; strapped to a handcart, it was.

It was honest come by – I do know that. It wasn't stolen or anything, and the handcart actually belonged to Pope. The two of them lugged the instrument into our front room – we called it the Spare Room on account that it was empty and had no furniture or anything. After Pope had gone, myself and five brothers and sisters were treated to a couple of hours of one-fingered exercises as dad plinked and plonked on the yellow keys. Some of the notes were flat, and the soft pedal squeaked on its levers, but gradually we recognized the outline of 'Nearer my God to Thee' and a few tunes of the day. Dad went to bed sober for a change, but well satisfied, full of music and proud ownership.

My dad was a strange tortured man – at times, only a hand's width from lunacy. A man who truly thought that a vengeful God was seeking him out for sheer spite, a man who, when a thunderstorm struck, would turn mirrors to the wall, hide bits and pieces of cutlery, then sit on the cellar steps with a blanket over his head, moaning and rocking back and forth. Thunderstorms and gypsies were what he was afraid of. The fortune-teller type. Once, when he had temporary work in the coal-mine, a gypsy told him not to go in next day because if he did he wouldn't come back. Next day he refused to go to his shift and there was this blarney of a row between him and mom. Even so, there was a fall at the coal face where he should have been working and five cutters were killed, including one of dad's brothers. I stood with dad by the great pit wheel-house as the bodies were brought up. Half the neighbourhood was there, women for the most part, all quiet and grim and intent under the arc lights and the lights from the miners' helmets. Dad kept saying over and over again 'O dear Lord, O dear Lord' with tears running down his face when he saw the mangled remains of his brother. For all that, the gaffers laid him off when he reported for the next shift, on account that he'd taken time off without permission.

These were days of mass unemployment with three men waiting in the shadows for every man in work. These were days of queueing up at street corners, waiting for the soup kitchens, with a few brothers and sisters mixed in the queue pretending not to know one another so's they could draw extra helpings. The Means Test days, with a stern-faced man calling at your house to look at your things, your bits and pieces, before he'd help you. 'You've got six chairs,' the man would say, 'you only need two, so sell the other four.' Or – 'You don't need that rug, or that lino. And you don't need that coat, it isn't winter. Sell them first, before you ask us to help.'

One Means Test man used to say which shop the stuff had to be sold to. We all knew that it was a fiddle, that he was in cahoots with the man at the shop. The man would buy the things dirt cheap and then sell at a fat profit to them who had got the money to buy; none of us doubted that the Means Test man got his cut; but the Means Test men were all-powerful, their word was law, and any protest or complaint against them would bring the wrath of full hunger onto the heads and bellies of the complainers. The Means Test people would strip you down to your soul before they'd sign the voucher which put a bit of food in your pantries. My dad was bitter about this, as were most of the men who had no work. Once, a bit earlier on, the Duke of Windsor made newspaper headlines by going into the cottages of out-of-work miners to 'comfort them'. The papers were patriotic enough about it, but men that I knew used to give it a belly laugh. 'The bleeder doesn't ask us to go and have a meal with him in Buckingham Palace,' they said, 'and he don't seem in the mood for handing over a few million quid.'

My dad would stand on the corner at the Labour Exchange and shout 'Soup Kitchens of the World – Unite'. It became a sort of local catch-phrase that covered anybody's absence. If a man were sent to jail for poaching, the locals would say 'He's gone to unite the soup kitchens of the world'. If a man walked out on his wife and kids, he'd 'gone after the soup kitchens'. Or (and I always liked this one) if one of the young men got a wench in the family-way and didn't want to marry her, he'd slope off for parts unknown and people would say 'he's had his bloody soup but he don't want to keep the ladle he poured it into'.

We didn't know then that protected days lay up ahead, the protection known as Social Security. National Health Service, National wealth service ... we didn't know then that a day would come when, if your belly rumbled with hunger, there'd be a queue of Good-intent waiting to fill it.

But these things didn't happen in my boyhood days. I used to watch dad and the other men in the Dingle Woods playing toss-ha'penny, often with coins robbed from their gas meters; playing with desperation to make a couple of shillings for home needs. Our house seldom had coins to feed the gas meter, so dad used to cut dummy ones with tin and scissors, or pieces of lead. He fed these into the gas meter so's we could get gas. When the man came to empty the meter dad had to scrape up enough money to buy back the counterfeits. If not, it was thirty days in the jail-house over in Birmingham. They were hard days.

Dad's piano started to get damp there in the spare room, so he dragged it into the kitchen. He kept it covered with an old army blanket when he wasn't polishing it or one-fingering it. I think it symbolised status to him; it was tangible, but out-of-this-world. Our house was the only house in the street to have a piano. We hadn't got enough chairs to sit on, we hadn't got a carpet on the floor – we hadn't even got a tin-opener, but used an old pair of scissors to open cans with. But we'd got a piano.

Dad would open the front door wide so's the whole street could share in stumbling one-fingered delights such as 'Abide with Me' or 'So Deep is the

Night'. Nobody else was allowed to touch it. It was dad's, every polished walnut inch of it. The brass pedals shone like soldiers' buttons, as did the candle-brackets sticking from the front, the sheet-music holder, and the lid lock.

I came home from school one day to see the Means Test man's bike leaning against our wall. He was inside, laying the law down to dad.

'You'll get at least a pound for it,' the man was saying. 'P'raps thirty shillings. You've got no right to expect charity from us while you've got that piano. Sell it.'

Dad was bitter, but such was the power of Means Test that his protest whined out rather than exploded.

'Who'll buy a piano?' he argued. 'Nobody wants a bloody piano. 'Sides, I want my kids to learn to play. Give 'em someat to look forwards to, give 'em a start in life.'

'Bloody liar,' I thought, 'you won't let us touch the perishing thing.'

The Means Test man sniffed official disapproval.

'You want to get such fanciful ideas out'n your head,' he said. 'You want to see about getting a job, you do. So's you can keep your own family, and not look to charity.'

I thought dad was going to hit the feller.

'Get a job?' he bellowed. 'Get a job? Wheer'm I going to get a job? Where's the other three million on us going to get a job? Eh? It's blokes like me who wants to work but can't that keeps bloody leeches like you in work.'

The man gave dad a demerit in his little book.

'Sell the piano,' he said coldly, 'and I'll see you in a fortnight's time.'

Dad was depressed. He didn't want to part with his piano. He might come home one night blind drunk and smash it into bits and pieces, but soberly he didn't want to part with it. As long as it stood there in the kitchen, an absurd luxury of uselessness, it was a cube of hope that present circumstances were temporary and would pass away to better days.

'Pope Tolley's in a bit of work,' he muttered. 'He might be able to lend me a quid. Then I could hide the piano in the back kitchen and tell the Means Test that ah've flogged it.'

I went with him to the great steel and iron foundry in Brierley Hill where Pope was doing a stint. Drop-forges hammered out shapes and masses from white-hot iron, a sprawl of railway sidings laced through the huge workshops. Hungry steam engines clattered streams of waggons and rolling stock. Somewhere, gaffers sat back with cigars and big dinners, sighing satisfaction. Pope Tolley was painted against a cloud of steam and smoke. He and four other men were fighting a coil of white-hot metal – three times the height of anyone of them – to make a giant spring. Jesse had one end caught up in a huge pair of tongs, and he heaved his end up to be clamped into the headstock of a giant's lathe. Another man shaped the glowing coils with a hook as big as himself, and gradually the tormented steel started to accept the shape it was meant for. The whiteness of near-liquid heat started to redden and ease away, leaving angry hotness and solidity. The men slipped the coil from the mandril to prevent it from shrinking and locking on. Then the whole mass was caught up by the men and dropped into a vat of oil. The metal went mad, spitting and screaming and bubbling like the torn-out entrails of some monster. The heat and the anger and exhaustion and sweat symbolised hard times better than a thousand voices.

Pope fell back to a cool patch of space, mopping his brow with his sweat-rag. When dad asked him for the money, Pope shook his head sadly, the unalterable 'no'.

'Ain't got it, Bill,' he said to dad, 'and this job packs in tonight. Gaffer's putting more men off. And he's dropped the rate by a penny an hour for them as he keeps on.'

Dad and me walked home from Brierley Hill over the Clock Fields. Past the deserted brickyards which waited for trade, past the clay mines whose pit-wheels and derricks stencilled themselves against the sky. Past haunted men who mooched desolate among the scene of work gone dead, themselves bitter and curdled to see the waste of it all, the stagnation. Dad was silent, plodding, stern in thought and movement. I walked behind, watching the still-present arrogance of his head, with outward jutting jaw.

'Never mind,' he suddenly muttered to himself, but loud enough for me to hear, 'I'll have the money tomorrer. You bloody well see if I don't.'

Next morning he woke me early.

'Want to come to the Wake, over in Cannock?' he asked, and I blinked up at him unbelievingly. The Fair – the Wake, we called it – was a million miles of dream away to most of us kids. Most of us only knew of its existence through grownups telling us about it. About the canvas tents, the side shows, the coconut stalls, the hoop-la's, the rifle-ranges, the big-dippers and round-a-bouts, the sawdust and glitter, the steam-driven things which were the playthings of Paradise, with hurdy-gurdy music and barrel-organs filling the shining mind with tinsel and happiness.

'Don' tell your mam,' my dad said. 'Let her think we'm going over the tip to picks bits o' coal.' From some magical fold of his pocket he took three pennies.

'That's for yoh,' he said, 'to spend at the Wake.'

We went on his bike, with a cushion tied on the cross-bar for me to sit on. The tyres of the bike were packed with rags to make the battered frame less bone-shaking, because dad couldn't afford inner-tubes.

The Wake grounds were packed – mostly farm workers and their families, mixing business with pleasure by bringing saleable produces as well as their offsprings. In-work coal miners were there, visiting between shifts. Children of the unemployed wandered about, ragged, amazed, envious and excited. I wanted to spend my threepence on everything I saw, but my dad kept homing in on the boxing booth whose surrounds were packed tight with spectators. Heavy iron moulders, colliers, brickyard men, canal navvies and bargees. I didn't understand dad's interest until a really big fair-ground bruiser took his place in the ring; big and insolent he was, stripped to the waist but with black tights on like the old-time boxers of Corbett and Tom Sayers.

They were strapping Black Country men clustered round the ring, with many a wench to spur them on, and I saw Big Stud Hathaway from Pensnett iron-mills climb up to take the challenge. He didn't even land a blow – the big man put him down with a single punch. Another man, a collier by the look of the blue coal-scars on his face, took Hathaway's place. But he didn't last ten seconds. My dad was flexing his hands and muttering over them.

'Ah dangled 'em in the piss-pot all night,' he told me, 'and then vinegar and turpentine, to get the knuckles tough.' The fair-ground barker was agitating the men, prodding and urging them.

'Black Country born, Black Country bred,' he sneered, 'Strong in the arm and weak in the head.' He chivvied at the younger men, holding them up for ridicule in front of their wenches.

'Now you look a promising starter,' he said, pointing. 'Young and strapping ... come up here, lad, and take my feller on. If you win you can buy that lass of yours a new dress. Eh, lad? Fancy your chances?' The lad didn't. He blushed and looked down at his feet. The girl turned from him, partly contemptuous. The Barker called out that he'd pay five pounds to any man who could stand five rounds against his fighter ... and believe me, five pounds was a king's ransom. The condition was that the five pounds had to be covered by the spectators, a shilling each in the cap. Five pounds to the winner, the rest to the Barker, and he was also willing to take side-bets from them as wanted.

There were almost three hundred men thronging the booth, all anxious to see blood. The Barker went amongst them, collecting coins into his hat. Satisfied, he went back into the ring.

'Who'll go three rounds with the Turk,' he blared; 'a fiver to the bloke who can stand up to him for five rounds ... *and seven pounds to the bloke who can knock him out.*'

I saw Pope Tolley pushing his way forwards, but my dad beat him to it. He was flinging his jacket at me for minding even as he went.

My dad was a bloody awful dad, he was no bloody good as a dad at all. But I knew one thing of him, and that was that he had no fear of anything on two or four legs. If God kept out of things with his thunder and lightning, and if fortunetelling gypsies kept their distance, my dad would tackle anything or anybody. As he stepped into the ring, the Barker muttered to him to pretend to be wrestling with the Turk if a copper came into the booth, because bare-fisted prizefighting was against the law.

The Turk made the mistake of taking dad for a smaller man; he made the mistake of not seeing through the collarless shirt with throat-knotted kerchief that dad was wearing. If he had of done, he'd have seen whipcord muscle and not an ounce of spare fat on belly or arms.

My dad beat the Turk.

He knocked hell out of the Turk. He bounced him off the ropes so fast they twanged like banjo strings. He kept his man spinning so fast and furious, with short jabs and uppercuts, that the feller must have thought half a dozen were onto him. Then my dad stepped back two paces, lifted a punch from the floor, connected to the Turk's button and the man went down in a daze and a panic. Dad rubbed his shredded knuckles, wincing at the pain in them. He turned to face the cheering crowd, and the Turk rolled over and kicked his legs from under him. He shouldn't have done. Dad went berserk – he dragged the Turk up and clobbered him hell for leather, hit him and hit him till the man's eyes were closed and puffed, and his lips cut against his own teeth as he spilled his gum-shields. The crowd went mad with cheering, and there was me climbing up one of the tent poles to get a better look. The Barker tried to drag dad off the Turk. Dad let go of the Turk and walloped the Barker; when he'd recovered, the Barker promptly disqualified dad from the winnings.

Dad stood quiet and still, disbelieving. Then, as the portent of the disqualification dawned on him he went berserk again. It was foolish of him, yes. Had he put it to the crowd, they would have made sure he got his money. The Barker wouldn't have argued with a frenzied mob, he'd have paid up. But dad wasn't waiting for reason – he started to wreck the boxing booth, pulling struts and guy-ropes loose, overspilling the desk and cash-cubicle (and a surge of men went scrabbling over the floor, grabbing at the spilled money) ripping canvas and smashing seats and chairs. He went out like a bull on the rampage, wrecking other nearby stalls and props. Fairground men started to pour at him from all points of the compass, but suddenly Pope Tolley was there with him, laughing like a madman and swinging punches which could blind. Two of his brothers joined in, fighting wicked with boots and bits of paling wood. As the excitement spread other Black Country men mixed in and wallowed deep with fists and boots. The fair-ground engineers stopped the music, stopped the wheels and dippers and all the mechanical movements, so that oceans of gold-scrolled horses and dodge-'em cars were frozen at peak points of motion. I could hear women screaming above the shouts of men – but above all I could hear Pope Tolley's voice laughing out loud and strong – 'Give it to 'em, our kids. Give it to 'em, Bill,' and snarling yapping dogs made a mad chorus to his powerful solo.

Then someone gave up the cry that the police were coming, and a mêlée of men and women panicked to get from the fair-grounds. I could hear my dad calling – 'Art, am yoh theer?' but it was Pope Tolley who scooped me up in his massive arms as he, his brothers and my dad pulled away to hidden safety as the police came up. Pope and his brothers had borrowed a pony and trap to come to the fair, and they piled me into the trap with them. Dad rode his bike, holding on to the side of the trap as it spanked along the sun-dusted roads. The hooves of the pony lulled me with rhythm, and the smell of strong men was a safety to trust for always. Drowsily I heard Pope talking to my dad.

'Yoh won fair and square, Bill,' he was saying, 'but the Barker bastard wanted a loop-hole to duck out of. And yoh lost yoh're thirty-bob side-bet, as well.'

I could hear the wheels of my dad's bike whispering like a low warm wind beneath the hooves of the pony and the hum of the trap. I drowsed nearer to sleep, warm against the holding man's chest, content in a nest of tobacco smoke and beer fumes....

... and then a thought lanced me awake.

Where in hell had my dad got thirty shillings from to place a side bet?

When we got home, I went straight to my bedroom and lifted the loose floorboard. I took my money tin out, opened it. The money I'd saved was all gone, and only a clog of spilled cigarette ash stared up at me.

My bloody, bloody, bloody dad had taken my money. I'd got to start saving all over again.

That night, he sold the piano for fifteen shillings and went out and got truly pissed with the money, and then came home and started a row and thumped my mam from one wall to the other. When I tried to stop him, he just threw me away like I was an ounce of nothing, and after a bit he sat down by the fire and fell asleep, snoring open-mouthed like the drunken pig he was.

Chapter Five

My best pal in those pre-war Black Country days was Caggy Scrivens. My own age, he was, but built sturdier and an inch or so taller – good shoulders and arms on him. 'Got a bit of lard on his bread,' his mom would say admiringly, in between clouting him for some misdemeanour or other. We called him Caggy because he was left-handed, caggy-handed. There was only him in the family besides his mom and dad, he'd got no brothers or sisters; and during school holidays I used to stay at his house for week-ends.

The Scrivens's house wasn't posh, not by a long chalk, but it was clean and tidy.... I think my own mam envied it. 'They'm silver sand people,' she'd sniff, spelling out more envy than criticism. See, it was still the practice in some areas to put sand down on the back-kitchen floors. The back-kitchens (brew-houses, or brew-'usses we called them) mostly had slate quarried floors, no carpets or oil-cloth or anything. The poorer people used to sprinkle common red sand over them, to give a bit of grip to the feet and to hold down the dust. Posher folk, them as were a bit uppity and had a shilling or two to splatter, well, they used silver sand from the glass works. Invariably the silver sand people were more prideful than the others. They had standards, they kept up appearances even when their men landed in the dole queues. You could walk down long streets of back-to-back houses and see evidence of self-respect. Those that cared would red-polish their front steps so that they glowed rich and warm like a punnet of cherries; they'd pipe-clay the lintels of their doors so that they stood out like a soldier's harness, and sometimes the gleam of a brass knocker played ping-pong with the sunlight.

But despite this, the streets were bleak and dingy and far too long for childhood to walk through; they were built back to back in long lean squares, as if defending themselves from external attack. They didn't stand, these houses. They hunched and squatted and squabbled in solid squares of brick and concrete, and windows had been stuck in them, and doors.... there were no gardens in Caggy's street or mine. Each house had a small fold (fodes, we called them) to front or rear. Each fold was the size of two bed sheets put together. The floor of the folds were made from blue-bricks, or slate quarries, and a four-foot wall fenced each space in.

You had to go through the folds to get to the front doors, but more often than not you walked up the entry and went through the back. Every house had got its entry, carved like a tunnel through the mass of bricks.

Caggy's house was built like t'others. You went down the entry and 'round the back'. Four paces from the kitchen door was the brew-house, a small kiln-like shed whose one corner was occupied by a huge washing boiler with a fire grate under it. Standing in another corner was a wooden tub, and against it was an upright cast-iron mangle. Mondays were washdays all over. You'd come home from school with a sinking heart, seeing clouds of steam billowing out of the brew-house, hearing the thud of the wooden dolly (a wooden gadget which looked like a milking stool with a long handle stuck on) as the woman of the house plunged it up and down in the wooden tub, pounding the clothes clean. And in all my boyhood I never saw a mangle that didn't squeak and put my teeth on edge; sometimes the brew-houses were used for the purpose from which they got their names, namely brewing ale. Caggy Scrivens's mom used to brew up two or three times a year. There was always a bit of a fiddle to start with, as you can imagine. For a start, if you wanted to brew you'd got to buy an excise licence; so the neighbours used to take it in turns to pay for a licence, or dub together to raise the money just for one of 'em. One would buy the licence and all the others used to brew up under cover of the Legal Smell which found its way for a good mile radius, causing men to look at the docks and lick their lips. The washing boiler had to be scoured bright-dean, jugs, urns, bottles and pitchers had to be scaled out; hops, yeast and malt had to be measured to exact quantities ... they earned their drink, by the time it was ready.

Squeezed in between every pair of brew-houses was a smaller shed, sort of tagged on as an afterthought. These were the lavatories, one between every two houses. Usually hanging from these, one on each side, were long coffin-shaped tin baths which came into use on average once a month. To have a bath you had to fill the washing boiler, light a fire under it, and syphon off as needed. If it were a large family for bath-night, there'd be a bit of doubling up. Two to a bathful. The cleanest in first, and then the dirtiest; girls were separated from boys mostly by a towel round the waist.

Inside Caggy's house, as with countless others, you came into the kitchen first. Painted cream and green with a two-inch band of red dividing the two colours, so that the whole looked like a wrapping paper out of Woolworth's. Sticking from the wall over the fireplace was the gas burner with gas mantle attached. No electricity in slum houses; only gas for cooking and seeing by. The gas mantles were a sort of fine-spun day, shaped like an egg with one end sliced off. They were very fragile, like tight-meshed cobwebs, and many the one would have patches of holes in them so that the gas hissed out in pencil flame, giving the appearance of a lit-up porcupine. I always envied Caggy because his family had got a wind-up gramophone in the kitchen. A good one in a polished cabinet. It was great to sit in Caggy's kitchen playing the records with the gaslight hissing a *warm* hiss, and a bank of fire in the ash-grate. Him and me listening to the music while his mam and dad went off to the boozer. We'd have mugs of rich brown cocoa to slurp over, and a wedge or two of cheese to bite at the tongue, maybe an onion between us. Suspended from the trivet over the black-leaded grate, a couple of herrings hanging in the smoke to make them into bloaters for supper. The heat from the coals wafted up to them, caused little gleams of oil to drip from their scales into the flames where they burst and splattered into miniature explosions. The voice of John McCormack brought lumps into our throats as he told us of Mother Machree and Kathleen Mavourneen ... our hearts bled for 'Two Little Girls in Blue, Lad' and puzzled at 'one was your mother, I married the other, but now we have drifted apart'. Caggy and me reckoned that when we were a bit older we'd find the 'Two Little Girls in Blue, Lad,' marry them, and live happily ever after.

When Caggy's dad and mam came back from the pub, I always had a warm feeling in my belly. Mr. Scrivens was never nasty in drink, nor moody; not a bit like my own dad. He was jolly and easy and the beer stain on his breath was healthy and like early morning woods, like the smell of a loved grandad with pipe and tobacco. Mr. Scrivens would come home draped all over with packages and parcels, a boy's pleasure of fish and chips sharing with a man's world-smell of ale. He'd unwrap the parcels, line the contents up on the table. Sometimes, rare times, bottled whisky would glow amber-warm; gin stood transparent as cellophane. More often than not bottles of stout hinted at dark gut-warming comfort. Or a trussed chicken, cooked and golden, jutted proudly from the newsprint in which it had been wrapped. Wisps of steam rising from it like traces of cigarette smoke. Odds on, despite the beer he'd already drunk and would drink before going to bed, Mr. Scrivens's first words would be, 'I last got the kettle on, lads?' But Mrs. Scrivens could be a right tartar when she wanted. She and him used to squabble like a mad pair ... but even so, the gleam of humour never left her eyes, as if she weren't serious. When my mam and dad rowed, all the street had the privilege of listening in. The privilege part meant they could put cotton wool in their ears if they'd a mind to. Mr. and Mrs. Scrivens would argue in whispers, if they thought they'd disturb anybody.

To look at, Mr. Scrivens was only two penno'rth of coppers. About five feet six, he was, and as scraggy as a ferret locked in a coal house for a week. He was what he called 'self-employed'.

'That means he hasn't got a job,' Mrs. Scrivens would explain, 'and that he doesn't very much want one.' Mr. Scrivens, being a self-made man, could dismiss such criticism with the proof of things.

'I'm me own gaffer,' he would boast. But Mrs. Scrivens would have the last word.

'That's why he allus looks a bit puzzled on a paynight,' she'd murmur, 'when other fellers come home with a week's wages and he's got nothing.'

Sure enough, Mr. Scrivens hadn't got what could be termed as regular employment. He'd tried it, but the dole-queues of the day stretched halfway round the world ... and the other half had been without employment since the world began.

So he was a tatter-man, he made his living that way – and a fair living it was, by any body's standards. He'd got a pony and trap which he kept in a farmer's field, and he'd built a shed in the same field to keep his heavier bits and pieces in. Three times a week he'd harness the horse to the trap and 'do his rounds' from door to door, street to street; collecting old rags, bits of scrap iron, old oddments of throwouts to do up and sell. Caggy and me used to do a bit for him when we could, earning mayhap threepence or sixpence apiece. It was good enough without the coppers in our pockets, us sitting on the tail end of the cart with our feet dangling over the edge, and the pony spanking along. Another thing Caggy and me did was to go over the tip some evenings, carrying small magnets and large sacks. We'd put the magnets on all the bits and pieces of metal which were mixed up with the refuse – and if the magnet didn't stick we reckoned the metal was worth putting in the sacks and carting off to Mr. Scrivens. There was usually a lot of women over the tip, picking and sorting gleads (cinders, like coke) and half burned coal to load into their broken-down prams for the home fires. We had to be careful that they didn't catch on to our magnet trick and do us out of business. Strange women, the cinder bank women; they wore sacks round their waists instead of aprons, clogs to their feet, men's caps over their hair ... strong as wrestlers most of 'em, and no face powder or lipstick to make them half-way attractive. But they could have been anybody's mothers ... most of them were. You got the feeling they had to rape their menfolk to get anywhere, you couldn't imagine the men volunteering to serve them just out of appetite.

Mr. Scrivens didn't live by the pony and trap alone; he was the local saltman as well. Twice a month he delivered yard-long blocks of salt to fish shops and grocery shops, canteens and cafes. He had a special salt-float, a small four-wheeled cart which was spotlessly clean and painted over with flowers and scrolls … nobody would buy salt from a dirty float. It had to be clean, as did the man who used it and the pony or donkey which drew it. Mr. Scrivens hired a donkey for the salt work, and it had crimson harness with brass buckles on it, and a small Union Jack on its collar. In the Black Country a donkey was always called a Gornal Cuckoo … don't ask me why, because I don't know. On top of everything, Mr. Scrivens also made a 'bit on the side' from cheek and light-fingered cunning. You see, they were strange crippled days we lived in. Poverty was extreme.

People had to steal in order to live. Steal from the land, from the coal wharves, from the game-woods, in order to supplement what they hadn't got. Looking back, I'd say it was an era of non-violent theft. Mr. Scrivens was no exception; he could manage nicely through tatting, but he wasn't averse to a bit of bonus. 'Fiddling', he called it. He was among the best fiddlers in the district, he made music all over. Mostly discord, like people ever complaining that they'd been robbed of this that or the other. When Caggy was younger, his dad and mom would take him for long walks along the canal, in his pram. And Caggy always came back on his two feet but the pram would be wheezing and groaning under a load of potatoes or fresh vegetables, a farmer's soil and loving care still clinging to 'em. Mr. Scrivens had a simple, poignant philosophy. 'We come into the world with nothing,' he'd say, 'and we go out with nothing. What we use in life we only borrow. So I'm not a stealing – I'm only a borrowing.' Mrs. Scrivens would purse her lips.

'You'd better borrow some turnips next time, then,' she'd suggest, 'we'm getting a bit low in the larder.'

The weekends I stayed at Caggy's house were always highlighted on Sunday mornings when we went up to his granny's. We'd ride in the pony and trap through Silver End where the Tolleys lived, past the early morning fishermen, past the rusting and rotting canal barges which fretted and waited for trade, and into Pensnett. Down old Bluett Street where Caggy's granny lived, little warren-type houses which I reckoned the King ought to come and have a look at, then see if he could sleep peacefully in his hundred-odd rooms afterwards. The Bluett Street houses did have patches of gardens, though, instead of concrete folds. A few flowers bloomed, or a green of privet; but mostly old wood and corrugated iron sheds and wind-leaking kennels and pigeon pens. Bits and pieces of salvaged poverty – bicycle wheels and frames, pieces of pit-props, mounds of bricks waiting to be dressed and re-used, piles of junk and brokenness.

When we went inside Mother Scrivens's house we had to get used to the inside dark. Sunlight, and very little daylight, had ever got inside, not since the roof was put on. The room was small, cramped; but clean and neat as a new pin. A wholesome fire burned in the gleaming grate. Brass kettles and urns glinted a welcome, while a steel kettle steamed a bubbling greeting from its trivet. A tea pot sat on the hob, warming its bottom. A smell of camphor and linseed oil and herbs permeated everywhere. On the walls were faded sepia photographs of young men in trench puttees and uniforms, swanking from a man's world of ammunition pouches. A picture of Queen Victoria frowned down on everything, the picture itself draped with two silk-embroidered over-coloured union jacks. Above the narrow door which kept the steep stairs from toppling into the room were two long, beautiful glass walking sticks. A matched pair, each four feet long, with a white and blue spiral-twist running inside the entire lengths; and the handles were moulded in tiny red roses and green leaves along the full sweep of the curves. The firelight threw back from them, as if the roses were rubies, as if the blue and white spirals were slim snakes matching curve to curve.... I knew with half my mind, even before Mother Scrivens told me, that Billy Swingewood had made them. My friend Billy.

Mother Scrivens would always be sitting in the same chair, just as if she hadn't moved since the last time, a chair which matched the horsehair sofa. She'd be surrounded by sweets and biscuits and cake, always complaining that she couldn't eat a thing. She'd always got her teeth out. They'd be resting on the dresser, laughing out at the world.

'Can't eat a thing,' she said. 'Not a thing I can't eat.'

Caggy watched her.

'You've eaten six chocolates, two humbugs, a piece of cake and a biscuit while we'n sat here,' he said.

'Not really eating it,' murmured Mother Scrivens. 'I'm just a playing with it. Can't eat a thing, really. Don't reckon as I'll last much longer.'

'That's what me dad was saying, coming up,' Caggy agreed with her. 'He reckoned as he didn't think you'd last much longer. He said you was on your way out.'

'Shurrup,' Mr. Scrivens muttered to his son. 'You'll get me into trouble, else.'

Mother Scrivens merely toyed and played with another pair of chocolates, popping them into her toothless mouth and clamping her gums down hard.

'There's some humbugs on the dresser,' she told Caggy and me. Then, to Mr. Scrivens, 'Is it all fixed up, then?'

Mr. Scrivens nodded. 'It's all fixed up, ar,' he said. 'What about your end?'

Mother Scrivens wiped chocolate drool from her chin. She stirred her camphor-smelling skirts and looked as mysterious as mystery itself.

'I've cleaned and scalded the hopper out in the brew-'uss,' she said, 'and there's plenty of sacks on the floor to catch the drippings. Billy Clegg has lent us his knives, on condition he gets a mouthful or two. It's the noise I'm bothered about,' she added, clamping and chumping on another biscuit.

Mr. Scrivens fixed Caggy and me with a stare.

'Two blokes 'ull be here in a bit,' he said. 'Couple of fellers I know. Them and me will be doing a bit of business in the brew-'uss, and I want you two to keep watch for us. Got it?'

'Watch what for?' I thought to ask.

'For anything unusual,' Mr. Scrivens said. 'Anything suspicious.'

'How'll we recognise what's unusual or suspicious,' Caggy wanted to know. 'Unusual from what, for instance?'

Mother Scrivens hammered her deep blue eyes at the pair of us.

'By suspicious and unusual,' she explained, 'he means anything that

65

looks like a policeman, a Council Inspector, or just a bloody tettle tattle of a copper's nark. And that's all *you* need to know about it.'

There came a rap on the door, and Mr. Scrivens went to it. I could hear him talking in low tones to a couple of men, and standing with half my face pressed against the pane of the small window, I could see that the men had a large sack between them that was giving them trouble. The sack was almost as big as either one of them, and it wriggled and flumped around like it was alive.

'Come away from that window,' Mother Scrivens said to me sharply; 'the less you see of this lot the better.' I could hear Mr. Scrivens's voice climbing the scale by an octave.

'You didn't say it 'ud be alive,' he complained, shouting in a whisper. 'You said it only had to be cut up. For God's sake, get it in the brew-'uss and lock the door on it. Stay with it – and for God's sake, keep the bloody thing quiet.' He came back into the room.

'It's alive,' he said to his mother. 'The bloody thing's alive.' He sat down, shocked and bewildered. Caggy and me, we wriggled inside our skins trying to guess the secret of what lay in the out-house.

'Bloody well alive,' repeated Mr. Scrivens.

'We can soon alter that,' his mother said, ever practical. 'The knives are sharp enough.'

Mr. Scrivens shuddered. 'Who's going to do it?' he wanted to know, 'I can't – I've never killed one before … and this one's a thumping big 'un.' He shuddered. 'I just couldn't do it,' he whispered.

Mrs. Scrivens took command. 'Caggy,' she said, 'you and young Archie nip down the street and over the cut-side to the Tolleys' house. Ask if Big Pope's in, and if he is tell him I want to see him straight away. Tell him it's urgent. And tell him it'll be worth his while.'

Mr. Scrivens's face lit up with hope. 'Tell him to bring his four-ten shot-gun as well,' he said, 'but to keep it under his coat til he gets here.'

Caggy and me went off to find the Tolley. On the way out I looked inside the brew-house, and could see the two men trying to keep the sack quiet. A pig's head kept poking out of it, and one of the men kept clouting it on the snout to make it go back in.

We found Pope Tolley and gave him the message, and he said he'd follow us back on his bike. Twenty minutes later he was sitting on the horsehair sofa arguing with Mr. Scrivens.

'A live pig's no good to you,' he said. 'It's got to be dead before you can eat it.'

'As that pig is now,' Mr. Scrivens informed him, 'it's a whole pig. But it'll whittle down to half with you at it.' He turned to his mother for support.

'He wants half the bloody pig just for killing it,' he said.

'Half a pig's better than no pig,' Mrs. Scrivens murmured, and we all trooped out to the brew-'uss, went inside and closed the door behind us. Pope unslung his shot-gun from under his coat. In two halves, it was, each half fastened under an arm-pit. He locked the two halves together and put a cartridge into it.

'Let the pig out'n the sacks,' he told the two men. 'Let's have a look at it.' The men did as they were bid, stripping the sacks away but holding the animal firm with string and rope wrapped round its feet, and its jaws clamped together with a muzzle made from more rope. The pig screeched and whimpered out of the sides of its imprisoned mouth.

'John,' said Pope Tolley to Mr. Scrivens, awe in his voice, 'it's a bloody big pig, is that. I'd say it was a bostin' big pig.'

'For God's sake shoot it,' Mr. Scrivens implored, 'else all the street 'ull hear it, and we'll have the law on our backs.'

'Wheer'd it come from?' Pope wanted to know.

Mr. Scrivens ignored the question.

'Bolvie's farm is my guess,' Pope Tolley figured. 'John, I reckon you'd best get this pig cut up into bacon afore old Bolvie himself finds he's one short.'

'Shoot it,' Mr. Scrivens pleaded. 'Don't just stand theer – shoot the bloody thing, quick.'

'You must be saft,' Pope told him. 'A four-ten shot-gun won't put that thing down. You'd need an army rifle, or a heavy twelve-bore. My bird shot 'ud just bounce off it.'

'Cut its throat, then,' Mr. Scrivens said. 'Goo on, cut its throat.' He passed Pope the biggest knife.

'It's a bostin' big pig,' Pope said, eyeing the knife with doubt. 'I've never cut a pig's throat before.'

'Goo on, you can do it,' Caggy's dad encouraged.

'There'll be a lot of blood,' Pope said. 'A lot of blood.'

'A lot of blood from a pig's a good thing,' Mother Scrivens said, 'we can collect it in one of the buckets to make black pudding.'

'It's still a big pig,' Pope muttered. 'A bloody big pig.'

'Kill the bloody thing,' Mr. Scrivens was almost pleading, 'afore the bluebottles get wind of it.'

'We'n got no licence to kill it,' Pope objected. 'You haven't got an official licence, have you?'

'Since when did you bother about what's legal and what isn't?' Mr. Scrivens snarled, 'and if it comes to that, we haven't got a bloody certificate of ownership either.'

'Old Bolvie doesn't know we've got it,' one of the men mentioned; 'we got away with it afore daybreak this morning.'

Pope seemed to consider this. 'How'd you get it away?' he wanted to know, 'without it squalling the place down.'

'We crep' up on it,' the other man said. 'We crep' up to it and slapped it over the head with a paling of wood. That's the mark just over the eye. We knocked it out, got it onto our handcart, and here it is.'

Pope thought it over, came to his decision. 'That's it, then,' he said. 'My gun won't even make a dent in it. We'll poleaxe it, that's what we'll do. Then while it's out cold we'll slit its throat and finish it off. Get the hot water ready for scalding its bristles off, Mother.' He went off for a while, returned with a long stave of wood with a ten-inch nail knocked through one end so that the point stuck out for a good six inches.

Mr. Scrivens bundled me and Caggy out of there, told us to keep look out. I stood on a brick instead, stared in through the window and watched what they were doing. The two men kept the pig on its side, on the floor. Pope took his jacket off, rolled his sleeves above the elbows to show a giant's muscles. He picked the fierce home-made bludgeon up, hefted it, lowered it to touch the pig's head lightly. Then he raised it high, stood on tip toe, and crashed down with it. The pig shuddered, and then lay still, a trickle of blood oozing from the small hole in its head. Pope was satisfied.

'You can untie its legs,' he said, 'and get it on its back so's I can slash the bloody thing's throat.' The men did as they were instructed, unlacing the animal's legs and heaving it round. Pope reached for the long sharp knife.

The pig shuddered again, squealed and grunted, then suddenly scrabbled to its feet and shot away for the half open door. Pope was amazed, dumbfounded.

'Catch it, quick,' Mr. Scrivens shouted. 'Stop it.'

One of the men dived on it as it passed but it tossed him away and belted hell for leather out of that place.

'Catch it,' Mr. Scrivens bellowed at me; but I let it pass, snorting and bleeding, into the street. Caggy gave a scream of terror as he saw it coming at him, and scrabbled up a wall for safety. The pig hit the street at a fair pace, making enough noise to wake the dead. People stared after it with drop-jawed wonder. A couple of dogs went after it, nipping in at it, barking and snarling. The pig squealed the more, until its swift passage up the street had gathered a wake of dogs, boys and unemployed men – all shouting and swearing and laughing, while from the front doorsteps the drab women screeched encouragement.

'Go it, Tommy boy. Grab it by the balls.'

'What'n you chasing your mother for, Sammy …?'

'Bring us a slice off its bum, Bert.'

At the top of the dingy street the pig met a lorry. The lorry was moving at high speed, and so was the pig. The lorry continued to move, but the pig didn't. It lay huddled and bloody at the kerbside. A group of silent people collected, stood staring. They started to move away when the policeman came, fetched by a shaken lorry driver. But when the policeman started his questioning, nobody knew a thing. Everybody had heard the noise, heard the crash, the braking of wheels. But that was all. Nobody knew who the pig belonged to, where it came from. It just happened.

69

Mr. Scrivens was heartbroken. 'All that bacon,' he said, 'all them spare ribs, the crackling and chitterlings. The fry, the ham, the trotters. The brawn and the dripping. The black pudding. All that lying there.' He lingered last, all the others melting away to small dark rooms in the terrible street.

'Now that's not right,' the policeman said, pointing, 'that's not at all right. That lorry never did *that*, I know. Whose bin at it, then?'

I don't know much about pigs, but even I know it has four legs and not two. And even I know that a lorry can't slice whacking great slivers off a pig's haunches as clean as a butcher can. But this dead pig was minus several bits and pieces, all taken during the excitement and mêlée.

To this day I don't know who helped themselves. But I did see Pope Tolley ride away on his bike with pockets bulging, and a drip of something drooling from a pocket.

Chapter Six

'It's the bloody Governing Rich against the bleeding Governed Poor' seemed to be a slogan on everybody's lips. It seemed to me that I'd been born to the chant of the slogan, and that it remained with me almost forever, like an extra heart-beat. When I was aged seven, in 1933, a man named Hitler had come to power in Germany, and the men who I knew – who'd fought in the Great War – grumbled and muttered about him, and said there was another big fight on its way. But these things were 'political', and had no real place in a boy's mind. I remember the dole queues more. They seemed to stretch round every street corner, village to village, town to town, city to city. Some parts of the country were less affected than others; ours, being an industrial area, was hit very bad. People in the country, or them as had got sizeable gardens, could live better than them in the towns, where there wasn't room to grow a cabbage.

We got used to seeing knots of idle men brooding on street corners, their muscles aching from the fatigue of no work. In a way, they all looked the same, like as if they wore a uniform of patched tatters, and their discipline was to slump and lounge, all in exact contradiction to parade-ground soldiers. Those of them who'd fought in the Big War used to sneer at the patriotic snips and pieces which appeared in the newspaper – news items which said that the Duke of this or the Duchess of that was doing this, that or the other.

'We fought a bloody war so's we could come back to a land fit for heroes', was the general message of the sneers; 'but what we fought for was *them*, so's they could keep what *they'd* got.' It seemed that the Americans were in the same boat, rowing with oars of discontentment. Evidently *their* leaders had told them that once the war was won they'd have a car in every garage and a chicken in every pot.

Well, our heroes didn't come back to a land fit for them, that's for sure. The piece of land *we* lived in wasn't fit for cattle, the grazing was that thin. Saucepans filled with free soup and wedges of bread was what we seemed to get most, queueing up to get it and then warming it up when you got it home. Them as didn't need to take from the soup kitchens seemed to draw away from those as did.

It's like as if two different sets of 'working class' emerged. Them as took free soup and Means Test were the lower strata, them as could manage without it were the upper, the 'monty-sods'. The 'monty-sods' became fair game for the soup kitchen lot; the eternal war of the Have-nots against the Haves. If a load of coal were delivered to a 'Monty' house, tipped up in the road, you could bet that a good third would disappear to the 'Soup' lot if the owner wasn't on constant look-out until the man of the house got home and shovelled the coal into the cellar. I often used to walk the streets with Caggy Scrivens, looking for loads of coal in the roadside. We'd knock on the door and offer to get it into the cellar for threepence. Sometimes we were lucky and made a shilling each in one day, but then other lads started to knock the bottom out of the market by undercutting our prices. By the time the price was down to a penny a ton, Caggy and me decided it wasn't worth the effort, so we packed it in.

There was one woman in the street next to ours, young she was and fairly pretty, who was a whore. The grown-ups didn't *tell* us she was a prostitute, but we knew. A sort of code existed between the women. When they spoke about the whore they'd sniff, tighten their shawls round their shoulders, and say – 'Her's no better than her should be,' or 'Any wench can win her bread by lying on her back,' and things like that. This code the women had between them was a sort of hangover from the days of

Queen Victoria when nobody would call a spade a spade, but call it an 'agricultural instrument'. Our women didn't come straight out and say things like – 'Martha Higgins up the street is going to have another baby,' they'd say, 'I see Martha Higgins is in an interesting condition again.' For some reason I never found out, straight talk about sex was strictly taboo; it was always referred to from an angle – except when family rows broke out and then a torrent of 'Fucks', 'Bastards', 'Whore-gets', 'Buggers', 'Sods' and 'Bloodys' would roar out like an over-volumed wireless set.

For instance, you'd never see girls' or women's knickers hanging out on the clothes-line, no matter how poor and 'cheap' the family was. Knickers were dried in some secret fashion indoors; it's likely that most of the women went about in half-dried drawers, they were that reluctant to show 'em any daylight.

Another piece of this woman-code was when they'd had some argument or disagreement with a person in authority, such as the rent man, the Means Test man, or somebody up at the town hall. They'd go into every detail of what *he* said – 'he said this, he said that' – and at the end of it all they'd say proudly, 'Mind you, ah didn't say any thing – *but yoh should have seen the bloody look I give him.*' Sometimes one woman would call upon another, troubled about an event which was scheduled to take place some nine months hence.

'Ah want's yoh're advice,' would be the opening preamble, in a low voice which you could hear from upstairs if you kept your ears tuned. 'Ah wants yoh're advice about last night.'

'Last night?'

'Ar. Last night. Yoh knows.'

'Now let's see … now, ah don't quite get what yoh'm on about …?'

'Yoh *knows*.'

'Ah doh. Yoh'll atta tell me a bit more.'

Pause. Then –

'Well, yoh knows ah've got five kids.…'

'Ar. I do know that. And yoh *does* look after them, ah will say that.'

'That's not what ah'm on about.' The woman needing the advice would look meaningfully at any menfolk or kids in the room before giving the key to the code.

'My bloke comes home drunk last night, while ah was in bed. Now do you see?'

The penny would drop, and the adviser would nod sagely, and herd the kids out of the room, menfolk as well if she could exercise any authority over them. If not, the two women would go across to the brew-house.

Our young ferret-like ears would home in on the conversation. 'He did it, see,' the seeker of advice would explain, 'and there was no, er, what you might call precautions. No precautions, see.'

The other woman would nod, make tutting noises with her tongue. 'Yoh can't stop 'em having it,' she'd say, referring to the men, 'unless yoh cuts it off for 'em. But yoh'd think they'd tek like what yoh said, precautions, like.'

'Ar.'

'When bist yoh due?'

'The monthly curse, yoh mean?'

'Ar.'

'Next week, ah think. At least by my reckoning.'

'Ar, well. We'll have to wait and see, won't us. If yoh misses, yoh'll know yoh've clicked. Now if yoh *have* clicked, what yoh've got to do is get a half pint o' gin, put it in a saucepan and let it simmer gently. Yoh has to be careful, otherwise it'll set on fire, just like petrol. Now when the gin is hot, yoh has to put a cabbage leaf in – the greener the better – and let it stand overnight. Next day, drink it all down. All in one go. It'll mek yoh feel a bit tipsy, of course, but drink it at a time when yoh can have a lie down for a couple of hours. The gin and the cabbage leaf 'ull stop it.'

If the woman concerned hadn't got the money for the gin, she'd make a bundle up of some odds and ends and pop them at 'Uncles', the pawn shop.

But if any of us kids had listened in on the conversation between the two women, a gang of us 'ud be sitting on a fold-wall waiting for her husband to come along. As soon as he was level with us we'd all shout at him, 'Yoh're missus is going to have a babby,' and run like hell before his dropped-jawed amazement turned into anger.

Caggy and me were mooching about the street where the whore lived – (we pronounced it to rhyme with 'war'; we'd come across the word in the Bible at school, and a bunch of us stood round the word, as it were, sniggering; grown-ups called it ' 'Oo-er'. So if one of us fell foul of a grown-up and got a tongue or belt lowking we could get our own back by calling him or her a rude word. We'd rub the sore part of our bodies and say 'Oooo-er' as if in pain, but our minds inside gloated over the fact we were calling the offender a Whore).

We were going past her house when her front door opened, and there she stood. Pretty as a picture and dressed to the nines. 'You boys want to earn a shilling?' she called, and Caggy and me stopped dead in our tracks, half-scared to death. 'I just want you to help me move a sideboard,' she said, 'it's a bit too heavy for me.' She laughed, and added – 'I haven't got a man about the house at the moment.'

Caggy and me went inside with her. It was posh and scented, a nice smell of scent everywhere. Thick carpets on the floor, and she asked us to take our shoes off and leave them in the passage before going into the room where the sideboard was. It wasn't really heavy, just awkward to get hold of. The three of us eventually got it where she wanted it.

'You're strong, both of you,' she said, and we puffed our chests out like bantam-pigeons. She gave us the shilling, then added another sixpence. From a drawer in the sideboard she took a block of chocolate, broke it into exact halves, giving each of us an equal portion. We went back into the passage and put our boots on. She opened the door for us and as we went past her she stooped and gave us both a sudden kiss. She put mine on the cheek, but caught Caggy full on the lips.

'Thanks, boys,' she called after us; and then, laughing – 'P'raps I'll still be around in about ten years' time, if you're passing.' We couldn't fathom the meaning of that. Caggy was a bit frightened, having been kissed on the mouth.

'What'll happen if she has a babby?' he asked. I stared at him in amazement.

'You don't get babby's by *kissing*,' I told him; and I told him the facts of life in full.

He was very thoughtful on the way home.

'When I grow up,' he said, 'I'm going to marry a whore. They look better and they smell better than the ordinary sort.'

We sat on a wall and ate our chocolate, and agreed not to tell our mams that we'd had any, nor that we'd got ninepence apiece. The coming Saturday there was a Tom Mix cowboy film on at the Odeon, and we decided we'd go and see it.

We sat on the wall chewing the brown melting sweetness. The wall was part of a lane which we called the Cliff, because it was high. From it we could see the heart-pulses of the Black Country, although the pulses were now weak and at low ebb. We could see the iron-foundries and glass-works, the strange mutilations of geographical areas where brick-kilns and pit-heads jostled shoulder to shoulder with small wild patches of natural beauty in the shape of handkerchief-sized meadows, fields and wooded coppice-land; we could see the dark sombre canals running alongside clean streams which sprang from the earth, and often the cough-making tuberculosis in men's lungs clashed with the song of free-winging linnets, high up in the skies. We sat and chewed our whore's chocolate and gazed out at a world of sweat and toil and throbbing iron, little patches of these still, despite the unemployment; a world sometimes of hunger, vice and darkness, and desperate poachers stalking the woods of Wordsley. We looked out at our world, looked down on it, this my boyhood land. And I knew then how much I hated and loved it, both emotions tangled up together, like tangled balls of wool of different colours.

Caggy kept fidgeting on the wall, brushing flakes of chocolate from his trousers. They were new. I looked at them and envied them, my own being patched and mended. Caggy had once tried to give me a pair of trousers that he'd finished with, but I turned on him savagely and wouldn't have anything to do with him for weeks after. He saw me looking at his new trousers. He finished his chocolate, jumped down from the wall.

'Come on,' he said.

'Where to?'

'To see some monty-sods up at Hagley.'

'What for?'

'Yoh'll see.'

Off we set for a good five miles' walk there, and another back. A round trip of ten miles. Once we were clear of the built-up areas we felt freer, light-hearted, with sunlight dancing through our blood and through our senses. We cut stout sticks with Caggy's bowie-knife, and used them as walking sticks, like we'd seen hikers do. Once, we passed a gypsy settlement at the side of a lane. The caravans were shaped a bit like the prairie waggons in the cowboy films, but the gypsy ones were nicer to look at. They were painted all over, just like the canal barges, and brass-headed coach bolts shone like jewels as the sun glanced off them. Horses were picketed at the grass verge, cropping the grass and at the same time feeding the next crop by dropping blobs of manure. Bare-footed kids mixed in and out of the caravans. Caggy and me crossed to the other side of the lane to get past, but we idled and stared with curiosity. The women were dark haired, dark skinned, as were the men. The weather of summers and winters had burned them brown. Most of the women wore their hair braided, in pigtails, sleek and glossy as if the strands had been combed in oil. The men idled around, scarcely giving us a passing glance. They were light men, light and lithe, but the corded muscle of their arms gave indication of how strong they were, how tough. Some of the women were squatting round a pile of thin willow-tree branches, making clothes-pegs which they would hawk from house to house in the nearest town or village. Their fingers were quick and sure and urgent, and the idle men watched them, puffing at clay or hand-made pipes. A delicious smell of herbs came to us as we lingered, wild herbs plucked and dried for smoking. Sitting on the stoop of one of the caravans was an old woman, an old crone, also smoking a clay pipe. Caggy and me decided there and then, in whispers, that she was a witch. All of the women seemed to be wearing black, dark skirts – but each had some blaze of colour, like a scarlet shawl made from wool, or wooden clogs painted with designs like the caravans, or a bodice embroidered in coloured silks and pearly beads sewn on. All the women wore heavy brass earrings, as did one or two of the men. Some of the gypsy dogs bristled and snarled as we drew abreast at the other side of the road, but a curt word from one of the men startled them into silence. The man called for us to wait a minute, and we were nervous of him as he came across. His mouth smiled at us in friendship, but his eyes were quick and darting, taking in every inch of us. His accent, when he spoke, was different to any I'd heard, and it took a bit of time before our minds could tune in with him.

'Where you going?' he asked, only it sounded like 'Werra ya gorn.'

'Just walking,' I answered; 'just having a walk around.'

He nodded, eyes looking past us – not 'shifty', but wide awake and alert.

'Who owns yon woods?' he asked, pointing.

We told him.

'Hast he any keepers?' the gypsy wanted to know, and all of a sudden I felt relaxed and easy, as if I could read the man's mind and found it was in tune with mine. Fear of the man went away, and I felt that I *knew* him from hundreds of years back.

'He's got no keepers,' I told him, 'but he's got four men working for him. They usually take it in turns to "keep" the woods and the spinneys, and they carry twelve-bore shot-guns when they do. One barrel, not two. Now, see that tree? Just to the left is a spinney. That's where he raises his pheasants. Not many. Just enough for him and his mates.'

The gypsy eyes were laughing into mine, strangely blue and clear as a calm sea which had good depth to it. The man squatted onto his haunches, and Caggy and me did the same. I took a piece of stick and drew a map of the area in the ground, showing the man where farms lay, how they were protected, how many keepers, how many dogs; for good measure I told him where each policeman's house was, and the times of the night when he could expect the police to be at their most alert. I gave him all the information I'd got stored in my head, and all the time his eyes laughed into mine, as if he too had known me before my life began. When I'd finished he stood up, looked down at me, jaunty and nature-arrogant. He said something loud and clear in a language Caggy and me didn't know, like a chant it was, and all the time he said it he'd got one of my hands caught between the two of his.

Caggy was scared. 'It's the gypsies' curse he's putting on you,' he whispered to me, as the man turned to go.

The man heard him. 'Not so,' he said, 'it was the gypsies' blessing.'

The blessing must have worked, because when we got to Hagley Caggy's purpose in taking me there became crystal-clear. Just on the outskirts of the village was a posh house with a wide, long back lawn. Washing was spread out on the clothes line.

'Wait for me in the hedge,' Caggy hissed, and slipped away from me. I saw him appear among the washing on the line, and then he was back with me in a flash, urging me to 'run like the clappers of hell and devil takes the hindermost'. We ran. I don't know what for; nobody was chasing us or shouting after us. After half a mile of running, Caggy let up, and we slowed to a walk. He'd got a bundle of clothes jumbled up under his arm, and he pushed the bundle at me. I unrolled the stuff, and saw a pair of almost brand-new trousers that would fit me nicely, a good shirt with an *attached* collar, and buttons on the cuffs, and a jersey. I thanked Caggy humbly and he grinned at me, cock-of-the-walk.

When I got home I told my mam that the stuff had been given to me by one of my school-mate's mom, because he'd grown out of them. I reckoned my mam knew the truth, though, because she dyed them from grey into brown before letting me wear them.

Chapter Seven

I reckon even now I could live off the land as a poacher. I had good teachers, the world's best. Black Country men all, with long ancestral memories and skills to call on. I trained under old Conquer Rabbit – he reckoned he'd conquer any rabbit this side the size of an elephant. I remember how he got his name, or at least I was told about it. His brother was a bit on the dull-witted side and when the pair of them sat down to table he wasn't quick enough a time or two in scooping other than potatoes and gravy into his bowl. After two or three such disappointments, he raised objections.

'Dun yoh know,' he said, 'theer's someat wrong somewheer. Yoh gets all the meat and I only gets the gravy and spuds.'

Big Brother winked at him.

'It's alright, our kid,' he soothed, 'yoh conquer the spuds and ah'll conquer the rabbits.'

The name tagged on. Conquer Rabbit. But everybody called him Konk for short.

In those pre-war days rabbit stews were plentiful for those who had the ability to go out poaching … but woe betide the 'ockard bugger', the awkward non-expert who tried to capture feather, fin or fur. The keepers and police were sharp as weasels, and there was ever a queue outside the magistrate's court. Most families whose men were out of work had to make do with gruetty-puddings or bony stew. Two penn'orth of dog bones from the butcher, let 'em simmer till nigh on melted, then potatoes added and thick heavy suet dumplings. Mothers would encourage their offsprings to get bulk into their bellies by saying – 'Them as eats most dumplings gets most meat'; and the kids would get stuck into the potatoes and dumplings, racing each other for the prize of meat which didn't exist. But even if it *had* of been there, there'd have been no room in their bellies for it. Mothers of the slump days were crafty, and did their best.

Black Country men never call meat 'meat'; they always call it 'mate'. Old Konk used to tell me a story time after time, thinking each time was the first. He said there was a bloke fishing along the cut-side and all of a sudden he races along the towpath and grabs a copper. 'Quick,' he says, 'my mate's just fell in the river.' The policeman went with him to the spot, took his tunic and helmet off, and went in. He swam around for a bit without finding anything, then swam to the bank and clambered out all dripping wet. 'I cor see him,' he said, shivering with cold. 'Wheer'd yoh say your mate fell in about.'

'It's not a him, it's an it,' said the fisherman. 'Me mate's in the cut. It fell off me bread.'

Konk roared with laughter every time he told me, till the tears ran down his face. He was full of tales, quirks, tall stories and half jokes. He told me one about the Great War, in which he fought.

'There was me and Eli standing guard on the firing step,' he said, 'with the battalion of the Staffordshire Regiment at rest in the trenches. Then all of a sudden Eli gives me a nudge – whass up, I ask him. Eli puts his mouth near my earhole. Yoh knows that young officer what's joined us, he says, do yoh reckon he tells the truth? Why shouldn't he, I says back, he's an officer, in't he ... Well, whispers Eli, do you reckon he was a telling the truth when he said he'd give erra one of us a pound note for every Hun soldier we captured alive? Ar, I says, I reckon he's an officer, and he'll keep his word. Eli puts his finger to his lips. Ssshhh! he says, – doh wake t'others up, 'cos there's ten thousand quid's worth coming towards us right now.'

I'd heard that one before, but thought it concerned Irishmen. 'Not on your bloody life,' Konk said. 'The Irish pinched it off the Black Country. Like they pinched most things,' he added, 'including the reputation of being the best navvies in the world. 'Twarn't so. The best navvies came from here. Strapping fella's, my feyther and his afore him worked as navvies. They'd only let the Irish do the scivvy-work. But the navvy was the man, big and bold and didn't give a cuss for owt. Shift twenty ton of muck in a day's stint, with nothing but pick and shovel … but they'm scattered now, such men as them. They moved on to America, or Canada, or other places.'

Konk was proud of being a Black Country man. He was a mine of information about its history. It was in the mid-'thirties when I knew him, and he was turned sixty, then. So he was born in the late eighteen-'sixties, early 'seventies; and through his father and grandfather in turn, could span direct memories back to the start of the nineteenth century. Almost the dawn of the Industrial Revolution.

'I'm telling yoh,' he said, 'the British army was bogged down at Sebastopol, and they wanted a railway building, to get supplies up. And over a thousand Black Country men went over on the boats, and they built that railway with a shovel in one hand and a musket in t'other. And while they was there, they killed more bloody enemy soldiers than our regular army did.'

Another time he told me:

'Yoh've read about the Roundheads and Ironsides at school, haven't you? Yoh've read about the battle of Worcester? Well, what the books don't tell you is that it was meant to be the battle of Birmingham. Only the Black Country men got fed up with two armies squaring off at each other on their own doorstep, and they marched out on 'em with picks and shovels and palings of wood and drove the buggers off. So they had their punch-up at Worcester instead of Brum. Not that I've any use for Brummies,' he said, spitting.

Many's the time, for the odd pheasant or rabbit, I'd stand guard for Konk and the two Tolley brothers he took with him from Silver End. The three of them went after the game together, with me tagging on like an afterthought. We went for pheasants, rabbits – anything reasonably portable which could be skinned, plucked, roasted, boiled, fried or sold. Most of the pre-war Black Country men worked in small gangs; at one time they even paid into a fund so's fines could be paid when they got tumbled by police or gamekeepers.

The youngest Tolley, Benny, was twenty-three and his brother Pope (my dad's mate) was ten years older. They were rough, tough hilly-billy's who would run a mile to get into a fight and laugh like madmen in between punches. They were strapping 'bostin' men. Benny stood about six feet, but Pope topped him by two inches. They had chain-strikers' muscles, muscles which twitched and rippled like boa-constrictors trying to shed skin. Yet Konk was the recognized leader – not because he was bigger, he wasn't; it was just that he knew more about rabbits and pheasants than the pheasants and rabbits did themselves.

Old Konk was strict about one thing, though, and that was guns. He wouldn't allow guns – shot-guns or air guns – on any of his operations. Catapults (flirters, we called them), sling-shots, nets, snares, clubs, strangle wires, clappers – yes. Guns, no. But he did welcome a good trained and disciplined dog, like a lurcher or Staffordshire terrier. He'd never own one himself, but he encouraged the others to get and train them. It was Pope told me that Konk gave up having dogs some years back, when the keepers shot the one he'd got. According to Pope, the dog – a Staffordshire terrier – was more than three parts human; and when the keeper shot it, the others had to hold Konk back because he would have done for the keeper. Pope said that Konk's dog would carry game as gentle as a retriever, without bruising the flesh, and that it would drive hares into a net and pounce on them before they could scream. And it could smell keepers a mile off, giving warning so that the men could pull out. Once, the dog brought down an assistant keeper by nipping at his ankles. But the best thing of all, when the night's bag was over, the dog would take a different direction home from the men and pretend not to recognise any of them if they chanced to meet on the homeward journey. Konk had spent days and months training the dog, and deliberately chose to train a terrier because that was about the last specimen that a keeper would expect. When the keeper *did* tumble it he put two barrels of twelve-bore into its back, breaking it but not killing it. The dog lay moaning, and Konk tried to get at the keeper but the others held him back, and the keeper slunk off because he was suddenly afraid. One of the men finished the dog off quick and neat with his skinning knife, and Konk would never own a dog after that. He used to tell me about the 'lawing of the dogs', I think it was called, way back in the twelfth or thirteenth century; when the King's men used to go round the country to literally 'put 'em through the hoop'. The hoops were of a certain size, and if a dog could pass through it easily, it was okayed. But if it couldn't, if it were too big to pass through the hoop, then the King's men would produce a sort of wooden clog with the front end open. Then they'd put one of the dog's front paws in it, and cut half of it off with an axe. The idea was that if it were above a certain size, the dog could be used to hunt the King's game. With half a foot missing, it couldn't....

Konk welcomed a good dog along, but it had to be a good 'un before he'd let it 'come for a walk in the moonlight'. The devil of it was, once you got to rely on a dog, farmers and keepers took to shooting them at the least provocation. Time was when the dogs needed more protection than virgin daughters. See, the excellence of a dog was in its groundspeed. It would raise a hare, head it into the waiting nets, pounce on it and quieten it before it could scream. Rabbits never screamed ... but my golly, a hare would scream like a banshee sitting on a splinter if you didn't muffle it in time. And if the keepers were staked out in the woods, waiting, they'd hear it clear as a fire alarm, and move in.

Konk wasn't a big man, but he was tight-muscled and strong. And like other men of the district he was filled with inarticulate rebellion, rebellion of the 'have-nots' against the 'haves'. Yet men like Konk and the Tolleys, and to some extent my dad, well, they merely stepped back a couple of hundred years in time, into history. And did what their forebears did. They lived off the land; whose land didn't matter a damn.

'There's a little bit of larceny in all of us,' Konk would tell me, dead serious, but the laughter-lines round his eyes creeping about like ferrets.

'My oath,' he'd say, 'me and a good many more fought for this bit o' land, so we'm entitled to a bit of the fruit from it. Never mind if the fruit's got feathers on.

Konk did a bit of bird catching on the side, like my dad did. Konk knew I didn't like to see the birds captured … it wasn't the capturing of them which hurt me, it was the absolute captivity which followed. The imprisonment. I wanted only to hold and touch, and then let go again.

'Birds in cages, or lions or tigers,' Konk muttered, 'I don't call the tune, me lover. I only pays the Piper. A man's got to live.' Konk taught me one thing – that poaching game (or 'filling the pantry' as we called it) was an art. Not just a matter of stopping your car in a quiet lane, lifting a twelve-bore at a road-strutting pheasant, and picking the pieces up after. Nor was it stopping a truck near a farmer's meadow, dropping the tail-gate, shooing a dozen sheep in, then high-tailing it for London at fifty miles an hour. That was *thieving*.

Poaching was *man*.

But to me, poaching was *boy*. I poached with the men because my legs were fast and my body slight. I could hide in the shadow cast by a blade of grass; I'd got a pair of eyes the gypsies called 'lucky eyes', I'd got extra-wide vision. I could sense the slightest sound that smelled of danger to our pantry-filling, and my eyes locked onto the slightest movement. I learned a trick early on – in the dark, if you think there's something there, don't look at it direct. Look at it slightly to one side, and whatever it is, man, animal or object, will come into focus. If you stare hard at what you think is there, your eyes will blur and you'll end up seeing nothing until a keeper's shot-gun touches you in the back, or he catches you a wallop with his club.

But mostly I could see the movement of a keeper out in the darkness almost afore he made it … and I could pipe my warning to my fellows then flash off in an opposite direction, drawing the keepers with me, while the men flitted away with the sacks and the nets.

Some keepers weren't too bad. If they caught you first time round, they'd warn you off. Second time round they'd spoil your nets. Third time round, it was the high jump in the magistrate's court, and thirty days in

Brummagum jail. Yet other keepers were vicious, hard when they had no cause to be. There was one up at Wordsley woods – him and two more caught a poacher on his own, and beat him black and blue. So from time to time we'd poach his credit and his reputation. When a keeper killed a stoat, weasel, a crow or any other form of carrion, he'd hang the skin or carcass on a bit of wire, just like washing on a clothes line. Then when the master of the land came round, he'd want to see the keeper's credit – the amount of non-game vermin he'd killed. The keeper would show him the skins and carcasses, and if they were a fairish quantity the owner would know that his keeper was on his toes. And the owner was no fool – the keeper couldn't keep any credits over from one visit to the next, the owner would know all right. Anyway, from time to time the men would take a walk over to Wordsley and pinch the credits (and by implication, the keeper's reputation) so that when the gaffer came round he'd see next to nothing hanging from the wire, and think his man was flagging.

As well as using nets for hares and birds, we used them to take partridges as they slept in covey. Two men would hold the outer edges of a long net, a third holding the rear end, in the middle to prevent it snagging. You'd come up-wind of the birds, quiet as a drifting feather yourselves, then the moment you heard the first fluttering of wings scrabbling to take off, you'd all drop the net and capture, on average, a dozen partridges. For woodcock you had to stretch nets between two trees, at an angle to the ground, and in direct line of flight of the woodcock when they were deliberately raised from their perches. Their own speed entangled them in the meshes of the nets, and then it was a matter of picking them out.

To catch rabbits, Konk used small purse-nets or clapper-nets – nets which consisted of two hinged halves which would snap shut as the rabbit entered. For 'slow' traps we used strong wooden pegs, twelve to eighteen inches long, pointed at one end to be driven into the ground. Then a running noose of baling-wire (piano wire was best; if you could get it) was fastened to the peg, and the noose opened out wide enough for a rabbit's head and neck to pass into. These 'slow' traps were then fixed in front of the rabbits' bury, covered with twigs and bits of grass. They were called 'slow' traps because the results weren't immediate. You'd set the traps one day, then go back the next to see what you'd caught. But an additional risk was that a keeper might be waiting for you, having spotted the traps for himself; or if a rabbit had strangled itself in the running-noose, stoats or weasels might get to it before you yourself did.

With Konk and the Tolleys, I learned that the best way to catch rabbits is when they're all in the bury (or burrow) and not in the open where you have to drive them into the nets, with their white underbellies flashing dangerously clear for a keen-eyed keeper to see them streaking away, and coming across to see what they were running from. Once they're in the buries, you have to block all the exit holes up except two. By the one stands the poacher with a club. Down the other, a ferret is passed on a long line. Long before the ferret reaches the centre, the rabbits are panicking to get out – they rush for the exits, turn and twist as they find them blocked, then make a beeline for the only one left open. As they come out, the club gets them. No noise, no white bellies showing up against the fields, no pain, no suffering. Thump, thump, thump. And there'll be rabbit stew tomorrow. Your own belly rumbles in anticipation.

I liked working the ferrets, perhaps because I liked the creatures themselves. Yellow and brown-flecked, they blended with almost any background. Pink eyes, ever twitching nose, small heads and long sleek bodies – close brothers to stoat and weasel. But if you didn't handle them right, they'd have your fingers off. Once a ferret drew blood, if a buck rabbit got cornered there under the ground and tried to fight his way past, the ferret would go for his throat. And once he'd done that, he'd do it every time. So Konk used to put a small leather muzzle on the 'killer' ferret, like a whippet's muzzle cage, and that way the ferret couldn't kill. But likewise he couldn't fight back if he cornered up with a rat … I saw one of Konk's best ferrets come back up dying, his throat ripped by a rat. Some poachers preferred to send their ferrets down 'free', that is without lines; this allowed them to have free range of the inner bury, and there was no risk of the line tangling with perhaps a hidden root. But often when a ferret was allowed to free-range, he wouldn't come out. He was maybe stuck, or down there gorging himself. So then it was a tough choice whether to let him stay, or get a shovel and dig him out. If you had to dig, you left signs which even a blind keeper could read.

Before we poached at nights the lie of the land had to be explored by day. Young Tolley did this, taking a girl with him so they could saunter arm-in-arm like lovers through woods and spinneys; but the Tolley eyes would be ploughing the ground and foliage for smoots of hares, rabbit-runs and the droppings of pheasants. Everything he saw would enter map-like into his memory, and moon or none to light the way he would bring us to that fertile place. If it were hares, we'd up the nets on the opposite side of the smoots (those gaps in the hedges which are a hare's 'right of way') then pincer round the wind and drive them against the wind. When a hare makes for his smoot he'll never go direct; he'll always angle up to it, this way and that, criss-cross and overlap, weighing the safety up. Then, when he's sure the way is clear he'll go through like a thunderbolt – with old Konk waiting on him as he struck the net. Konk, always swift and clean, never brutal. And Konk always carried a bit of fresh sheep-pelt with him, scrounged from the slaughter yard at Brierley Hill. He'd rub the pelt over the net-pegs, round the smoot, obliterating all smell of human presence.

We used nets for pheasants, too. Nets on long poles, spread out like tennis-nets. Gently push them up in front of the roosting pheasants, then startle them into sudden flight so that they hit the nets in a tangle and the whole lot rained down, so that all was left to do was click their necks and pop them into the hungry sacks. If birds were plentiful in the pheasant line, and there was no wind and no presence of keepers to spring us, we'd burn sulphur under the roostings. The fumes rose and partly stupefied them. Then we'd have our pole tackle ready to take them. The poles were long, like fishing rods, with a length of thin wire running up the full length of them, leaving a loop at the top end before returning back down the pole to the right hand of the poacher. The poles were gently thrust upwards to where the stupefied birds huddled, the wire loops dropped gently over their heads then the wire was pulled sharp to tighten the noose, and down would come bird after bird in this fashion. You could strip a branch of a dozen dozing birds, one after the other, as easily as taking apples off an unresisting tree. 'Crowing time' was the best time of the year to take pheasants, the months of February and March. Nights often sharp with frost or muffled in mists. If the frost was hard, we had to be careful not to cross open spaces, since our footprints would be impressed on the ground.

Another thing Konk wouldn't allow on the night-runs was bird-lime. This was a sticky black substance, and if it were smeared on roost-perches or on sprigs and twigs among the feeding grounds, birds – large and small – would tangle up in it. It would get into their feathers, stopping them from flight. Konk wouldn't use the stuff because he said it was cruel, that the birds could still run and hide, but would be prey for stoats or weasels, being ground-tied as they were.

One time – winter it was, with deep snow underfoot – Konk took me over Kinver woods. We walked well against the hedges so that our footprints didn't stand out like a grin on a blackman's face. Konk had got a bottle with him, an empty wine bottle with a slow-tapering neck. We saw pheasant droppings in the snow. 'Sithee, me lover,' Konk said; and I watched as he pushed the bottle neck-first into the snow, until its glass bottom were level with the surface. Gently he pulled the bottle out, leaving its hollow upside-down impression there. He scattered a few raisins and grains of corn near the hole, with a stepping-stone-trail leading up to it. Then he poured half a handful into the mould, and the pair of us went and hid among the hedges. After a while a cock-pheasant came for the bait. He pecked it up, dainty as a girl stepping out to her first dance. Nearer and nearer it came to the hole, put its head inside, clucked and gobbled at the contents. But, as the amount of feed grew lower and lower it had to stretch its neck deeper in. Then what Konk anticipated, happened. The bird lost balance, over-toppled. It was jammed there with its feathered behind waving at the sky. Konk grinned, pulled it out and clicked its neck, then stuck it in an inside pocket which was half as big as a haversack.

We were poachers for all seasons; on windy dark nights that gusted the weeping rain, perhaps we were less poachers and more thieves. We kept to open farms, me as look-out, and raided the hen roosts. But too often the farmers had yard dogs on wide looping chains to give the alarm, or a goose among the chickens – and a goose is the best alarm 'dog' you can have. Once it starts its cackle and screeching, any farmer worth his salt will be out of doors at the double, stopping only to pull his boots on and pick up his twelve-bore.

But on clear starlit nights we kept to the spinneys and woods for rabbits and pheasants, loaded down with piano-wire traps and mayhap a ferret or two. The two Tolleys would be quiet, serious, almost as efficient as Konk – and they never drank before 'filling the pantry'. Konk wouldn't wear it. But once the work was done and the game disposed of, what they drank between them would float a canal barge from Kinver Edge to Hagley Wood. Yet none of them was ever nasty tempered in drink, like my dad was.

Well, there came this time when we'd poached the night out and got a good bag, and the day was hard with morning light when we decided to give it best. Konk was deciding how to get the stuff home, and figured it best to get it hidden near the canal tow-path and a mate of his, a bargee still in work, could pick it up and hide it on his barge up to Stewpony lock, where Konk could get it back again – well out of range of keepers. But Benny Tolley put his nose in it proper. Earlier on he thought he'd heard a dog snuffling deep in the thickets and he swiftly sprinkled pepper (which we carried in a leather bag) across what he thought would be the line of attack. Thought it was the keepers, see, with their dogs. If he'd have been right, the dogs would have snuffed in on the scent, picked a cloud of pepper up, then sat down to sneeze it out while we got away. Only the snuffling Benny heard turned out to be a hedgehog, false alarm.

But, as we were coming away from the grounds, Benny slipped and went sprawling and got a faceful of his own pepper ... and it was *him* as did the sneezing. It sounded terrible loud, there in the morning-hushed woods where we'd no right to be. I never saw the policeman come up. I think he'd been mooching about in the vicinity for a long time, trying to get wind of us. It was the sneezing which homed him in, like a pigeon to its loft. Konk and Benny managed to get their masks up before the copper saw their faces. The masks were bandana-like neckerchiefs – almost all the poachers wore them. They covered up their faces if they were in danger of being recognised, knowing full well that positive identification were needed to convict them in the magistrate's court.

Benny Tolley's mask kept flapping and blowing under his sneezes ... the policeman didn't see me. I was hugged into the bushes, well hidden from his first appearance.

Big Tolley, Pope, faced the policeman square on. He was laughing. 'Yoh'm trespassing, John,' he said to him, 'this is private property.' The policeman didn't answer straight away. He was weighing the odds, looking at the two men with masks round the lower parts of their faces.

'Tell yoh're mates to tek them rags off,' he said to Pope. Pope shook his head, no.

'It's yoh're business, not mine,' he answered. 'Meself, ah'm only here waiting for a tram.'

'Tek them rags off,' the policeman said to Konk and Benny, going towards them as if he were going to do it for himself. Pope stood in front of him. The policeman hesitated.

'Ah know who they are, anyroad,' he said at last. 'It's old Konk and yoh're kid, Benny.'

'But you can't swear on it,' Pope told him. 'Thinkin's not evidence, me lover.' The policeman put his hand down towards his tunic skirt, reaching for a side pocket in his trousers. Pope Tolley shook his head.

'Ah wouldn't, John,' he said, 'not if ah was you. If ah was you, ah'd leave that bit of wood in my pocket. Otherwise ah shall bend the bloody thing round your head.' I could tell the policeman didn't like the odds. Not three to one and devil take the hindermost.

I knew the copper – he'd lifted my dad a time or two. He was only young, but by God he was keen. Big built, he was, and able to tame any Saturday night boozer punch-up. Both him and Pope stood well over the six-foot mark in their stockinged feet ... and I knew it was corning. Pope nodded his head as if agreeing with somebody, but it could have only been agreement with his own thoughts, because nobody else had spoken.

'Will you fight me, John?' he asked the policeman. The copper considered, not liking it, but thinking mayhap he stood to risk with all three of them if he couldn't come to some agreement.

'Ah'll fight *you*,' he said to Pope, 'if t'others 'ull keep out on it.' Pope nodded, stripped his coat off. The policeman shrugged out of his cape and tunic, folded them and put them down. He put his helmet on top, then he drew his truncheon and handcuffs and laid them alongside. The two of them closed … and the simple truth of it is that Pope was the better man. He swung hard and fast with his fists until the policeman couldn't get up and stand; but then Pope did a very silly thing.

He threw his head back just like a fighting cock and *crowed*. Then he picked the policeman's truncheon up and hurled it away through the trees. But even this wouldn't have been so bad if he hadn't of picked up the handcuffs, clapped the bracelets round the dazed man's wrists, locked them and sent the key spinning after the truncheon.

'Yoh'll have some mithering to do when yoh gets back to the station,' Pope said, wiping blood from his cut mouth. 'Ah bet yoh'll never hang *yoh're* head up again.'

Pope and Benny slipped away through the woods, taking some of the bag with them, leaving the rest for Konk and me. The policeman clambered and splayed to his feet unsteadily, hands manacled in front of him. I came from hiding and stood loyally with Konk. 'He shouldn't a' done it,' Konk said, flaming mad and angry. 'Pope shouldn't a' done it. Shouldn't have handcuffed him, it should a' stayed a fair fight. The copper would have let it stood at that, it was fair till Pope buggered it up. Now the bloody blue-bottles 'ull be hiding under our beds o' nights.' I helped him to search for the handcuff key, but it was lost forever. I thought Konk would have moved on home then; but no, he didn't. He put the policeman's helmet back onto his head, fastened his cape round him in the now shivering woods. Then he folded the man's tunic and gave it to me to carry. He helped and supported the policeman out of the woods and along the tow-path of the canal, to get him back to his station by the quietest route. When early morning workmen passed, Konk tried to save the copper from embarrassment by pretending to be handcuffed to him; but it must have looked a bit queer even to a half blind man, because neither Konk nor the policeman seemed to notice that Konk's face was still half-covered by his mask.

I walked behind like a puppy-dog, carrying the policeman's tunic.

Well, the police didn't come for Konk. They left him alone. But they went after the two Tolleys and there was such a riot it took nigh on a dozen of them to manage it. Pope drew the heaviest sentence, he got sent down for eighteen months' hard labour. His brother Benny caught twelve months' of the same.

And there was no more poaching with Konk. He packed it in. The only real poaching we ever did after that, other than the odd 'accidental' touch, was to sit on his back step and talk about it. I don't think he ever put hand to net after that, nor threaded a ferret from a line, or came up-wind at the back of a sleep of pheasants.

'It's all done with,' he brooded, dark inside himself. 'The good poaching days am over and done with, me lover. It's gone when they starts playing tricks on the Law like that. Pope finished it. The copper lost in a fair fight – ar, and he'd a been fust to admit it. But Pope dirtied it. He dirtied every hare and pheasant and rabbit this side of the bloody pantry …'

I know one thing. It must have broken old Konk's heart every time he passed a coin across a butcher's counter – and not for the sake of parting with the coin, either. Because Old Konk was a craftsman who adhered to the rules; but, as far as he was concerned, once the rules were broken, the game was over.

Chapter Eight

This once, a thing called Opportunity gave a thumping big knock on our front door, and came in and sat down. It stayed with us for almost a month, then left and never came back again.

It happened with dad coming home with a pony and trap. Not really a horse trap, but a sort of light cart with two seats up front. Dad got permission to keep the horse and trap in a field just the other side of the railway track, and there was a falling-down barn for him to put the trap in. Once he'd got the horse and trap into the field, dad rummaged around with paint tins and brushes, sending me to Woolworth's to buy a thre'penny can of yellow paint, and six pennyworth of nigger-brown dyes which were usually used for dying clothes.

When I got back with the stuff, dad had put his paint tins and brushes into a bucket, and he motioned me to follow him. We went over the wooden railway bridge (footer-bridge, we called it) and into the field where the horse and cart were. Dad gave me some rags, half a bottle of turpentine, and some sandpaper. He told me to clean the cart all over, wheel-spokes as well, and then to give the paintwork a rub down with the sandpaper to take the gloss off the existing paint. The cart was painted blue and white. I got to work as ordered, seeing my dad gathering sticks to make a fire and wondering what for. As I worked away at the cart, I watched him. He'd got a good fire going at the side of the shed where he couldn't easily be seen by passing loafers, and he fetched water in the bucket from the horse trough, which was filled to overflowing. Then dad boiled the bucket of water over the fire. From time to time he came over to see how I was doing, pointing out bits and patches that I'd missed.

Then, when the bucket of water was bubbling away I saw him take the packets of nigger-brown dyes and pour the stuff into the boiling water. He stirred it all in with a stick. Then he brought the bucket into the bam and set it down to cool. I carried on working, but watched him as he rolled a cigarette and stood there smoking it. When he'd finished he carefully pinched out the glowing end between thumb and forefinger, and put the butt-end back into his tobacco tin. He took the paint, tipped it into a bigger can, added a drop of turpentine for thinners, and stirred it well. Satisfied, he came over to me with paint can in one hand and paint brush in the other. 'Now,' says he, 'paint every bit of that trap yellow. Don't miss a bit. All yellow, see? Don't spread it on too thick, else there'll not be enough to go round. But at the same time, doh get missing any bits.' I took the brush and paint and got to work without questioning him. The set of his jaw told me I'd get no answers, anyroad.

I got to work with the yellow paint, completely obliterating the true colour of blue and white. While I worked, dad fetched the horse – more of a pony than a horse – into the bam. The animal was dirty-grey in colouring, and I watched in amazement as dad started to change all that. He got a wad of rags, dipped the wad into the bucket of dye, and rubbed it into the pony's coat. Gradually the dirty-grey colour disappeared – it seemed to me the whole bloody pony disappeared and a new one took its place. When dad had finished, a nigger-brown horse stood there, with just a fleck of grey in tail and mane, front socks, and a small blaze on its forehead. Dad tethered the pony to the side of the bam.

'Yoh'll have to stand theer for an hour or two till yoh'm dry,' he muttered; and then he took the brush and paint from me and finished the cart job off.

We'd started out with a dirty-grey pony and a blue and white trap; we ended up with a nigger-brown pony and a yellow cart.

My old man pointed a finger at me.

'Mouth shut, yoh,' he said. 'If yoh breathes a word of this to erra body, ah'll break every bloody bone in yoh're body. Sithee?'

I nodded. We packed our tools together in silence, and went back home. A while later, maybe three or four hours, I had to go back with him to the barn where the pony was, its re-coloured coat now dry and natural-looking. Dad took a bottle of almost white stuff from his pocket.

'Coconut oil,' he said, pouring some onto his palm. 'Now ah'll work this side, and yoh work that – and rub the stuff well in. Leave his head to me. Yoh might get some of this stuff into his eyes, else.' He started to rub the oil into the pony's coat, and I did the same my side. When we'd finished, the pony's hide gleamed like gun-steel. Sleek it looked, sleek and shiny. It snickered warmly as I stroked its head, pushing its nose into my neck. Dad was lifting its hooves, one by one, peering at them and muttering. Suddenly I heard him say – 'Ah, theer it is.' I walked close to see what was doing, and me dad had got one of the pony's back hooves lifted from the ground.

'Sithee?' he said to me, pointing; and there, burned into the hoof, I could see a number.

'That's it's owner's identification mark,' the dad said. 'And we'll soon bloody well alter that.' He let the hoof rest back on the ground, took a stub of black cobbler's wax from his waistcoat pocket, and a box of matches. He melted the wax into the burned-in number on the horse's hoof, until the whole hoof was smooth and unbroken by any identification marks.

'That cobbler's wax 'ull hold,' he said – only he called it by its old name, 'heel-ball', not 'cobbler's wax' – 'And once it's bin scuffing in the field a bit, it'll tek the shinyness off.' He'd restarted the fire in the barn, got it glowing. Then he put the end of a small soldering-iron into the heat, and when it was red hot he took it out.

'Hold the hosse's head,' he told me, and I took hold of its halter. I winced as dad put the hot iron to the horse's other rear hoof – it smelled like burning bone – but the pony never flinched. The dad finished what he was doing, then piddled on the fire to put it out. 'The hoss couldn't feel anything,' he said. 'Its hoofs am only made of the same sort of stuff yoh're fingernails am made of. Yoh has to go high, into the quick, before yoh can feel anything.' I looked at his branding-work done with the hot soldering-iron. It was a completely different number he'd burned into the hoof. I didn't need a college education for me to know that my dad had pinched both pony and trap.

And I didn't need a religious vow of silence to stop me from telling the dad that I *knew* he'd pinched them.

One thing was for sure, though; they hadn't been stolen locally. My guess was that they'd come from Bromsgrove market, or Kidderminster, or maybe Lichfield over the Potteries way. Or the dad could have lifted it from outside a pub within any part of a twenty-mile radius, while the owner was getting sozzled at the bar, making a dent in his market profits.

Anyroad, the Hill family suddenly went up in the world. We'd got a hoss and cart, which was only one step down from owning a motor-car. Suddenly, too, the Hill household got painted with a miracle. We were still living in the Comper at this time, opposite the skin works. We'd got two rooms downstairs, and a kitchen. We lived and ate in the kitchen – the other two rooms were 'spare'. Which meant they hadn't got any furniture. Well, like I said, this miracle came and lived with us for a bit, after Opportunity had knocked on the front door. The dad was suddenly half a dozen men rolled into one, all of them sober and busy. In the 'spare' room which overlooked the street, he started to fit shelves and a counter. Some of the timber he stole from building sites, other bits and pieces he begged and scrounged. Gradually the 'spare' room became a shop, even down to the detail of a home-made till, and all it lacked was things to sell.

But the dad, determined to earn a 'honest' penny, soon altered that. He took the pony and trap out on a couple of trips, and came back each time loaded up with vegetables stolen from outlying farms. I had to go with him each time and keep watch, and hold the horse still while he loaded the trap up.

So it came about that we started to sell vegetables at about a quarter of the price proper shops were selling at. And mam had a brainwave. She started making meat-faggots and peas with some of the money from the sale of vegetables. The smell of faggots and boiled peas was delicious, and she'd open the front door and some of the windows so that the smell could drift out and about, and bring the customers in. And come they did, with platter dishes, jugs, saucepans, crocks and all.

'Two penn'orth of faggot and peas, missus.'

'Give us a tanner's worth, missus.'

'Missus, me mam says can yoh let her have a shilling's worth and her'll pay yoh at the weekend?'

Mam made the meat-faggots in the kitchen, wrapping the minced meat and chopped onions in cattle membrane bought for next to nothing from the butcher's. Then the faggots and peas were cooked in the boiler-hopper out in the brewhouse, and dished up and sold as required. Hungry men from the skin works started to come in for penny, twopenny or threepenny portions, and trade really started to roar.

Then this one time I came home from school, there was this strange smell. A smell of something new, something I couldn't lay name to. I walked from the kitchen into the 'shop', but there was nothing different there. Then I went to the other 'spare' room, opened the door, and got the wild impression I'd stepped into a green meadow. Everything was green. A green miracle had taken place. Green curtains at the window, green oilcloth on the floor, green sofa and two matching green armchairs. In a corner, a brand new sideboard with a green cloth on it. One big mass of green, with here and there a bit of brown wood showing. It was like stepping into a bloody field. Pieces of newspaper were spaced out on the oilcloth, each a pace away from the other, the idea being that the paper would stop anybody actually treading on the new floor covering. Perched on the edge of an armchair was me mam, with a piece of newspaper under her bottom to prevent the chair getting dirty. In the other chair was me dad, a piece of newspaper under his bottom as well. On the sofa, but without newspaper under their bottoms, were me Aunty Liz and Uncle Jim from Tipton. Me dad's sister and her husband. All four of them were balancing cups and saucers on their knees, sipping tea, all as uncomfortable as somebody who wants to go to the lavatory but is too shy to ask.

'Doh get coming in here,' said me dad, as I stood in the doorway, looking in. 'Yoh'm not to come in here, none of you.'

Mam aided and abetted him, that flattering fawning note in her voice which always made me wince, and always stuck in my mind like the mental tick of a clock. When she was in this sort of mood, and not at loggerheads with dad, you could reckon on a new baby nine months to the day.

'This room's for yoh're dad and me to get a bit of peace away from yoh lot,' she said, 'we doh want you lot under our feet all the time.' Dad grunted his approval, and Aunt Liz and Uncle Jim made sympathetic noises in their direction.

'Put the wood in the hole,' me dad said, 'and bugger off.'

I wished I could bugger off for ever. I wondered then how I'd ever get away. When I'd run away before, earlier on, I'd got no fixed idea in my mind. I'd got no destination, no prospects; if I went off again, I knew I'd get no further than Llangollen, like last time. It seemed only important to get to that place, because my grandad was buried there, my mam's father. A kind beautiful man with a poet's tongue and hands which stroked music into a violin. He'd been dead a long time now, I could hardly remember him, only little wisps of kindness of him and his long white flowing hair and beard, like an ancient Druid; and the way he would dance me round the room or pipe me out into the sudden-changed world with a penny whistle at his lips and the twinkle of Father Christmas in his eyes. My grandad Jones, my own hugging, kissing beautiful kind old man who had gentleness in every ounce of him, in every word of him, in every shadow that he cast upon the ground. I remembered the way I'd catch my hands to his waist as he penny-whistle-piped me into the street, the dismal street, and how other kids would leave off their play and quarrels and string on, hands to waists, like a crocodile of happiness, like my grandad was the Pied Piper of Hamelin. And even grimy neighbours would peep from behind equally grimy curtains and smile, and enjoy some sweet flash of childhood memory for a heartbeat or two.

Sweets he'd bring us, this Welshman who was my mam's dad. Sweets and kindness, and little triangles of cheese wrapped in silver paper. And sometimes, when he looked at how we lived, his brow would frown over, and he'd gently herd us from the room and from behind the closed door we'd hear him speaking sternly with my mam. But it always ended up with her telling him to bugger off back to North Wales, and stop interfering. And away he'd go, sad and gentle, putting shiny new pennies into our eager hands.

If I left home again, North Wales was the only place for me to go. To find his grave and sit by it and talk with the memory of him, and ask him where all the music had gone.

Our faggots-and-peas and vegetable trade flourished for almost a month. What a month. Three Saturdays running, mam and dad went to market with the pony and trap and came back all laden with carrots and potatoes, brussels sprouts, wet-fish for supper, apples, pears, damsons and plums. Into the shop with them, ready for sale. The family of us eating the fried fish for supper, and tea with sugar and proper milk in it instead of condensed milk which had to serve for sweeteners as well as colouring. Three semi-delicious weeks, with storm clouds disappearing behind the horizon. We started to get new things. A shirt here, a pair of boots there, knickers for my sisters so that when they bent over they no longer had to show bare bottoms. Little bits and pieces started to come our way. On top of it all, the mam and dad took to respectable drinking. A glass of stout with their dinners, and a few glasses of whisky before bedtime.

For three weeks not a scold or a shout or a thump up the ears or a kick in the ribs or backside, not a theft from a coal wharf or a farmer's field, not a row in the night with the bits of kitchen furniture being smashed and the mam wailing and screaming and the dad roaring like a bull at a flag.

The kitchen was still a mess, where us kids lived. But it was a mess with a purpose. Faggots and peas to be prepared, pigs trotters to be prepared, tripe and onions to be cooked – oh, yes; the Hills were very much up in the world. True, us kids still weren't allowed in the 'new room' which had got the greenery; but we sometimes had a peer in to make sure we weren't dreaming, and for three weeks it *was* there, every bloody green inch of it.

Then this one Saturday came and mam couldn't go to market with the dad because the latest baby was a bit on the sickly side, so dad went to market on his own.

He didn't come back for a week. He had sold the pony and trap up at the market place and he didn't come home again till he'd pissed every penny of it against the wall. Couple of days later, a furniture van came and took all the green-room away. Armchairs, sideboard, sofa, oilcloth, the lot. The gaffers of the shop repossessed it for non-payment. The vegetables in the room we'd used for the shop had all gone rotten and stank the place out. So me and a couple of younger brothers had to load it all into sacks, stick the sacks on an old trolley-cart we'd made between us, and take the lot over to the rubbish tip.

In less than no time things were back to normal. Squares of ripped up rags round the fire, drying, nappies for the baby. Scoldings, quarrels, bellowings. The old man getting his drink money from some place and staying out till pub-closing time, then coming home to rip the place apart. He came in this time, and mam had got the baby on her lap feeding it titty. She said something to the dad, he snarled back, she shrieked and cussed him, and then he landed her a belter which threw her half-way across the room. The baby dropped from her lap into the fender, and I thought it was dead; but it started to blart and squeal, and my sister picked it up and ran upstairs with it to get it out of the way. Dad had got mam by the hair, banging her head up and down against the floor, and she wasn't making any noises now, and I knew she was unconscious. But the dad wouldn't let up. I jumped at him, onto his back, but he threw me off.

'I'll bloody well kill you, you Welsh bitch,' he kept saying to my mam, all the time he was thumping her. 'I'll bloody well kill you.' I grabbed the next brother to me, next in age, and told him to belt up the road fast and get the policeman. I knew too well that the neighbours wouldn't come and interfere, they'd never interfere in things like this.

'It's Family,' they'd say, meaning that it was a personal family matter into which they couldn't poke their heads. I could see mam was bleeding at the mouth, and I grew really scared that the dad *was* killing her. I looked around for a weapon, saw the poker in the fire-place near the ash-grid. I picked it up, held it high, brought it down towards the old man's head. Instinct told him, despite the beer he'd drunk. He moved, so instead of hitting him on the head, I brought the poker down on his shoulder. He took it from me like you'd take a rattle from a six-months-old baby. Then he hit me – not with his fist, but with open hand. I felt as if my head had been ripped from my shoulders. He stood over me.

'Ah said ah'd half murder any kid of mine who lifted a hand against me,' he said, 'and yoh just did.' I tried to roll away from him, but his boot toe-cap caught me just below the ribs. I felt this thick pain, and my lungs were gasping for air. He kicked me again, almost in the same place, and the kick itself sent me skidding along the quarry stones of the kitchen floor. I could see him unfastening his belt. I rolled up into a tight ball, just like Pope Tolley had taught me; head down between my knees, knees up to my chin, arms wrapped round myself, presenting as small a target as I could. The leather of the belt bit deep, red hot it felt, and it kept coming strong and fast. I think I passed out for a bit, but only for a bit, because he kept hitting me and the pain brought me awake again. I kept trying to squeeze tighter into the corner, but his boot pulled me out every time so's his belt could get the fullest spread. I started to be sick, and it came up thick all down my belly and legs because I was still doubled up. The pain from the belt didn't seem as much now, and I think it's because the body can only absorb so much pain, and then it shuts off and numbs itself.

After a bit I realised that the dad had stopped hitting me; and I was aware that somebody else was in the room. I lifted my head and looked, and this copper was standing there, looking all solid in cape and helmet. His mouth was set in a thin straight line, tough looking, like I'd seen Tom Mix once, from the threepenny stalls at the picture-house. I watched the policeman take his helmet off, and even in my pain I thought how young he looked, and clean. Then he took his cape off, and I could see he'd got good strength to him. 'Come on,' he said to my dad. 'Ah'll risk my fucking tunic for yoh.' Dad was alert to it. The drink had worn off – and despite everything, he was no coward when it came to fighting men of his own size or bigger.

'In the yard?' he asked the copper.

'The backyard 'ull do,' the copper answered, and the two of them went into the back fold. The copper, fit as he was, had a hard time of it. Dad kept him rocking with hard punches, jabs, uppercuts. Twice the copper was knocked to the floor, but he got up each time and mixed it. And then his fitness, youth and training showed through. He put the dad on the receiving end. Once his first burst of energy was done with and spent, the copper could have put dad down for the count any time he'd wanted. But he didn't. He kept hitting him where it wouldn't show, mostly in the belly area. He kept the dad on his feet, hitting him all the time, long after a professional fight would have had the towel chucked in. He made a good job of it, did the copper. My dad had never had a good hiding like it in all his life, it was a good hiding to remember to the grave; it was a bloody, bloody good hiding. And then, to round it off, the policeman put a straight right to the chin which seemed to lift dad inches off the ground, and he was unconscious before he landed flat on his back, the policeman catching him at the last second so's dad's head wouldn't crack against the yard quarry slabs. The policeman was breathing hard. He went back into our kitchen, put his helmet and cape back on. The skin was missing from all of his knuckles. Mam was sitting down on a chair, rocking herself back and forth, moaning with pain and misery. The copper looked at her anxiously.

'Bist yoh alright, missus?' he asked, and she looked at him dully, but nodded a 'yes'.

The policeman awkwardly took two half-crowns from his pocket and put them into her hands.

'Buy someat for the kids with it,' he said, 'and doh let that bugger outside get his hands on it.'

He stopped at the door, adjusting his chin-strap. 'He'll probably leave yoh 'uns alone for a bit, now,' he said, 'but if he starts again, come and fetch me, alright?' I nodded, worshipping him with my eyes. I heard his step, strong and sure, going down the entry. And suddenly I knew what I was going to be when I grew up. I was going to be a policeman. *That* was going to be the consuming passion of my life.

Soon after, the dad came staggering in and flopped himself down. He'd taken a right pasting, I could feel my face gloating over it. The policeman must have made a phone call, or stopped by the surgery, because the doctor came. He sent us 'uns out of the room while he examined mam, and when he was finished he called for one of us to bring the baby to him. I went upstairs, got the baby from my sister, and took it to the doctor. He examined the baby, said it was alright. Then he looked at my dad. He snapped his bag shut. 'As far as you are concerned,' he said coldly, 'it's not ointment I'd like to give, but rat poison.'

Dad didn't even have the heart to make reply. He just sat there, head in hands, sore inside and outside from the policeman's fists. Dad's pain made mine endurable. Mine didn't matter, but *his* did. It mattered a lot. The only pity was that time would nurse it away.

I went to bed that night filled with dreamings and imaginings, like a swarm of bees at a hive, thinking and longing and wishing for the day to hurry up and come so's I could join the police force. My sister could be a whore if she wanted, but me – I was going to be a policeman.

Chapter Nine

By the time I was nine years old we'd moved house eleven times to my knowledge. Dad would get into arrears with rent, and we'd move out one night when it was dark. Always with a borrowed handcart which I think belonged to Pope Tolley. Dad would push the handcart loaded up with bits of mattresses and sticks of furniture, with the youngest of my brothers and sisters wedged in here and there. Mam coming behind pushing a pram that had two tyres missing from the front wheels, with a load of other bits and pieces, and a couple of babies crammed on top. My elder sister and me would tail behind, and off we'd go for a mile or two until we arrived at the 'new house'. That's how we got to the Comper, a street of joined-on houses opposite a skin works whose stink was enough to send you crazy. The River Stour actually passed through the works. Before it went through it was clear and clean, but when it came out the other side it was thick yellow with chemicals and scum. For two or three miles on, no fish could live in it. Not until the muck and impurities had filtered into the ground, and other, cleaner riverlets, fed the main river like a blood-transfusion. The house we lived in was dirty, musty, decayed; it had been waiting for the bulldozers for nigh on a hundred years, as had the rest of the houses in the Comper. Running alongside the Stour, on the opposite bank to the skin works, was a railway siding and all night long you could hear the steam engines clanking up and down, and coaches and waggons bumping spitefully against each other. To top it all, two huge gasometers reared fat bellies against the sky, and when the wind swung our way – and our way was its favourite position, you got the stink of that as well; stink of burning coke and leaking gas.

Caggy Scrivens lived in the Comper, but he was up the far end which had a bit of dignity about it, and clean curtains at the windows once a month. We didn't have curtains. Our front yard looked like a herd of moles had been playing football on it, and when the landlord saw the door was missing he swore blind we'd burned it for firewood. We had, as a matter of fact.

The school I went to was a tough 'un; and a hundred yards from it was the King Edward Grammar School, where the 'monty-sods' learned French and Latin and Chemistry and stuff, and whose dads were at least foremen in safe jobs – or even higher in rank and position. When I went to school, I had to pass through a herd of these fellers, all the youngest being a bit older than me. There were three that I tried to avoid, but seldom did. They'd get me in the middle of them and play me off one another like a football. Then, when they'd got tired of it, they'd give me a belt up the earhole or a kick up the backside to show the unemployed working-class where it belonged. This one time they did it I lost my rag, and threw a punch into one of the fellers which made his nose sprout crimson like a turned on tap. The other two gave me what for, and I went home battered and ripped, but not crying. Seeing the state I was in my dad lifted his paw to give me another wallop, then realised I'd been in a fight.

'How many?' he asked. 'How many of them was there?'

'Three,' I said. 'But I only duffed one.'

'We'll bloody well see about that,' dad said.

Next morning he took me to school.

'Which am they?' he asked, as we passed the Grammar School lot.

'Them,' I said, pointing; thinking my old man was going to bang their heads together. He cornered all three of them in the vee of two walls.

'Yoh'm the lot, bist?' my old man asked them. 'Yoh'm the lot as give him a thrapin'?'

The Grammar School kids were self-conscious, ashamed of being seen talking to one of the soup kitchen lot, a man with patches on the backside of his trousers, no collar and tie, cloth cap, and boots with string in 'em instead of laces.

'Righto,' said dad, pointing to the biggest. 'Yoh can tek yoh're jacket off for a start.' The lad hesitated, and dad helped him roughly, tearing the jacket down a seam as he did so.

'Now yoh,' dad said to me, and I took my jacket off. Dad drew a line in the dirt with his boot-toe.

'Come up to scratch,' he said, and stepped back, holding the other two so's they couldn't run away. The Grammar School kid was bigger than me, but if I didn't give *him* a good hiding, I knew my dad would give *me* one. I went for the kid's nose. Pope Tolley had told me to always go for the nose.

'Once yoh flattens that,' Pope had advised me, 'and the blood starts to come and their eyes is filled with tears, yoh'n got 'em wheer yoh wants 'em.'

I'd got this one, alright. Both his nostrils were pouring blood, and the tears were there alright, like he'd been peeling onions. I clouted him around a bit, got a couple of good 'uns into his well-fed belly, then landed a sizzler on his chin. His head banged against the wall, and he sat down all dazed as if a tram had hit him. Satisfied, I turned to put my jacket on. Dad wasn't having any. He pushed one of the other boys forward.

'Now this 'un,' he told me. 'This 'un' was a bit more wary. He'd seen what I'd done to his mate, and he came in boxing clever. I knew bloody well he was a better boxer than me, that he'd keep me away with long punches and wouldn't mix it. So, as he stepped back to circle me I shot out one of my feet and trapped one of his. It spoiled his balance, and I got in close to mix it. I ended up sitting on him, banging his head up and down on the floor. He was crying.

'Now yoh,' dad said to the third kid, and pushed him at me. He was the easiest of the lot. He was the one who munched me more than the others when he got the chance; he was brave enough when he'd got his mates to back him up. So this one I really decided to work over. I knocked a tooth from his front uppers, split his lip, hit him in the belly till he doubled over sicking his breakfast up. Then I grabbed him by his hair to rub his face in it. My dad grabbed me and pulled me away.

'That'll do,' he said. 'One coat o' paint's enough, yoh doh have to whitewash the whole bloody town.' I didn't go to school that day.

That night, two dads turned up on our doorstep. The dads of two of the Grammar School kids I'd scrapped with. The third one didn't come, I don't know why; only the two of them came.

'What'n yoh want?' dad asked them, the tinder of his temper glowing well under the flint and steel of me mam's nagging.

Both blokes were well spoken, what we called upper-bracket silver-sand people. One owned a tobacconist's shop, t'other worked for the town council.

It all ended with dad kicking the shop-owner's backside down the street, and then trying to throw the town council man into the River Stour. It took four men from the skin works to stop him. Thirty minutes later there was a policeman on the doorstep.

'Self defence,' dad assured him. 'They tried to come barging in here so ah chucked 'em out. An Englishman's home is his castle, yoh knows that.'

'Some bloody castle,' said the policeman, staring in; then, staring at dad, 'Some bloody Englishman. Strikes me yoh was brought up with the Red Indians.'

'Self defence,' dad repeated, 'and yoh cor prove otherwise.'

'No,' said the policeman, turning away, 'and ah'm not going to bother trying, either. When ah gets yoh, bloody Billy Hill, it'll be on a big 'un. With a rope round yoh're neck eight o'clock one morning up at Birmingham prison, like as not.'

The Battle of the Comper didn't end there. I'd still got school to face next day, with no excuse for my absence. Nothing went right that day. To start with, I had to go to school in a girl's blouse since the only reasonably good shirt I'd got had been torn to shreds in the fight with the Grammar School kids.

As soon as I got into the playground I was jostled and laughed at before going into assembly; by the time I got into the hall with the others, the blouse was ripped, my face cut, and a couple of the other lads had got black eyes from the weight of my fists. On top of it all I swear I'd got one ear longer than the other where one of the masters had pulled me out from the fight, him swearing that I was the culprit. There was another thing about school as well. Ever since I could remember, I used to blush easily. I'd blush if anyone as much as looked at me, outside the family. I lived in sheer hell because of this blushing. My face would colour up and the more I tried to control it, the redder it became. I'd got no reason for it, it just happened. Sometimes, if I saw a group of other kids hanging around a street corner, I'd walk a mile off my way to get round them. Not because I was afraid of them, but because I was afraid that I'd blush. It was agony. I took to carrying a pen-knife with me, and when I felt the blush starting I'd open the blade and dig the point into my palm so's the pain of it would keep the blush away. Sometimes my hand was as messed up as a squashed orange.

Every morning, before school started, Bingley the headmaster would have us all in assembly for prayers and hymns, and to lay the law down. One prayer, one hymn, and then lectures about conduct, appearances, misconduct, honesty and thefts of a petty nature from desks and cloak rooms. This time, after I'd got me girl's blouse ripped in the playground, he started to go on about something or other stolen from the girls' cloak room – which was situated at the far end of the school, and out of bounds to boys, anyroad. Well, as he started to go on about it I started to blush. I don't know why. I just did. Some of the kids round me started to nudge and giggle in my direction, and this made the blushing worse. Then I saw a teacher looking at me, frowning, suspicious, and I hung my head to hide the blush. Old Bingley went on about the stealing, and about a 'wicked element being at large in the school', and wave after wave flooded my face. Dark and crimson blush and me guilty with the shame of *it* and not in connection with the thefts. I could feel my breath panting and hurting inside, like I'd run a long way, and more teachers were looking at me, and more kids. I'd look at my boots and I wouldn't look at *them*, and everybody was looking at me queer and suspicious. Old Bingley's voice tailed off and there was a silence so deep it hurt. Then he dismissed all the assembly but told me to stay where I was … and all the kids went out, whispering and looking back at me … and I was taken to the headmaster's study and they all stood around, all the teachers did, while Bingley accused me of the stealing. And I blushed and blushed and started to cry, but the bastard headmaster wouldn't wear it, wouldn't believe me. Innocent people don't *blush*, boy, he said; only guilty people blush. We've had our eyes on you, oh yes we have. It's guilty people who hang their heads in shame and sweat with fear when they're found out.

I switched off inside.

I heard one of the teachers say, 'His dad's in and out of prison. Like father, like son.'

Bingley stood with feet apart, motioned me to put my head between his legs, picked up a cane. I stared at him, swallowing hard. Wondering whether to run for it or take the licking and forget it. There were too many teachers around to run for it, so I slowly put my head between his legs and decided to take it; but when the first stroke cut into my rump I went mad with the injustice of it. I bit Bingley on the inside of the leg, high up, and he screamed like a woman and let go of me. I was out of his study in a flash, racing down the corridor then into the street and home. I hung about outside for a bit, wondering how I was going to explain myself. But I felt nothing was worse than I'd get when I *did* go back to school. Dad was there in the dirty kitchen, Pope Tolley sitting with him, the pair of them planning some moonlight devilment. I told them what had happened, why I'd run away from school. Pope looked at my dad.

'Bist going up to the school about it, Bill?' he asked. The dad laughed.

'He can wear that one for hisself,' he said. 'Ah copped wuss than that when ah was a kid.' Pope worried at it like a dog with a bone.

'Yoh'd best get up to that school and sort that bleeding headmaster out,' he said. 'Ah would, if it was my kid.'

'He got hisself into it, he'll get out of it,' my dad said. 'Ah'm buggered if ah'll molly-coddle any kid of mine.' Pope stared at him, and his lips tightened. He picked his cloth cap up, put it on his head, rakish, couldn't give a damn.

'Come on, young Archie,' he said, 'let me and yoh tek a walk.' He took me back to the school, straight to the school. Bingley wasn't in his study, he was in one of the class-rooms. Pope and me walked down all the corridors till he saw him talking with one of the teachers in a class-room. He barged in without knocking. 'Come here,' he said to Bingley. 'Ah wants yoh.'

Bingley started to splutter his objections, but Pope took his arm and made him walk on almost tip-toe back along the corridors to his study.

'Wait here,' Pope said to me, and took Bingley inside. I never heard Pope Tolley's voice raise by half a beat. I only heard Bingley spluttering and snarling that he'd call the police. Then after a bit, his voice fell quiet and I could only hear the rumbling hum of Pope's voice. After a bit he came out of the study with Bingley. It was all Bingley could do to keep the hate from his eyes when he looked at me. He had to fight to keep his voice level when he spoke to me.

'Alright, Hill,' he said, 'we'll say no more about it. You can go back to your class-room.' Pope shook his head, no.

'Hang on a tick,' he said, 'there's someat yoh'n forgotten.' Bingley gulped, and if looks could have killed Pope Tolley would have been nailed to the wall.

'Er, that is,' Bingley stumbled. 'Some misunderstanding. Sorry.'

Pope smiled at him with his mouth, but not with his eyes. 'That's better,' he said; then, to me – 'Goo and get yoh're learning done, Archie. But if this little bugger comes it again, come and tell me. And ah promise yoh he'll spend the rest of his life in a bloody wheelchair.' He didn't even try to hold Bingley's stare of hatred, just let his eyes flicker across him with contempt, then off he walked across the playground, jaunty and tall and arrogant as muscle-strength itself.

'Go to your class-room, Hill,' Bingley said gruffly.

I was grateful to Pope. But it didn't stop me blushing. So I found a trick to disguise the blushes. Every time I felt my face going red for no reason at all, I'd pretend I was going red with anger, and pick a quarrel with some boy or other standing near-by to make the anger real. Then there'd be a fight, and the teachers would drag me off to the headmaster, and he'd lash into me with his tongue but never the cane, not since Pope came to the school. They'd all say I was no bloody good, that I was a thug and a tear-away … so one day I thought to hell with the lot of them. If that's the reputation they want to give me, I'll live up to it. So I started to pinch things. Black-board dusters, boxes of chalk, paint brushes. Anything. And you know what? I stopped blushing. When Bingley read the notices out in assembly I used to look straight back at him and grin. He knew that I'd done the pinching, and I knew that he knew. But it didn't matter one little damn. It was my fight, and I handled it the best way I could, and devil take the hindermost.

Even so, the remedy often back-fired. This one afternoon we were having gardening lessons in the school grounds, and I was playing around with a garden fork. I tossed it into the air, like it was a javelin, and it came down prongs first and went straight through a boy's hand, pinning it to a wheelbarrow. It was a sheer accident, based upon an act of stupidity; but it spread like wildfire through the school that I'd done it deliberately, and instead of coming to see my dad that night the police came to see me. When I told them how it happened, they believed me and went away. But you'd have thought my mam and dad had been disgraced forever. 'What'll the bloody neighbours say?' screeched my mam, 'what with the police and all?' My dad sided with her. They often came together in jangling disharmony when somebody else was the target. 'Yoh wants a bloody good lowking,' me dad said, righteous indignation in his face, 'fancy bringing the police here.' I could hear them talking about me down below, and I felt this knot of anger burning in my belly. I went to the head of the stairs and started shrieking down at them.

'Who the bloody hell are you to talk?' I shrieked. 'What sort of bloody saint are you? You're nothing but a bloody fucking jail-bird yourself.' It was the first time I'd ever used *the* word out loud. I could see my mam and dad's faces down below me through a swim of tears, and then my dad was up the stairs and I was across the bed, and the big leather belt was raising ridges on my backside.

'I'll kill you, you bastard,' I told him. 'When I'm bigger. I'll kill you.'

I wouldn't cry, not till he'd finished and gone. And then I cried. I knew then. It was all a prison. Every god-forsaken minute of it, and you could never get away from it. Only take it with you forever and ever. It was a lopsided system, and all you could do was build muscles inside your mind to keep the world at bay....

Dad got beer money from somewhere that night and came home drunk. Then he broke every stick of furniture in the house, room by room, with a devil's orchestra of screaming children following him around. I knew if he cottoned on to me I was for another lowking, so I crept out to the brewhouse and made a bed for the night on a pile of old clothes waiting for the dolly-tub. Some of the neighbours complained to the police, and two of them came and took him away, and he got seven days in Winson Green. For three days we'd got nothing in the house to eat, and then from somewhere mam got three hard, stale loaves. If there'd have been enough of them, we could have used them to build a house, they were that brick-hard. We watched mam soak the loaves in water, squeeze them rough-dry, then put them in the fire oven to rebake so that when they came out they were crisp new. We tore into them, filling our bellies with starch. The next day to this, Konk and Pope left a rabbit on the back step, and a carrier bag of spuds.

When dad came out of prison we did another move, a mile further on. The house was near a lane by the iron foundry where I did my spare-time pocket money work. It wasn't a large house, but the first time I saw it I thought it was beautiful.

Dad felled the lilac trees, tore up the lawn and flower-beds. He spoke of bloody useless flowers and all that rubbish, and talked manfully of table produce – potatoes, brussels sprouts, cabbages, turnips, improvement. But instead of potatoes and cabbage and runner-beans we had weeds and mounds of earth, scrub and piles of burned up gleads, old bicycle frames, pigeon pens, scrap-iron and old bedsteads. The house we lived in now squatted in the middle of a refuse tip, and let in the growl of industry, rumble and shrill of traffic, the constant bickering of railway waggons.

They're all against you, all down the line. You can't win, you can only keep on fighting ...

After dad had wrecked the house and gardens beyond repair in the space of a week, we started to get free gas. There was no electricity in the house, only gas to cook by and see by. We'd got no money for the gas meter, and dad decided that he didn't want to go back to prison for putting lead or tin coins in, made by himself. So from somewhere or other he borrowed, begged or stole a great length of small-bore rubber hose. Outside our house was a street lamp. When it was dark, dad used to make a stirrup of his hands for me to climb up. I'd open the little side-window in the street lamp, blow out the flame, cap the jet with the rubber hose, and then we'd play the length of it through our front window and fix the other end to a gas jet. It gave a light about as strong as a dozen candles, and we could see by it, and boil a kettle. Many's the night we sat down to bread-crumb tea through the unconscious generosity of the local gas board. We'd get some bread, peel and fumble it into crumbs, put these in a tin can and bake them black as charcoal against the gas-jet. Then we'd grind the burned crumbs to powder, put half a handful into the no-handled teapot, and pour scalding water over it. When it was 'brewed' we'd drink it. Bread-crumb tea, with a dash of condensed milk in it if we'd got any. What with gas from the street, coal pinched from the wharves and vegetables from the fields, we did manage to survive somehow. But without family love and unity; without loyalty and respect for one another.

It was at this house that I learned I had part of my dad's mad temper and savagery in me. I'd found a dog wandering, a bitch. Thin ribbed and weary, and hollow eyed. I took her home and loved her back to strength. I let her sleep in a knocked together box out in the brew-house, where she eventually settled down to deliver a litter of pups. I doted on those pups. Straight home from school to make sure they were alright, plenty of scrounging from the butcher's for offal and bones and throw-aways so that the mother could have strength to keep them fed. Then this one day I went to see them and all the pups were dead, their clean smooth pink bellies turned to the sky.

But the horror that hit me was the mother. She was calmly eating one of her own pups. She looked at me calmly all the time she was eating it, and I picked up an old garden spade and killed her with one blow, there and then. When I'd finished, she was only a heap of broken bones, and I took that and the dead pups and buried them in a far unseen corner of the dead orchard.

It was about this time that I ran away from home. I was around eleven years old. Dad had come home blind drunk and there was this hell of a row between him and my mam out in the street near the iron foundry, with all the workmen and neighbours looking on. A lorry loaded with scrap-iron was trying to make its way through, and there was my mam standing in front of it calling on the world to witness that she was going to commit suicide by throwing herself under the wheels. But for every inch that the lorry moved forward, she moved back the same distance. A sort of delayed action suicide. Eventually the lorry had driven her almost up the entire length of street and the neighbours couldn't see her anymore, she was that far away. So she let the lorry pass without getting its tyres bloodied, and came back into the limelight. The dad had got some fish from some place, big ones, unwrapped, unsealed and ungutted. He took them from the pockets of his jacket, all covered with bits of fluff they were. He kept roaring for my mam to take them inside and cook them for him. She kept shouting back – 'You bloody drunken pig, cook the bloody things yourself.' And there he was, running round in loping staggering circles, trying to wallop her with his fist. But he couldn't catch her, he was that drunk. Eventually one of the neighbours called out – 'Cook the bloody fish for him, missus. So's we can get some peace.' So mam took the fish inside and cooked them in stale, smelly fat, just as they were. And the dad sat down and ate them sweet as a nut – scales, fins, heads and guts, complete as the moment they were hooked from the water. The beer had made him maudlin and he sat there crying with self-pity, his mouth and chin covered in glistening fish scales and gut slime. He started to tell me how my mam had always been a rotten cow and that she'd rather sleep with the tally-man than him. And my mam screeching back at him – 'At least he does a better job in bed than yoh does' – and then the old man's on his feet tipping the table over and smashing the bits and pieces again. I took a chair, hefted it, then crashed it down on him. He lay on the floor snoring, like as if he'd decided to have a natural sleep.

I'd got a bike I'd built for myself from discarded bits and pieces picked up from scrap-yards and rubbish tips. I'd collected the bits over a long time, and assembled the thing in our backyard. For inner-tubes, I packed the tyres with bits of rag and grass, like my dad did his.

This night, I wrote a letter to my mam and told her I was going. I propped the letter on the mantelpiece about four in the morning and went to get my bike. It was raining. As I went up the entry my dad came out at the front door. He'd just got an old overcoat on. His feet and legs were bare and dirty. I kept the bike between him and me in case he should lash out and land me a wallop. 'Yoh'm off, then?' he said more than asked, and I nodded. Afraid to speak in case my voice sounded like my sister's.

'Yoh'n thought about it?'

'Yes.'

'It's flat and final?'

'Yes.'

'Ar,' he said. 'That's the way on it, then.' And he went back inside and shut the door, and I mounted my bike and rode off out of it. I slept in hay-ricks and barns for a week, stealing raw eggs for swallowing from farmers' poultry runs, apples from orchards and raw vegetables from fields. The only pair of socks I'd got were those I was wearing, and they got so hard with caked sweat through pedalling that I had to throw them away. Then I ripped the sleeves out of my shirt and put these over my feet, turning the open ends under. At the end of a week I was picked up by the police and taken home. I'd got as far as Llangollen in North Wales.

'Ah suppose yoh could do with a cup o' tea,' my mother said to me, as if I'd never stepped out of the house, and I think it was the only time my heart honestly warmed towards her.

When I asked where the dad was she just shrugged. 'Slung his hook again,' she said, 'buggered off with the dole money. Yoh's best goo and see the gaffer in the foundry, chap, and see if he'll let you do some work again. There's no money comin' in, otherwise.'

When I went back to the foundry some of the moulders had a whip-round for me, amounting to fifteen shillings in all.

'Now hide that away,' one of them said to me, 'an' keep putting a bit with it. And next time yoh buggers off from home, doh come back. Yoh get yoh're feet under somebody else's table, chap. Yoh get yoh'reself out'n that bloody mess yoh'm living in.'

Chapter Ten

It's the men of the Black Country who ever held me in bond, the native born. Between them, in a sort of composite form, they provided me with a substitute father. The simplicity of them, the strength, and sincerity. And their pride of self in personal craftsmanship which nothing, not even the dark days of depression, ever seemed to daunt for long. I always feel that, whenever Black Country men move on, when they have diluted themselves to 'modern manner', the last threads of old Anglo-Saxon England will be no more ...

You can tell a Black Country man's trade just by looking at him. The iron-moulders, strong men, heavy and sure. Every movement methodical, economical, flexible from the waist up, firm-planted from the waist down. The stance of his work-bench is well ingrained. When you note the glassblowers in repose, you note the sunken cheeks which swell into little balloons when they laugh or purse their lips, because the muscles of their cheeks have stretched through constantly blowing mouth-air through the long hollow tubes to which the molten glass adheres, waiting for shape; the glass-cutters, with hands as white and soft as well-bred ladies, soft and delicate and flowing with unconscious grace. The skin of their hands is kept pale and soft through the use of pumice at their work, and the graceful hand-gestures are a result of the slow intricate contours which they put the table-glass through on the cutting wheels.

Without exception, almost, these men would work well – and second to none when they were allowed to. And they drank hard, as well. The heat of the work made this understandable, perhaps. It was always the pub, the 'local', which formed the hub from which they radiated their sports and pastimes. A Black Country man rarely 'visited' a public house, he always 'used' one.

'Do yoh know wheer ah can find Tommy Oakley?' someone might ask, only to receive the answer,

'Ah doh know wheer he lives, but he uses the Green Man boozer down at Lye Cross.'

Publicans could usually set their clocks by their 'regulars' when there was money about; and regulars were loyal, seldom giving their business to any other pub in the district. When times were hard, the publicans took to selling 'bum-clink', which was stale beer often watered down, which could be sold at next to nothing; but it kept the publican's 'regulars' there until such time that money would circulate again, and his till could ring out a more cheerful message. The men would sit and sip the 'bum-clink' and talk of better days which lay just round the corner, or would talk of their sports and hobbies.

Dogs and racing pigeons were the Black Country man's pet hobbies. (If you know your way around, you can *still* come across the odd cock-fight, despite the fact that it's illegal.)

'Ar, owd man,' Billy used to tell me before he died, 'The law says it's wrong but *we* doh agree. Anyroad, as long as the Top-'uns can run after a fox with a load of dogs, they can't tell us 'uns what to do, can they?'

He had a point, did Billy. The fox doesn't want to fight, especially against such odds; but fighting-cocks are natural born enemies, worse than two male pheasants fighting for territory and mating-rights. Cocks fight to the death, on sight, without encouragement, just like they were a cat and a dog. But when we went 'cocking' we had to do it quietly and secretly. Rough men need violent safety valves from time to time, and cock-fighting supplied this. Better than exhibiting a need for violence over miles of open public landscape for fifty or more hounds to rip a fox into pieces at the end.

And dressing up to do it in white breeches and scarlet coats. When our men fought the cocks, they wore cloth caps, baggy patched trousers, collarless shirts but with gypsy-like neckerchief at the throat, and boots like as not soled and heeled from pieces of old motor tyres scrounged from the tip.

When we knew that the men were taking their dogs 'ratting', a whole troop of us used to follow. Men, boys, women pushing prams. We'd all herd up and follow. The rats were mostly nesting in the tips, and the idea was to find the whereabouts of a colony of them. When this was done, men and boys would build barricades round the spot – breastworks of earth, ashes and gleads. Then the diggers would get to work with their spades, digging down to expose the nests. When the rats were uncovered they were driven squeaking and spitting into the paddock which had been built to receive them, then all escape routes were closed to them. Anything from one to five hundred rats would be captured in the paddock. The men with their dogs would be waiting for betting arrangements to be settled among the organisers. If people had got money to place bets, they'd do so. If they hadn't, they'd bet with pledges – candlesticks, old ornaments, Woolworth's jewellery – anything at all which could lay claim to having some small value. The organisers would examine each item and set a price tag on it, so's the owner would know how far he or she could go in the betting stakes. Dogs of all sorts and descriptions would be there. Lurchers, terriers, mongrels, bulldogs with legs as bowed as a cowboy who's spent all his life in a saddle.

The owners of the dogs were ever feeling and probing at them, letting their fingers test the reliability of muscle and sinew, checking paw-pads and teeth, rubbing grease on to their ears and around the fur-ruffs of their throats so's the rats couldn't get a hold of them. Although all the men clustered there were friends, workmates or acquaintances, not one would touch another man's dog. It was the unwritten law. One dog, one master – and no petting, fondling or touching, otherwise the rat-fight wouldn't start but a fist-fight would.

One of the men, an out-of-work glass-blower, had a dried out rat pelt which he kept showing to his Stafford terrier, close enough for the dog to smell. The terrier kept whining and struggling, blood up and ready to go.

The other dogs too were whining and squirming in their owner's arms, or pulling frantically at their leashes. The rats, nigh on two hundred of 'em, were all squatted up in one corner of the paddock, squeaking and climbing over one another. Only the very young ones wandered about, whiskered snouts quivering, not knowing what all the fuss was about. Children who were trying to peer over the breastwork of the paddock were hauled back by their mothers, who were well aware of the danger which rat bites carried.

The first dog in killed a dozen rats, but he wasn't a good killer. Wouldn't go in at the rat mass, but stuck to the young ones who gave little resistance.

'Time's up,' shouted one of the organisers, looking at his stop-watch. 'A round dozen in five minutes. No bloody good. No bloody good at all. Yoh wants to sell that dog or chuck him in the cut with a brick round his neck.'

The owner of the terrier retrieved him reluctantly.

'He's only a puppy, yet,' he muttered. 'This is his fust blooding.' The man handed over his shilling bit to the bet-taker. To win, a dog had to kill a minimum of thirty rats inside five minutes. Somebody put a bulldog in, and inside three minutes he'd killed twenty-two. But he idled the remaining two minutes away by locking his teeth into one huge rat, as big as a cat, and refusing to let go. This was the trouble with bulldogs. Once they got something large and chunky in their jaws, they'd hang on and wouldn't let go. A local story had it that a bulldog at Tipton had once grabbed a man by the leg and wouldn't let go. Rescuers actually had to kill the dog, but even when dead the jaws wouldn't unclamp. So they had to chop and hack at the head until the jaw-bones were busted, and the wounded man freed.

Another terrier was put into the pit. His whole attitude showed that he was an old hand at ratting, without having to see the scars and teeth-dents in his body, or the ragged ears. He ignored the young rats completely; he let them look at him, squatting back on their hind legs and cleaning at their faces with tiny pink front paws. The terrier went at the mass wedged into one corner. He went in fast, furious, scattering them. He saw the one he wanted, the King rat, the biggest around which the others invariably clustered. The big rat backed up, cornered, ready to fight. The terrier feinted with a paw, and as the rat went for it the terrier had got him by the back of his neck. He shook it side to side a couple of times, then jerked it up and high, over its back. We actually heard the rat's spine break, like a small twig crushed underfoot. Then the terrier went for the others. He dealt with them all in the same manner; feint, grab, toss. Well inside the five minutes he'd killed over forty rats. The proud owner called him, lifted him out of the paddock, checked him over carefully for scratches and bites. The man collected his winnings, put the leash on the dog, and started to leave the tip.

'The game's not done with,' one of the organisers called after him. 'There's more to go in yet. Yoh might as well play some of yoh're winnings back.'

'Not on my bloody oath I won't,' the man answered. 'Ah'n won enough now to buy a bit of beef for Sunday table.' He clambered up to the top of the tip, his terrier dog whining and hanging back, wanting to kill more rats.

'And yoh needn't worry,' we heard the man tell him. 'There'll be enough bones for yoh as well.'

Some of the men climbed into the paddock and slung the dead rats out by their tails. The mass of those still alive huddled up in another corner, a moving, writhing mound of vermin anxiety. One by one other dogs were played in, but none could match the kill of the terrier. The Staffords were quick and nippy, but their jaws usually lacked that vice-like compression of the bulldog. Some of the terriers were content with a single kill, then spent the rest of their time worrying at it, despite their owners calling out to them – 'Drop it, it's a dead 'un.'

Another dog, over ambitious, dived straight into the pile of rats, and came out bleeding from a dozen bites and scratches, and one eye missing from its socket. The owner took the dog away where we couldn't see, and then came back alone. We all knew that he'd killed his dog as quickly and as mercifully as possible.

Eventually, about a dozen dogs were put into the paddock at one go, and between them they destroyed all the rats. But then, with no more common enemies to go at, they started to fight among themselves, and the swearing, shouting owners had to go in and separate them. So it was that dog-owner started to quarrel with dog-owner, and man-fights were near to boiling-over kettle stage. But one of the women, sensible and practical and wise, shouted out that the police were coming; and the men quickly forgot their differences, scooped up their dogs, and got out of it. There were, of course, no policemen about. But the woman who had shouted her warning of them had done a good service, because if the men *had* started fighting, there would have been broken bones among them at least.

* * *

Caggy Scrivens and me had decided to join the Boy's Brigade, because we liked the uniforms and the pill-box hats. But suddenly, and from no apparent anywhere, troops of young men called Blackshirts started to appear. So Caggy and me, well, we switched our admiration to these. They looked so alert and virile in their black uniforms – the officer lot wore jackboots, like riding boots – that we longed to join. We used to follow them, trying to keep in step with them, admiring their black polished belts and cross-straps. For some reason me and Caggy couldn't fathom, our own men-folk were dead set against them. When they marched, groups and knots of our own men would walk against them, forcing them to break step and rank. Caggy and me just couldn't figure out what all the fuss was about – the Blackshirts were clean and well-fed, with good-looking uniforms, but our own men called them 'Fascists' and 'Mosley Pigs'. Sometimes fights broke out between our own men and the Blackshirts, and they were heavy fights, not light ones. Fists, boots, belt-buckles, staves of wood-anything went. But the moment the police started to come up, everybody would scatter, Blackshirts as well. Somewhere in a place called Abyssinia a war was going on, and men were talking in low voices about a man called Franco in Spain, and something about a civil war brewing up over there. None of it meant much to people like Caggy and me. All that belonged to man-world, not boy-world. Mind you, we liked hearing about war. The stories of the bravery of British soldiers. We liked to hear about the Somme, and Flanders, and Ypres and places like that. Pope Tolley had fought in the Great War. He'd joined up in 1916 at the age of sixteen, and fought through the last two years of the war. And how he hated the French – 'Froggies' he called them. Said they were unreliable to a man when it came to front-line action, and you could never depend upon them to protect your flanks or backs. He hadn't a good word at all for the Frenchmen, although he had many a good word for French women. When I asked him about this, he used to half smile as if he were dreaming of something miles away that was good to think on, and he'd answer – 'Yoh'll find out for yoh're self one day, ah shouldn't wonder. So I won't spoil it by telling you about it in advance.'

'You mean the French women are good to go to bed with,' I said openly and Pope roared with laughter.

'How old, bist,' he asked me. 'Let's see, yoh'm coming around twelve years old now. M'mm? But yoh still knows too much about life for yoh're age.' He kept chuckling about it, so much so that I thought I'd said something really deeply clever. Then Pope grew serious. 'Ah'm going to tell yoh a little story,' he said. 'A sort of joke-story. There was this rabbit, see. And his mother told him never to play down by the railway lines. Never. But the little rabbit thought bugger it, ah wants to see a bit more of the world. Ah'll go and have a look at them railway lines for starters. So off went the little rabbit, and he hopped up and down the railway lines. Then all of a sudden, as he was hopping across some points in the track, they closed on his little willy-winkle and cut it off. So the little rabbit ran crying home to his mam. What's the matter? his mam asked. Ah went playing down the railway lines, the little rabbit cried, and all of a sudden the points closed and cut my willy off. His mam gave the little rabbit a clump up the lugholes for disobeying her, and told him to go back and find his willy-winkle and she'd sew it back on. So off goes the rabbit, hopping all over the place, looking for his willy-winkle. Every set of points he came to, he popped his head inside to see if it was there. It wasn't. And then, as he put his head inside another set of points they closed on him and cut his bloody head off.' Pope was silent that long that I grew impatient to know the rest of it.

'Go on,' I insisted, 'finish it.'

'That's it, me lover,' Pope said. 'There's no more to it except this; *never lose your head over a bit of dick,*' and away went Pope laughing his head off, leaving me to puzzle it all out.

A hunger-march of miners from the Welsh coal valleys came through our area. Several hundreds of them. We stood on our doorsteps, all down the street, looking at them as they went by. They were like death-marchers, all silent and voiceless, just the sounds and echoes and re-echoes of their marching feet. They were going to London, marching on London, to air their grievances. Some of our own men joined up with them, men from the Cannock coal-fields, and a goodly more from other places and reaches. The marchers were grey-faced with weariness, they marched like puppets, like as if their bodies had no spirits in them. But even so there was a feeling of urgency about them, a level of desperation which did not weaken or falter. They passed down our street, and some of the women darted inside their houses and came rushing out again, giving pieces of bread to the marchers, pieces of cake – anything and everything they could spare. The leaders of the marchers called a halt, and the men sat down tiredly for a rest, leaning against walls, or spread out full length on the pavements. The policemen with them didn't interfere, but collected together in their own close-knit company, and rested themselves some twenty feet away.

Caggy's mother filled her huge boiler-hopper out in the brew-house, lit a fire under it, then sent me and Caggy from house to house along the street to collect spoonfuls of tea, sugar and milk and whatever else we could scrounge. Most of the people in the street had little enough for themselves, but each gave something. Even my own mam gave half a tin of condensed milk.

When the water in the hopper was boiling, Mrs. Scrivens added the tea, let it brew, then poured in the milk and sugar. The women in the street had organised themselves with cups, drinking mugs, and washed-out buckets. Some of the women went among the miners with the cups and mugs, handing them out, while other women followed with the buckets of tea. The men accepted it all gratefully. I did note that nobody offered the police any tea; but I'd heard the men talk about what the police had done to the miners in 1926, when they marched to Parliament. How they'd been beaten back by foot-police charges, and mounted policemen, charged and beaten and scattered as if they'd been an army of invaders, and not a marching collection of mainly honest men wanting to express their grievances to the Government, and obtain assistance for their families. Some of the London papers described these men as 'rowdy rabble', men who were anarchists, 'Commies' – anything but the truth. Some of the papers said that if men like the miners insisted in going on strike, they must take the consequences. But the miners never *did* go on strike, so Pope said. They were 'locked out' by the gaffers, because the miners wouldn't – couldn't – accept a lowering of their wages. As the men drank their tea, I made my way down the line to where Pope and a few more of our men were talking to the leaders. One of the leaders was saying how they'd stopped off at a farm a couple of miles back, Wordsley village side, and asked the farmer if the marchers could rest up and sleep for the night in a couple of his barns. The farmer had flatly refused, saying if the marchers came onto his grounds he'd lift his shot-gun at them.

Pope was angry. 'You wait theer till we gets back,' he said to the Welshman; he beckoned his brother Benny and spoke with him in low tones. Inside thirty minutes sixty of our own local men had collected, all with old bicycles to ride on. Pope and Benny borrowed theirs. The senior officer of the police came across to the group and wanted to know what they were up to.

'We'n just formed a biking club,' Pope told him. 'So's we can ride round the countryside and get some fresh air. Now bugger off and mind yoh're own business.' The policeman went. He'd got no hankering to start a riot.

Pope and his men started to ride off on their bikes, and I ran after Pope, caught up with him, hung onto the back of his saddle.

'Whass up?' Pope asked, looking down at me as I struggled to keep pace with him.

'I want to come as well,' I said. 'I want to come with you.'

Pope stopped his bike, sat me on the cross-bar.

'Yoh'll find it a bit hard on yoh're bum,' he said. 'But yoh'll have to put up with that.' With a few strong strokes of his legs, he soon caught up with the other cyclists.

'We doh want him along,' one of them said, pointing to me. 'He's only a bloody babby yet. This is man's work we'n got to do, not kids.' 'It's our bloody world today,' Pope answered, 'but it's hiss'n tomorrow. Let him alone with me, he's alright.'

The sixty men were spread out like gaggle on gaggle of geese, their old bicycles squeaking and protesting, some of them bumping along on flat tyres, some with no tyres at all but running along on the bare steel wheels, rattling and clattering like a convoy of tin cans. Some had no brakes, and the riders had to slow them by pushing a foot forwards, so that the wheel rubbed against booted foot, which acted as a brake.

Eventually we came to the farm which had denied barn-bedding to the marchers. The farmer had seen us coming, and he stood grim-faced there in the yard, flanked by two sons, all of them holding twelve-bore shot-guns. Pope dismounted his bike, and the others did likewise. The whole group of them walked slowly towards the farmer and his sons. As if they'd been given an order on a soldiers' parade ground, each of the three men lifted his shot-gun and snapped it into closed position ready for firing.

'Yoh can put them bleeding things away,' Pope told the farmer. 'There's nerra one of us here come to harm you, only to talk to you. So break them guns and point 'em at the floor, because I'm telling you if erra one lets fly, yoh'll just wish yoh hadn't. That's all.'

The farmer hesitated, looking at the sixty men facing him. Then he slowly lowered his piece, broke it at the breach and removed the two cartridges. He motioned his sons to do likewise.

'What is it you want, then?' he asked Pope.

'Two barns for the night,' Pope answered, 'for tired men to sleep in. Two barns for one night. They'll be no trouble, and they'll be away again early in the morning.'

The farmer spat. 'If yoh'm on about them Taffy's as tried to stop here later back, the answer's no,' he said. 'Ah won't have 'em on my land. That's flat and final.'

Pope let a long silence hang. Then he pointed to the men behind him.

'See that lot?' he asked. 'They'm not Taffy's. They'm locals. And almost every man jack of 'em has seen the inside of Brum jail for poaching and thieving from farmers. Did yoh know that?'

'What's that to do with me?' the farmer wanted to know, 'it's got nothing to do with me.'

'It will have,' Pope assured him, 'if yoh refuses them marchers shelter for the night. Because if yoh don't let 'em sleep in yoh're barns, ah promise yoh that between us this lot here will strip yoh're land of every pheasant, rabbit, hen, egg, lamb – the bloody lot. And the moment yoh gets a few acres of corn ready for cutting, we'll set fire to every inch of it. We'll come by night an' we'll bost every bit of farm equipment yoh've got. Ploughs, tractors, the lot. We'll open every gate and let all the cows out, all the sheep and all the hosses. Think about it, ust?'

The farmer had paled under the wind and sun tan of his face.

'Ah'll bring the police in,' he said. 'Ah'll report it. Ah shall have the police with me.'

'Piddle on the police,' Pope told him, 'us lot 'ull run rings round them any day. Yoh'd want a hundred coppers on twenty-four-hour duty to anywhere near stop us – and do yoh reckon the gaffer of the police can spare that lot? Just think on it.'

The farmer went into a huddle of talk with his two sons. Eventually he turned to Pope. 'Alright, then,' he said. 'They can use the barns for one night. But they'm to leave my livestock alone, and no smoking where there's straw in the barns. If they want to light a fire, they'n got to light it outside the barns, well away from everything.' He turned away with his two sons, went back to the farm-house. We all climbed back onto our bikes and rode back to the marchers, where Pope went up to the leaders and gave them the news. The marchers climbed wearily to their feet, formed up, and marched back to the farm where at least a roof awaited them. The contingent of police stayed with them; some up front, some along the offside flank, some to the rear.

We watched the silent men go, and even after they had passed from sight behind a hill in the road, the sound of their dogged marching feet came back to us. Soon after, while the men were sitting on doorsteps moodily talking about things beyond my comprehension, things like 'monopolies', 'Public Ownership', 'Share-holding profits' and that sort of stuff – half a dozen spanking Blackshirts passed us, going to a meeting at their drill hall up Dudley way. They looked neat and clean, strong and virile. Most of us kids couldn't wait to grow up to be old enough to join. The Blackshirts' uniforms were better in every way than those of the Boys Brigade, or even the Boy Scouts.

The men watched the Blackshirts pass. 'Fucking fascists,' one man called after them, but they walked on untroubled.

'Every time ah sees 'em ah'm bloody choked,' Pope said. 'Ah'm bloody, bloody choked.'

That night there was a fight between Blackshirts and local men. Unwittingly, it was Caggy and me and half a dozen other kids who started it all. The Blackshirts held their meetings in a hut which had a corrugated iron roof, and a stovepipe sticking out from the wall. Since we couldn't join the Blackshirts, and perhaps because our men-folk held such dislike of them, we decided on a great lark. We went to their hut, the entrance door of which opened outwards and was kept locked with a padlock threaded through two hasps. First of all we coupled the hasps together with a piece of coach-bolt rod, so's the Blackshirts couldn't get out. Then one lad climbed upon the shoulders of another and stuffed the protruding stove-pipe up with bits of rag and stuff. Then we hauled off and started throwing bricks onto the tin roof. It sounded like a herd of bullocks trying to dance a polka. We kept the fusillade up, and inside we could hear the Blackshirts coughing and snorting as smoke filled their hut. They smashed a pane of glass at the back of the hut, but we didn't hear it, nor hear them climbing out of the window, because we were all too busy throwing our stones onto the roof. The first inkling we'd got of their escape was when a flying wedge of them came tearing at us round a corner of the hut. We took to our heels, with the lot of them trampling after us. When we reached the well-lit high street they were still after us, and one of the boys fell, and they caught him. They held him against a wall and started to belt him.

129

Some of our own men saw what was happening, and a great surge of them went for the Blackshirts. The fight was open, anything went. Some of the Blackshirts took their heavy-buckled belts off and started to use these as weapons. So the chain-strikers and iron-moulders did the same, and used theirs.

The fight gathered in volume. Blackshirts seemed to be everywhere, kicking and clawing, punching and some had got knuckle-dusters; Pope and Benny Tolley were there, weaving in and out, punching and clobbering. I saw Pope pick up a Blackshirt – big and heavy *he* was, too – lift him high, then throw him at a group of Blackshirts who were fighting and struggling to get their backs against a wall. They went down like skittles. Then the police came up with batons swinging, hitting no matter where, heads, faces, shoulder-bones.

Cars full of policemen kept arriving from outlying districts, going in at the fighting men with utter disregard for the damage their staves were causing. Men were falling cut and senseless, only to be trampled underfoot as the fighters struggled to and fro. Some of the local men started to mix it with the police; the police being dressed in black, and with helmets missing, were mistaken for Blackshirts, and got the receiving end.

And then, for no reason I've ever learned to understand, the police were fighting *for* the Blackshirts. They seemed to join forces with them, and fought our own men. And our men didn't like it – they fought back hard and furious, spilling across pavements and roads, fighting bloody and dirty as if they'd gone over the top like they'd done in the last war, and everything in a uniform had to be put down. But more and more police kept arriving, until our local men were utterly outnumbered. They started to fold up and slip away, running up back streets, getting away before the police could lay hands on them. A round dozen men lay badly injured about the battle arena. Blackshirts, local men, and two policemen all hurt bad. A Magistrate had arrived in a big car to read the riot act, and Territorial soldiers were arriving at the double, with bayonets fixed. But the fight was over, the local men dispersed. The police started going among the crowds of spectators, trying to get names of the men who had been involved in the fight. But not a one would answer, would give the information required. I was near one group of policemen who, between them, had recognised several of the local men, and now they were compiling a list so that they could go after them. I heard one of them mention Pope Tolley, and another said he'd seen Pope lay one of the badly injured policemen out. Ambulances had come up and taken the injured men to hospital; and then the senior officer of police started to give instructions to his men, telling each detail which local man they'd got to arrest. I felt a sneaky pride in me when he instructed eight coppers to go for Pope Tolley, yet only two to a detail to arrest the others.

As soon as I knew they were going to lift Pope I grabbed the nearest bicycle standing at the kerb, never mind whose, I thought, and I pedalled like mad to get to Pope Tolley's house at Silver End to warn him before the police arrived. His brother Benny was tidying up the cuts and bruises on Pope's face when I burst in. 'Pope, Pope,' I cried. 'The police are coming for you – eight of them. They say you half killed one of the copper's in the fight, and they'm coming for you.'

Pope muttered his thanks, got to his feet.

'Ah'll get me things together and sling me hook,' he said.

I pleaded with him to go now. 'They'll be here any second,' I told him. 'They'd got a car, and ah'd only got a bike. Go now, Pope, else they'll be here.' I had a brain-wave.

'Go hide in the osier beds by the Stour,' I said, 'the bit nearest Moody's field. When the police have been and gone, Benny 'ull put all your things in a bag and ah'll bring 'em to you. I'll whistle like a nope six times, and you'll know it's me.'

Pope nodded, ruffled my hair with his strong fingers to express his affection for me, and then he was gone. He beat the arrival of the police by three minutes – eight of them came charging up the entry and barged in without knocking. Benny had a go at them. 'Wheer's your bloody warrant?' he said. 'Yoh just can't come barging in here like this.'

'We can't come barging in here like this,' one of the coppers said to another. 'We haven't got a warrant.'

To Benny he said – 'Yoh shurrup, else we'll be teking yoh down the road with us as well.'

They searched the house from top to bottom, with Mrs. Tolley, Pope's mother, fat and wheezy, cursing them at every move. One of the policemen grabbed her by the neck of her dress and shook her.

'Wheer's that son of your'n?' he asked. 'Wheer's that bloody Pope?'

'He's slung his hook,' Mrs. Tolley wheezed. 'He beat yoh to it. He'll have jumped a coal train be now, and yoh'll probably find him anywhere between London and Glasgow.' The policeman shook her so fiercely that she cried out as the collar of her dress cut into her. Benny crossed the room in two strides, turned the copper round to face him, then hit him flush on the jaw and the man was out on his feet, with only Benny holding him up, with right fist drawn back to hit him again. The other policemen jumped Benny, got him on the floor and worked him over. I knew it was a bad work-over, because I heard Benny cry out with pain a couple of times, and I'd never known that before.

When the police finally let up, Benny's face looked like a half-boiled cabbage; some of the bruises were already green, and his nose was broken, some of his fingers broken, and one eye closed.

The police dragged him away, hands handcuffed behind him. Mrs. Tolley went upstairs, motioning me to wait for her. She came back down with a suitcase and a bundle of clothing.

'Pope's clothes,' she said, 'what bit he's got. If yoh teks 'em to him now, yoh'll miss the police. By the time they'n got Benny in a cell and start working things out, it'll be an hour at least afore they posts a copper outside the house to catch Pope if he turns up.' She put the clothes in the suitcase, adding shaving brush and razor, plus soap and a piece of towel. Then she went to the larder and rummaged around. She put half a loaf in the suitcase, a tin of sardines, and a box of matches. She picked her handbag up, looked inside at the contents.

'The rent-man will have to go hungry this week,' she muttered, and gave me six shillings.

'Now goo to him,' she told me, 'and give him the suitcase and the money. Tell him it's all ah'n got, but it might-hap help him get away.'

I went off into the darkness, down past the iron foundries, over the hump-backed canal bridge near Moody's field, to where the osier beds were. I whistled six times like a nope, a bullfinch, and then Pope was alongside me, noiseless as a ghost.

I gave him the suitcase and the money. I didn't say anything about his brother Benny being lifted, because I knew it would mad-worry him, and he was liable to go to the police station and take the whole lot on single-handed.

He stood looking down at me awkwardly.

'Well, Archie, me lover,' he said, 'we parts roads for a bit.' I nodded, lump in my throat.

'If ever ah'd got married and had kids, ah'd of wanted me a son like yoh,' he said, and then he was gone, caught up and melting in the shadows just as if he'd never existed.

* * *

Months later, I learned that Pope had crossed over to Spain and joined the International Brigade to fight the Fascists there, in the Civil War.

It was 1937 when Pope went to Spain, with me past the threshold of my eleventh year. One English king died, another took the throne but didn't keep it, because he wanted to marry an American woman but the Government, or somebody, didn't like her, so the king was given a choice. The woman or the throne, take your pick, but you can't have both. So he picked the woman and let his brother have the throne. There seemed to be months of celebrations, one way and t'other, between the one king going out, dead, and the other coming in. There seemed to be flags and buntings all over the place, everywhere you went. Union Jacks floating over every important building. Drinking mugs with the new king – George, his name was – and his missus painted on. Shawls and cushion-covers, embroidered pictures, handkerchiefs, neckties, portraits on the wall – they all had their shining hour. But for the life of me I couldn't see the sense in all this bloody fuss, all this spending and wasting of money. There was still near on three-quarters of a million blokes in the dole queues, and most of them *with* jobs had to pull their belts in a bit, because the money wouldn't go round.

There was a sort of unrest everywhere, a sort of held-down excitement, like a banked-up fire. The heat was there but you couldn't *see* it, only the smoke.

The Hungry Thirties were giving way to the Fighting Forties. There were more aeroplanes overhead, and officials were going about the country looking over private-owned horses, to call them into cavalry service if need be. Work for men seemed to blossom out, making guns and ammunition. More men started to come back from the Spanish War, and these were grabbed up and made into senior ranks because they'd got 'modern fighting' experience to pass on to others. I asked among them for news of Pope, and some of them had been with him 'over there' and said he was alright, the last time they saw him.

It was a Sunday morning when he told us, a September morning that had a nip of cold in the air, but with sunlight. I was doing my part-time work down in the iron foundry, collecting scrap-iron and riddling sand through a sieve at the work-stalls. One of the men had got a wireless set with him, plugged into a light-switch. There were a lot of men working that day. As soon as the announcer came on they switched off their machines, put down their tools, and quietly collected round the wireless set. Chamberlain's voice, full of dark and gloom, told them that war was here. After he'd done the men went quietly back to work, not talking, just thinking. During the next few weeks not many of the same men remained. They'd been 'called up'.

For almost a year before Chamberlain spoke on that Sunday most of us had treated the prospect of war as a joke.

'The bloody Hun hasn't got the guts to take us on.'

'We gave the bastards a good thrashin' last time. He'll not come back for more.'

'He'll come unstuck against the French. They've got the Maginot Line, he won't break through that.'

'Our navy's the best and biggest in the world. It 'ud tek more than a little bloke with a Charlie Chaplin moustache to bost that.'

Months before, we'd been fitted up with gas-masks. We were told to carry them everywhere, and if we went to school without them, we were sent home to collect. Out of school, the gas-masks were a joke to play with. To put on our faces, and play soldiers. When we'd got bored with them, we used to only carry the shoulder-bags, putting our school dinners where the masks should be.

There'd been a 'dummy-run' of siren-testing; an up-and-down wail for 'air raid', a long continuous one-pitch note for 'all-clear'. There was triumph in the 'all-clear', a sort of victory. But, until the day Chamberlain told us that we were at war, we got used to the sirens. 'Moaning Willy' most of us called them.

But after that Sunday morning we knew that the sirens weren't on 'dummy-runs', but they were blaring for real. There was menace, now, in the 'air raid' signal, and relief from fear with the all-clear. Food rationing came into being, and clothes-coupons; then petrol rationing for them as had got motor-cars. Blackout swept the country, private houses, factories, streets lamps – all got 'blacked-out'. Even the private cars still on the roads, as well as the building-up army convoys, had to have masks fitted to their headlights, sidelights and taillights. The masks were like partially opened Venetian blinds, so only a weak pattern of light could show the roads. Some private cars tried to get by without petrol, they had bed-size gas-bags fitted to luggage racks on the roof and fed the gas directly to the ignition-spark. But even these seemed to die out eventually, and only 'essential service' vehicles operated.

Back gardens were holed to accept Anderson air raid shelters, and public shelters were built on street corners. At first, when the sirens sounded, we used to go into our cellars. Then, when the Anderson shelters were put in, we slept in them. But the damp and the chill made us change pattern, and we went back to the cellars. Neighbours came together more, shared their lives and bits and pieces more generously. Two or three families would 'double up' to a cellar for company, taking with them what night-rations they could spare and 'pooling' it.

My lot, my family, used to go to a cellar a couple of hundred yards away. It was owned by a middle-aged couple, and I don't think the feller had got all his marbles. When an aeroplane was overhead, he'd shush us into silence, whispering that the German airmen could hear us through their wireless sets. He'd got the idea firm in his head that if the Germans 'listened in' and heard you 'running them down', you'd be their target for tonight.

In the end, I used to let the rest of my family go to the cellar and I'd stop in the house reading a book, until I heard the crump-crump of bombs on Birmingham or Coventry and the lighter blup-blup of anti-aircraft fire. Then I'd go to the Anderson shelter till the all-clear sounded.

The dad wasn't with us when war came. He'd cleared off a couple of months before. On my mam's orders, I'd gone with him to the Labour Exchange to collect the weekly twenty-five shillings. He gave me half of it, twelve and sixpence.

'Yoh can tek that to yoh're mam,' he said, 'and tell her ah'll not be coming back to yoh're house any more.' I watched the bugger walk off and away, and out of it. When I gave her the money, you'd think I'd walked out on her. She carried on at me, screeching and shrieking her head off, till I exploded back at her, using language the dad used when he was pissed.

'It's not my fucking fault,' I shouted at her. 'I couldn't hold the fucking bastard back. What you think I am? Father to this shower of shit?'

There was only my bit of money coming in from the foundry, plus a bit of Parish relief. If I buggered off, she'd not know what to do. I was thirteen when the war got declared, I'd just passed the Art School examination and taken my place in a New World which couldn't last because there was no way of sustaining its growth. Big Dreams jostled with Reality. Once I put charcoal and paint brush down, it was dash back home, grab a piece of bread and jam, and down to the iron foundry to earn the money. I was burning my fuse at both ends, and it couldn't last. On top of it all I was angry with my years, because I wanted to get into the RAF and join the scrap.

The big blow of Dunkirk had hit us. But then the miracle of the world happened. Rowing boats, motor boats, sailing yachts, tugs, barges, cockle-boats, fishing yawls – an armada of bits of wood, steel, engines and sail and blood and guts and courage which shined like a searchlight went over to Dunkirk and brought the British Army home. Men went over to fetch the soldiers in anything which could float and move at any speed, even a snail's pace, through the water.

When the men came back, they were no longer singing 'We'll hang out the washing on the Seigfried Line'; and those young ones who'd dashed away to join the 'Terriers', the Territorial Army, at the local drill halls, came back old and strained. From the cinema glamour of Tom Mix and his pearl-handled six-shooters to the reality of shell and bullet was a long, long step. But the Army came back, leaving its weapons on the bloody coast of Dunkirk. Overhead, a handful of young men; week-end flyers caught up in the swift machinery of war – were fighting the Battle of Britain. Theirs was a different war. They went up, they fought, they died or they won, and a couple of hours later were back in an English pub with 'popsies' and ale. The khaki-men, the soldiers, had already learned that war was not a high-spirited game with perhaps a bit of chivalry tagged on. They knew war for what it was, in mass, and not in single combat like armoured warriors of old. Hurricanes, to them, were the salvos of enemy heavy artillery. Spitfires were German machine-guns. And defiants were what they all were – defiant to a man.

The men came home, walking-wounded among them, dirty and unshaven and with lice in their clothing. Back to families for a little while to be nursed and mended, and then sent out again.

I got up this one morning and went downstairs to make a cup of tea before going to the iron foundry. I had to go across to the brew-house, and as I opened the door this figure, this man, was getting up from the pile of dirty washing which he'd used for a bed. I reached my hand out for some sort of club, alarmed and scared. Then I saw that it was the dad back. Only this time he was in a soldier's uniform, torn and dirty. We stood looking at each other, then I turned back to the house. He picked his haversack and rifle up, and followed me in. I said nothing, but I made extra tea and turned round to tell him to help himself, but when I turned I saw he'd fallen asleep in the spring-broken armchair. I went upstairs to my mam and told her he was back, then went to the foundry to do my stint. Only four more years to go, and I could get into the fight.

When I got back home, I found that mam and dad had 'made it up', and were getting along with each other like a pair of courting doves. Christ, I thought, there'll be nappies in front of the fire again before the dad makes Lance-Corporal. Now that she could see a bit of security coming her way by means of Army allowance, mam could afford to get stand-offish towards me. It didn't worry me, I was only marking time with my life, anyway.

I gathered from the talk that dad had come through Dunkirk. That explained his dirty, muddy and stained uniform. Tomorrow, he'd got to report to the nearest drill hall to be re-kitted. I could see from his forage-cap badge that he was 'in' the Royal Artillery ... and then I heard Pope's name mentioned. My eyes froze out the page of the book I was reading. From a dream world away, I heard dad telling how Pope had 'copped it'. Pope had become a three-striper, a Sergeant, owing to his experience from the Spanish war; and him and dad had crossed to France together, but Pope was still over there, and would never come back.

I felt horror inside me, thinking of Pope lying dead on the Dunkirk beach, his body rotting away and none to see to him.

'He needn't have done it,' I heard the dad say, 'but there's no holding Pope when he gets someat into his head. The Germans were fronting us and flanking us, and we'd got the wounded in the middle and we were all the rest of us bogged down and firing rapid ... that rapid, the rifles were hot to hold. And there's this young 'un caught up in a cross-fire a couple of hundred yards away ... and he's copped it in both legs. And Pope goes out to fetch him in, to get him into the middle. Jerry was putting the shells down amongst us and we had to spread ourselves as thin as we could, so's not to lose too many men. And Pope goes out there, ducking and weaving – ah could see him through the smoke and the dust, and a dozen of us try to cover for him as he picks the wounded kid up ... and then he's coming back to us with the wounded soldier wrapped round him like a scarf. But he don't make it. A Jerry machine-gun near enough cuts him and the kid in half. Pope never knew what hit him. He died in mid-stride, like a bloody rabbit to a twelve-bore.'

I swallowed rage inside me. 'Not Pope,' I shouted silently. 'Pope didn't die like a rabbit. Not Pope wouldn't. He'd die with guts. It should be Pope sitting there, and not you. It's you that should have "copped it", not Pope. He was a better man than you.'

I left my book and got my bike, and went to Mother Tolley's house. She was dressed in black, all black, veil as well. Benny was with her, a soldier now; they'd given him a compassionate forty-eight hours pass so's he could be with his mom. I sat down with them, chairs to the fire, and grieved with them.

'He was a good lad,' Mother Tolley said at last. 'Our Pope was a good lad.' Her sigh was like a spent cinder falling into the ash-grid. She reached to the mantelpiece and handed me the 'death' telegram received from the War Office; and then a short letter which had come that morning, from Pope's Commanding Officer. The words and phrases had only a numbed sort of meaning for me … 'he died painlessly and bravely. He made a gallant attempt to save a wounded brother-soldier from the gunfire of the enemy … and he lost his life in the attempt.… I was proud to have such a man serving under me … a fine soldier and a first-class NCO …'.

'He died brave,' the mother said. 'He died like a General.'

'He died like a hero,' Benny interrupted bitterly. 'He died like a soldier. Not like a General. There was no bloody Generals at Dunkirk, they was the first to fly from the roost. They got out of it quick … and they left men like Pope to watch their backs.' From somebody's wireless set up the street somebody was singing 'There's a long, long trail a winding …'.

I kissed Mother Tolley quickly and then ran away, because her tears were private, and they were all for Pope. So long, Pope. Good night, God bless.

Chapter Eleven

With war all around us, with surges of armies against armies all round the world, I came into an area of life where war seemed not to exist. I left Art School and the part-time foundry work – which was near enough full-time, the hours I put in. I left it all, and joined the watermen and canal bargees, and war seemed far, far away....

In all my Black Country days, none burned trails for memory more than those of the water-ways. The inland water roads we called 'cuts', or canals.

Rich, hard days they were. No man or boy could have wished for better; but now they are over and done with and nothing like them remains, and they will never come again. To walk the tow-paths was one thing, to ride the boats was another.

The long narrow boats with a small cabin tucked at one end, and the rest for cargo. No picture on earth greater to see than a tizzle of boats moored up together at lay-bys or wharves, like chips of wood in a logging yard, like a mass of fish caught up in a trawling net. The brass fittings of the boats gleaming like candle light, the brilliant painted emblems of roses and castles, scrolls and family crests jostling to catch the passing eye and hold it ... emblems and heraldry as proud as that of Buckingham Palace, and more hard earned. Women there on the small decks, scrubbing their washing, slapping their children. Shrilling and screaming to each other. Women with gypsy-dark faces, long plaited hair, burnished ear-rings and wide leather belts to hold up their skirts. Inside the cabins, nine feet by six, a division of curtains to separate the crowded bunks of children from parents; a small stove in a corner, and shelves of kettles and pans and horse-brasses and bric-a-brac. The canals drew me like a magnet ever since I was a boy old enough to keep pace with the barges as they carried freight through the Midlands Black Country.

But even in the pre-war days, the canals were closing down, having lost the more than a hundred-years battle with the railway. The navigable waterways were getting fewer, and for those which remained, the horses were being put off and engines fitted to the master-boat which in turn could tow another.

But engines couldn't make up for horses. Engines were dead spluttering things which smelled, and throbbed artificially. Horses were sure, strong, even in stride and temper, and they looked *right*, somehow, up there ahead of the boat with towing rope attached to collar so the strength of its shoulders could be brought into play. Horses didn't splutter and stink of oil, they were content to re-charge between stops at grass verges, or at journey's end go into stable and munch well-earned oats, with a handful of greens for good measure and to keep stamina high. Big horses they were, almost as big as Shire horses. But they knew their jobs. When to slacken off, or tighten up and give that extra surge to bring the boat through uncleared weeds.

When I was nine years old I ran away from home and smuggled myself onto a cargo barge leading out from Stourbridge and running on to Kidderminster. I was absent for three days, living on apples and bread I'd taken from my mother's pantry. During the daytime I had to keep low in case the barge master saw me; but at night, with him asleep and the boat moored to the bank, I could poke my head out under moon or starlight and ghost my mind over the still water with a headful of thought and imagination that was more urgent than a boiling kettle.

The police eventually returned me home with a sore behind to get along with, and a lowking from my dad's strap waiting for me on the doorstep.

But the experience closely allied me to long dead relatives who'd been navvies and pioneers on the canal cuttings. I'd travelled the way they'd made. I'd gone hungry. I'd been hunted. I'd been thumped and clouted, pushed around, kicked up the backside by officialdom. Ever after, men long dead leaned on their shovels or tillers and winked at me as I walked the cut-side.

I finished with Art School at sixteen. There was no point in going on, because college was a money-distance away. Besides, the spare-time work in the iron foundries was sapping my mind away – dulling any creative abilities I might have. So I went to work on the canals and came home only at week-ends and bank holidays. I was mostly on the Wolverhampton run, carrying coal and iron castings from the foundries, or red sand from the quarries. On board boat, they were splendid cramped days. The barges brightly painted as gypsy caravans, brass work richly polished as a church chalice, a whispering of passing water and green rustling of moorhens out in the reeds. On the bank, the solid plod of the tow-horses' hooves and a sing of wind along the tow-rope itself as if a muted violin were being played. Sometimes, if the horse were feeling a bit contrary, we had to tie a pair of old boots to the rope and let them dangle and scrape against the ground, so he'd think one of us was walking behind him all the time. At scheduled intervals came the flush and swirl of the lock-gates to lift us up or put us down to a different level; or perhaps tied up for a few hours, horse hobbled to splash of green grass, waiting for another barge to come up from the opposite direction and share the double lock with us to save water.

Great names the bargemen had. My master was called Tomato Juice on account he drank nothing but whisky; there was Tinkers Cuss and Contrary Harry, Bully Boy and Half-pint-Alan, Cock-o'-the-Walk and Oyster Sam. There was the Tipton Slasher and Quarry Bank Alf, The Wordsley Wonder and Stourbridge Lad ... it was *me* they called Stourbridge Lad.

It was the Stewpony Lock where I fell in love for the first time ever. Sure, I'd had gropes and fumbles – my hand up a skirt or down the front of a dress, and I'd once bedded two female cousins one after the other ... but this was the first time in love. Me sixteen and she, mayhap, fourteen or fifteen. I loved her for almost a year before we spoke a word together. Her father stood like a ten-ton weight between the two of us, never letting the distance between us reduce to less than five yards. Mind you, I will say he was right in some respects. More than one lock-house lass cuddled a helpless bundle and waited for her boat to come home, bearing him who owned half the bundle.

The first time I saw her she was floating high and low on a home-made swing in the lock-house garden. Corn coloured hair she'd got, and a face as sweet as a modern doll, and the breeze stirred a froth of lace at her petticoat. My heart was like a bumble bee in a jam jar, trying to get out. There's electricity between youth – I made to speak to her, to warm the air between us with a spark of greeting. But her dad stood like a blown fuse between us, against the contact, and Tomato Juice growled a warning at me.

'Don' get speaking to her,' he said. 'Her old man 'ull dump you in the cut, else.'

I kept looking at her while the barge came up to its new water level. Tomato Juice smoked his clay pipe in the stern, exchanging gossip with the master of the opposite barge which was going to Kidderminster with a load of pig-iron. The horses stood at rest on the canal bank, mare and gelding, rubbing noses in meaningless affection. The girl on the swing never looked at me, but she was aware. I whistled nonchalantly, posed outrageously, offering the coin of my youth – mint fresh – against the spending power of middle-aged bargemen. The lock-keeper packed her off indoors with a curt word and a long deliberate stare at me. Tomato Juice chuckled more with glee than sympathy.

'Hitch the hoss on,' he said, and we cleared the lock, 'We'n got more than an hour to catch up on.' The other boat bobbed away from us, six feet lower, clean and proud and simple. The lock-keeper crossed to the tow path side with bucket and shovel, collected the steaming horse manure for his allotment. I looked up at the bedroom window of the little house and she was there at the pane watching me, haunting and delicate in the soft shadows. I mooned about her all the way to the main wharf where we unloaded in a swirl of sweat and graft. We refilled with coal and I was anxious to turn round and push back to Kidderminster. Tomato Juice thought I'd gone mad; he trimmed his whiskers, washed and changed into cleaner corduroys, wrapped his best silk scarf round his throat and donned his old fashioned bowler. It was the cutside boozer for him, the public house where all the bargemen collected between runs. They'd sit and drink ale and whisky, or rough cider straight from the wood, smoke twist in filthy clay pipes, and swallow canal oysters by the dozen.

They'd sit with their dogs and talk of ferrets and whippets, of horses and cage-birds, pigeon flying and the good old days which, really, were only pipe-dreams handed down from olden smoke. They'd sit in the pub with its black-leaded grate and trivets, surrounded by personal pewter pots and wall decorations of horse brasses, and massive iron horse shoes each with a private history. And all the while they talked, their hands and fingers would be exploring their dog's sinews, unconsciously, in that inexplicable way of theirs – as if their fingers had separate knowledge from their brains. It's a peculiarity of Black Country men, this need to question with their fingers, to probe and burrow against the flesh of birds and beasts. Try to sell a Black Country man a dog for instance, and not even the biggest signed pedigree in the world will convince him, nor his own eyes. 'Let's 'ondle him', he'll say; let me handle him, let me put my fingers over him, and then I'll know the truth of it.

I drank my whack at the cutside pubs, despite my years. I'd drain a pint or two with any man, and the odd noggin of whisky.

When we came back from the pub Tomato Juice would fall into his bunk in the tiny cabin, but if it was warm I'd sleep topside on the cabin roof I'd be up at first dawn to fetch the horse in. Then back we'd go to Kidderminster, past the stifling built-up areas of towns, past the factories and foundries which hunched like black cripples in mountains of slag and coal, into the Stourbridge cutting and on to beautiful open Stewpony and past the green flank of Kinver. The bat of a father always passed us through the lock-gate, signed our schedule sheet, with a word or two for Tomato Juice but never for me. But I always caught a glimpse of her, mostly at the bedroom window.

After a few trips she'd smile down at me when her dad's back was turned. I got to leaving her presents. I left them at the approach to the lock-gates, nearest her swing where she couldn't be off seeing them. I left a bunch of wild flowers, once. Another time it was a swan's egg. One day I bought a book of poems for her and wrote 'with all my love' on the empty front page. After a while we were exchanging real love letters, and what we said in them was nobody's business but ours.

I started to win her father over, too. He'd give me a civil word for a change, and my gaffer Tomato Juice put in more than a good word for me, helping to put a bit of gilt on the lily.

'When they made my mate theer,' said Tomato Juice, 'they chucked the mould away afterwards. They doh come nor better than him.'

When we carried coal we'd leave a goodish pile at the lock-house for the fire. 'Coal doh only warm the house,' Tomato Juice said, helping in my interests, 'it warms the heart. Chuck him another lump, me lover.'

I think, if they'd have let me, I'd rather have worked through instead of taking days off for rest. After the cramped cleanliness of the barges, home was like entering shanty town. On the barge, I'd got my own narrow bunk and could sleep in privacy. At home, it was a shared bed with two brothers. I got fed up with it and got some timber struts and spans of canvas from the boat; I made myself a trestle bed and stuck it in the corner of the bedroom. It was mine; it was private and personal. At the main wharf in Wolverhampton I'd got me a locker in the rest room, with my own key, and those possessions which I accumulated of any value but couldn't carry around with me, I left there for safety. Despite the fact I was away from home most of the week, I gave mam thirty shillings every Saturday. The dad took to waiting on it, him sitting there waiting, coming on with a burst of artificial friendliness when I showed my face but his eyes foxing at the money I put on the table. It didn't matter to me much, then. A bit would go on food for the table, the other would be pissed against the wall. But I only regarded the money as severance pay from a family I didn't give two sods about.

One day on the cut-run we were three parts of an hour ahead of time and we had to wait tied up for the down boat. The lock-keeper invited us onto his patch for a mug of tea, and out we clambered – me trembling like a catkin because the feller hadn't told my sweetheart to clear off into the house. Tomato Juice greased the way for me a bit. He gave the man a pair of pheasants, two of six brace we'd poached I he night before when we'd moored up. The feller was pleased enough with them, but I saw the girl's face wince as she looked at the dead birds. Half a tear of pity stole from her eyes. When I got to know her a bit more I found she couldn't stand hurt getting to birds or animals – if she saw a swan with a matt of oil on it she worried her dad into netting it and giving it a clean down. There's nought as soft-hearted as a nice wench, and mayhap that's half the battle we love 'em for. Sheena was my sweetheart's name. Sheena.

A name with all the colours of the dragonfly in it, all the fabric of the kingfisher and the stitchings of the rainbow.

My mate, my gaffer Tomato Juice, he always measured the pace of the horse to allow us at least half an hour to spare at the lock-house. Him and the keeper grew into great friends, sitting there drinking their tea with a lacing of whisky in it, and me and Sheena never daring to trespass from her father's eye reach. Just maybe the touch of a hand to go on with, or a long look at each other when the men weren't seeing. Enough to keep the wheels of our hearts turning until we were old enough to do something about it....

Me, I begrudged the days and nights and hours spent away from the lock-house. But there was nothing to do about it except look forward to each visit, and hope the bloody horse would put a move on so we could spend more time at the best anchor point in the world. I'd grown up, these past months on the water-way. I was tough and brown, with one foot still in boyhood but t'other set well and truly on the porch-step of manhood. And I'd got me a sweetheart. A lovely high thinking wench who put kindliness and decency where they belonged – in use and not on a pedestal. I started to save my money against the day I could carry her off and marry her.

And I would have done. If it hadn't of been for the perishing cock-fight. News of it carried all over the water-ways, over every canal in the Midlands network. Bully Boy had got himself a fighting cock that was the talk of

Kidderminster – except the talk never got louder than a whisper in case the police got to hear of it. Up in Wolverhampton Oyster Sam reckoned he'd got a game-cock that would fight wild lions in pairs. The match between the two was fixed and settled to take place in an osier wood near where my Sheena lived, and back at the wharves bargemen argued and jostled and bribed so they could get to the fight.

We worked our hoss hard that morning, on the up run, to get to the lock-house with time to spare for the match. When we got there it was like a traffic jam. Barges everywhere, packed tight, and more horses grazing than you ever saw in a cowboy film. All along the tow-paths and banks, on hills and up trees spaced at regular intervals, were barge-boy look outs. All ready to give the alarm if the police or canal inspectors took our wind. Me and Tomato Juice tied our barge up – although it couldn't drift off, it was that packed in – and clambered through blackberry briars and hawthorn down to the osier beds. About twenty bargemen were already there, including Sheena's father. The gaffer from a canal public house had turned up with a small barrel of beer and some bottles of whisky, selling noggins at a fairish profit. There was tense, belly-clenched excitement everywhere. I put whisky under my belt with the others, felt it bubble through my blood the way I liked.

There was an unreal sense about it all. The sweeping green of the trees and fields contrasted strangely with the tight knot of men with their crouched bodies and excited faces. They were quiet, almost silent as Bully Boy took his fighting-cock from a wicker basket; the sun lanced against the bird's feathers, made colour there like a slick of oil on water. It was a beautiful bird, just out of stag-age. Two years of loving care had gone into its growth, fed on best corn and barley for strength. Plenty of exercise and fat insects, and rationed hard with its running of hens. It's wattles and comb glowed brick-red with health and fighting anger, and the black beads of its eyes glittered challenge across the clearing to where Oyster Sam's bird was being got ready. Sunlight glinted on lethal steel as spurs like needles were fitted. Both birds had been weighed and matched, with not a quarter of an ounce of difference between the two on 'em. Bully Boy fondled his bird, turned him arse-end round and blew against the tail-feathers. The flesh showed warm and red, a sure sign of fitness. The Umpire sketched a line through the turf with the toe of his boot, signalled for the two bargemen to pass their birds to the appointed handlers. The owners of fighting cocks weren't allowed to touch their own birds once the fight was on.

'Come up to scratch,' said the Umpire, 'Bring 'em up to the scratch.'

The handlers dipped forwards, hooding the heads of the birds so they should not see each other immediately. At a signal from the Umpire they let go and stepped back to give fighting room. The cocks stood still for the space of a heartbeat, then screamed hate and anger at each other. They both feathered for top position, tried to weigh each other down. Young as they were, neither used spurs for the mere sake of it. Some ancestral skill and knowledge had been passed down to them, warning them not to burn energy in abortive stabbing. They jockeyed, bantam light, for key position; circling and feinting, circling and fluttering, darting in for a sudden beak stabbing or clawing. Feathers drifted on the wind they made, breast and tail feathers. The men were hushed, anxious, silent in speech except for the code-like laying of bets. The time-keeper measured the hands of his stop watch and called the rest periods. Then the handlers moved in and parted the fighters, carried them back to neutral corners and bathed exposed skin with raw spirits, cleaned the rubble of feathers and down from gripping talons. Bully Boy smiled with huge satisfaction as he saw one needle-spur covered with blood along its three inches of length.

'You'rns got more than a graze, me lover,' he called over to Oyster Sam. 'Will yoh give mine best?'

Oyster Sam spat a tobacco quid into the turf. 'It'll tek more than a scratch to stop this'n,' he answered. 'You mark my words – he'll have your'n under him this round.'

The handlers took the birds back to the scratch line. Bully Boy's crowed once, loud and long and piercing. It stood magnificent, defying the world or owning it. Oyster Sam's bird wilted, drew back. The men groaned, a solid one-voice of dismay. Oyster Sam slipped his body towards the centre of the ring.

'Yoh'll be disqualified if you touch it,' the Umpire warned. 'Leave him to the handlers.'

But it made no odds. Oyster Sam's bird wouldn't face it; it scuttled back and back, ran in circles, trying to take off from the ground. It couldn't, not with its flight-feathers trimmed back since birth. The men were disgusted. They chivvied and jeered at the crestfallen Oyster Sam.

'It's a runner,' they said, 'A bloody quitter. Strikes me you'n been training a wood pigeon, old son.'

The winner crowed from the centre of the ring, full and square on the scratch line. The ruff of its neck swelled with pride, its comb bristled erect. It was sinking low to spring out on the vanquished, to put final spurs in, when Bully Boy reached down and gathered it in. He returned it to its basket, crowing protest and frustration. Money clinked and jingled as bets were paid off. Oyster Sam picked his bird up gently, shook his head over it.

'A fighting cock that runs away is no good,' he said, 'Just no bloody good at all.' He screwed its neck without fuss or ugliness, and the men nodded approval.

'It's all yoh can do with a cock that quits,' they said. 'No use letting it get at the hens.'

Oyster Sam threw the dead bird to me. 'Make a mouthful for your supper,' he said. 'If yoh wants to go to the trouble of tekking its feathers off.'

I followed the men up the bank and onto the tow-path, the dead bird dangling from my hand. Sheena was standing there looking down at me, tears streaming down her cheeks. I knew she'd watched the whole show. I smiled at her and went towards her, but she turned and ran away to the lockhouse. I hung around till all the boats had gone through the lock and it was our turn to go through. But she never came out to speak to me, nor did she look through the bedroom window. I left some daffodils for her, by the swing, but they were still there on the down-run, withered and dried and unclaimed. And I never saw my sweetheart again. She just avoided me, and her father shrugged his shoulders when I asked him about her.

A little while longer I travelled the water-ways with never a glimpse of her; and time was coming for me to wander off across the seaways of the world and circumstances for a goodly spell of my life ...

Now the navigable canals become fewer and fewer. The horses are all gone and diesel powers the remaining barges. The gypsy-painted patterns and designs are gone, and nobody gives a damn about a spit of polish on a bit of brass. And not many people walking the cut-sides can see the ghosts of long dead navvies and bargemen leaning on tillers or shovels, in calico shirts and peacock neckerchiefs, corduroy trousers with straps under the knees; leaning on shovel or tiller to give a friendly wink, then stooping to the work again. But I see them. They still give me a passing wink.

Oyster Sam and Tomato Juice, Bully Boy and Cock-o'-the-Walk ... they're all dead and gone now; and the world is a sadder place for their having gone. Their sons and grandsons have married 'onto the land', have let the rich traditions fade away, the 'roses and castles' and private boat-emblems are stored in crumbling museums, out of circulation. The railways and the motorways, the lorries and the mobile tankers have eaten the canals up in a giant's feast, it took a hundred years to do it. I came in at the last bite. But they were lamp-oil days, though. They were a man's days.

Chapter Twelve

I was coming up on eighteen when I went into the RAF. I celebrated my intention to enlist, that June in 1945, by patronising the Blue Brick public house in Brierley Hill, but first I went to the canal bargees pub in Wordsley. I took my leave of corduroy and clay pipes, horse brasses and coloured neckerchiefs, brown faces and oyster shells; whippet dogs and mongrels, poached game and black-leaded grate and bloater-smoking trivets.

It was time to go, to leave the old men and join the young before the war in Europe staggered to its standstill ... I left them all without a whisper of farewell, these people that I loved. I inched myself away from the tap-room bar, faded away from their vision and conversations bit by bit, until I could slip through the door and away for Brierley Hill.

'Yoh' m off, then,' Caggy said. More of a statement than a question.

'In the morning,' I answered. 'First light. I want to get to Brummidgeum Recruiting Office when they open at half past eight.'

Caggy was wistful.

'Wish ah was a coming with you,' he said, 'wish ah was.' Caggy wouldn't be called up. He was in a war reserved job. We finished our beer in silence.

'I'll see you, then,' I said, turning away.

'Ar,' said Caggy, 'keep in touch.'

That's what I like about Black Country people. No fuss, no bother. No lingering farewells, no sentimentality. Just 'Keep in touch,' no handshake of farewell, no strings, no suction, no leeching.

I walked home from Brierley Hill over the clock fields. Past the brick-yards, past the clay mines whose pit wheels and derricks stencilled themselves against the stars. A moon was lifting from the edge of the sky, a bomber's moon. Here and there a searchlight tested its beam, on and off, like indecent fingers poking up the skirts of the night.

I came home. My dad was there, swaying drunk among the poverty, and my sluttish mam was wailing her dirge of inadequacy for the neighbours' ears. I stood in the doorway looking at my terrified brothers and sisters. I stood in the doorway looking at my dad's green-eyed drunken rage; and I thanked God for the spare-time work in the iron foundries and the long hauls on the canals, which had put muscles on my arms. I was ready, now.

I pushed my brothers and sisters from the room. My mam cowered against the wall, whimpering the scene into an ever-fixed memory. She was bleeding from the mouth where the dad had struck her, and one side of her face was swelling up. Dad's eyes met mine as I moved in; his eyes flickered downwards, but I wasn't falling for that one. I'd seen the miners fight at Cannock Chase and I knew if I let my eyes glance away from my dad's, his fist would crash from nowhere and put my lights out.

He leaned against the fireplace almost casually, but I knew the drink no longer held him. His instincts and reflexes were wide awake. He bunched against the mantelpiece, tight coiled as the springs which Caggy was designing. I hit him hard in the belly before he could move. I took him fair and square, two stones lighter than he was – but he didn't have the hate that I had. I hit him time after time. His eyes went bloodshot, the breath whistled in him; but I'd got the bastard, I'd got him bang to rights, I'd got him where I'd always wanted him, on the receiving end. I started on his face, spacing each punch against a memory. I planned my anger so that it increased and multiplied, because I was breaking my father into pieces. This is what I had survived the years for. This was my appointed task; I had nursed my days for this. I hit my dad until I couldn't feel my fists. My dad's face collapsed beyond recognition. When he was unconscious I held him with one hand and hit him with the other. I had no tiredness, only wild freedom and dancing elation that the mighty were fallen. Cain was my brother; my heart sang into the wilderness and found him.

I used my fists to hammer at the wasted years, and my dad was nothing, and the fear of my life was lifted.

Then suddenly I felt my arm captured in the nuisance of a weakling's grip and I brushed it aside with a blow. I saw with indifference that it was my mother I'd struck. I let her lie on the floor where she'd fallen, moaning and weeping. Then I lifted my dad again, worried into him, intending to kill him. My mind was a pool of calmness and I had to destroy my dad so's I could go about my days untroubled by his influence. But then the police came and dragged me away. I felt the anger leave me. But the blood remained, the warps were not straightened. Two pigmies had fought, two insects, two microbes. I looked at the mess, and a broom and a towel would put that right. I sat among the debris of broken furniture and puzzled at life's contents. The policemen warned us both, me and my dad, then went away.

The sergeant turned at the door and looked at my dad. 'Yoh asked for it, Bill,' he said. 'By bloody Christ, you asked for it.'

I went into the kitchen and washed the blood from me, then made a mash of tea and carried a cup in to dad. There was no pride of manhood in me as I looked at his broken face; there was only a sickness and a cry of mind for neutral places. The fight was over between him and me; only the fight of self remained.

My mam cradled dad's head, she crooned and comforted him, her dark Welsh eyes when they met mine burning near to madness. 'Bugger off,' she said. 'Bugger off from here. You'm the trouble here, always was. We'm not good enough for the likes of you. Sling your hook, then. Bugger off.' A nest of hissing vipers fed from her tongue.

I went upstairs and got my belongings, then I left the house and went up the street and crossed the threshold into the Outer World. I rode a late bus into Birmingham, slept on Snow Hill station until the Recruiting Office opened, then signed six years of my life away into the keeping of the Royal

Air Force police. Soon, I packed all my memories into an ocean-going kit bag.

I served my full six years with the RAF, four of them abroad in the Middle East. When I arrived out there, the war was almost ended. The Big War, that is. Hitler had come to the end of his days in the Berlin bunker, the German army was broken, great movements of allied troops were taking place all over Europe as battle-tired veterans went home and fresh troops took their place, to police the outposts and occupied territories. North Africa and the Middle East were thick with British soldiers and airmen, and the remnants of German and Italian armies who had been herded inside POW camps, were waiting to be returned home. I took to the desert strips happily. It was a far cry from the Black Country, and Moascar and Fayid suited me better than did Coventry or Birmingham. I went point-to-point along Transjordan, Baghdad, the Persian Gulf. There was action, travel, independence, and these suited me. I earned two stripes, then three, remained sergeant until demobilisation, except for the final three months of service when I was dipped in rank for being drunk on duty.

Out East, I drank more and more. Alcohol was cheap. There was Stella beer – quite potent – Indian rum, and arak. When I'd been out there for two years, I was getting through two pint bottles of rum a day. By the time I was twenty-one, I was greeting every dawn with a long pull from the rum bottle; just to get me set up for the day. But I was young, and the abnormal consumption of alcohol did not as yet affect me. My system could cope with it. I just felt better, could communicate with others better, if I had a good warm slug under my belly. I didn't make close friends – I mixed in well enough, but became nobody's confidant, nor did I confide in others. Military friendships suited my nature. Friends were always coming and going. They were always coming up, hands outstretched in farewell, as postings took them further afield. The moment this happened, the moment the hand-clasp was loosened, the friendship was over. All bonds were severed. A remoteness and a privacy closed in; the other man became a stranger. Military friends didn't leave extensions of themselves lying round. Once their kit-bags were packed and shouldered, they were away and gone. No strings attached. They had no permanence, they left short memory of their passing. It was almost with relief that I saw old faces depart, and new ones take their places.

My years with the armed forces weren't important, they were a marking time, with various diversions littering them. The Stern Gang terrorised Palestine, three unarmed British sergeants were hanged by terrorists along Transjordan, hand grenades were hurled through NAAFI windows. The King David hotel was blown up in Jerusalem, killing over ninety British servicemen and their families. Once, I watched two Jews publicly hanged on the West Gate of Baghdad, by Arab Nationalists.

Looking back on my years of service, I remember mostly the brothels, the Stella beer, the wild drinking orgies in mess which sometimes carried on across the threshold of dawn. The armed forces did not mature me in any way – indeed, they catered to my excesses and social inadequacies. As long as I was well groomed and shaven, did my duties in accordance with the regulations, stood smartly to attention for commissioned authority, I was regarded as a reliable non-commissioned officer. My appearances counted, not my personality growth or lack of it. Perhaps the armed forces added to my personal warps. Bearing arms, there had to be an enemy ... even if that enemy consisted only of half starved arabs breaking into our camps to steal. Rifle or pistol became a symbol of power. It was focused on the enemy, and it discharged itself with violence, and the enemy was destroyed. It was impossible to do that at home in the Black Country. Here, in the Middle East, violence was not only permitted, it was encouraged. Even in mock battles, on the training grounds, the ingredients of Hate were brought to the boil. With the others, I'd scream and hurtle my way down the ramps with bayonet hungrily seeking its target. In it would go, straight up to the hilt, and the sand bag would be more than just that. It became my home life and background, mother and father, brothers and sisters, and every person who had hurt or slighted me. Authority stood on the touchline and only criticised if the bayonet wavered, or the lunge was not true, or lacked the power of hating. All the training I received – and passed on – was based upon hatred. Hate the enemy, no matter who that enemy was. I took to battle training at a time when my entire life was in emotional turmoil. Yet I knew, deep down, that a good soldier must be a bad citizen. The inconsistency loomed too large.

I got shot out on patrol one night. The bullet smashed my arm, and I almost went mad with fear when they told me it would have to come off. I fought them when they gave me the gas on the operating slab; fought them with twisting body and twisted mind. The air force surgeon saw hatred blazing up at him and he lifted the mask a moment to ask me, Why do you look at me like that, son? I'm trying to help you, not hurt you.

I damned him forever if he should cut off my arm. They saved it. It took a long time for it to mend, and even then the surgeon was doubtful, saying it wouldn't knit and grow strong again. But I knew different. I bought a small rubber ball and kept squeezing it every moment I had, until the muscles grew round the wounded limb, and it belonged to me again.

I was in military hospital in Fayid for a long time. My drinking increased – I even took to carrying a bottle of rum round with me, in the sling that supported my arm. Twice the hospital authorities reprimanded me for being drunk ... then eventually, because of my behaviour, they put me up before the psychiatrists. I only kept the appointment because I was dragged to it by escort. The head-shrinkers put my behaviour down to shock following gun-shot wound, and I was returned to unit mentally A1.

I was hoping the Medics would send me back to Blighty; but they felt that the desert climate would help the arm to knit better than the unpredictable one of England. After a bit, I didn't mind. As long as I could get hooch cheap and plentiful, it didn't matter where I was, really.

But even so, drunk or sober, the Iraqui sunsets were really something to see. The Western sky, with nothing in the way to interrupt the view, would merge backwards to the East from light blue to turquoise, then blend into full darkness. In the East, when you turned your head, you'd see the sky filled with night, and stars out bright and polished. But looking West you forgot the night and saw only the sunset colours. Great bold colours, nothing half-hearted and faint; everything bold and full of impact – sometimes it seemed over-painted – so vivid were those sunsets. The crimson slashes across the sky were like knitting needles keeping the clouds together. The clouds were small towards the sun, growing larger as they backed up – and the clouds were Walt Disney ones, with buttons of gold and silver stitched onto them, and veins like marble. The sun seemed to pull the clouds after him, as if each were on a coloured string. And then, when sun and clouds were gone, came the evening silence of the desert. Once, before my arm got smashed, I'd left camp early one morning, on horseback, deep into the desert. I drew rein and the horse stood still. And so did time.

Never in my life had I heard silence, experienced it. Complete, utter silence. Not a stir or whisper of anything – just silence, and a desolate landscape like the craters of the moon. Even the horse felt it, I think. Because he stood still, carved from silence itself. Not a creak of saddle-leather, not a jingle of spur or bit-chains. Nothing. Just silence.

Elsewhere, there may be hush and quiet, but never silence. There's always the buzzing of a bee, a sough of breeze in branches or grass, a bird singing, or waves washing away a shore. Silence exists only in the desert. Complete, utter, total. The Arabs have a saying which, roughly translated, means – 'He upon whom the Desert puts its spell will forever be haunted by it. No matter where he goes, the Desert will call him …'.

There is truth in the saying.

'Hearing' silence for the first time is strange and frightening; under it, you feel you are of no importance, or if you do have importance, it is only equal to that of the desert lizard. And in thinking that, you immediately raise the desert lizard to new heights of importance in the scheme of things, lest you walk the rest of life with an inferiority-complex that will show. Listening so, on the death-quiet horse in the death-quiet desert, a thought seeps into your mind, and then you know that if Jesus Christ had been born in any other place than the desert, he would not have been Jesus Christ. It was the desert which shaped and moulded him, it was the desert silence which taught him how to think and live …

There was a Chiefie, a Flight-Sergeant, with us who was ex-aircrew. He was a kind, thoughtful man; the half-wing badge with the letters

'AG' for air-gunner seemed out of place on him. He was more Chaplain material than warrior, I thought. I didn't get to know him very well. But I secretly admired him. He'd got an old fashioned wind-up portable gramophone, and a complete set of discs which were a violin concerto, I think by Mendelssohn. Sometimes he used to bring his gramophone onto the bungalow stoop and let the music wash the day away. Melody upon melody, haunting, sad, wistful.

I learned that the Flight-Sergeant had been a tail-gunner on bomber-missions. He was a top-notch tail-end-charlie, and any crew was glad and happy to have him along, because they knew that their backsides were protected by a gunner who was second to none. He'd left quite a few scattered piles of German aircraft debris over North Africa. It seemed he drank and wenched as good as he fired his guns ... until this one time when he was given ten days combat-leave. He air-hiked to the Holy Lands, having seen enough of Cairo and Alex, Port Said and Port Suez. He drank his way through a few days of casbahs and night-spots, the usual 'sports' of tired veterans who have 'seen it all', but keep on hoping that they may yet see something new. Then, this one night, he came to the Sea of Galilee; and he took a rowing boat onto the Lake, alone; in search of quiet and peace. And something happened to him out there on the water, and when he brought the boat back he was a changed man. A new man. Somewhere on the Lake he had his personal moment of truth ... but after a while none of the air-crews wanted him in that rear-turret. They could no longer depend on him to press the gun-buttons. He became the Jonah of his squadron, because the killer-instinct had left him, and he just could not press the buttons when an enemy aircraft came into his sights.

Eventually he was grounded, taken off 'ops' and put to general duties. Lack of moral-fibre, operational-exhaustion, battle-fatigue, 'Log-book-happy' – it all amounted to the same thing. He could not kill. The Sea of Galilee had taken his life and altered it. It was as simple as that. But the War-machine worshipped the God of War, and not Christ of Galilee. The Flight-Sergeant's moment of truth was an annoyance, and an incovenience, and after all, God-dammit, God was on the Allies side and not the Axis. Every bullet and tracer which ripped from the muzzles of air-borne machine-guns had God's blessing, if they were fired against Ities or Jerries. So the Flight-Sergeant was grounded; and as a result probably had more good influence upon more men's lives than he had flown with or blasted from the skies.

Chapter Thirteen

When my arm was mended and my overseas tour of duty ended, I came back to England for the remaining months of my military service. I was still with the Military Police, but engaged upon Special Investigation inquiries. I built up some reputation as a 'racket-buster', and was twice commended by the Chief Constable of the area for 'clearing up' crimes cluttering the civil police books. More and more I wanted to be a policeman when the Military were finished with me, and so, when demobilisation came, I joined the civil police of a Midland town. The career, so long waited for, so long ached for, was not to last. During my last six months of military service I'd met a girl and married her; what with a police house and a good solid career stretching in front of me there was little more I could ask of life.

But inside of two years I'd been sacked from the police, was pissed morning noon and night, and my marriage was as good as over. I had got a couple of years to limp into divorce – thank God we had no children.

I'd now reached the ripe old age of twenty-six. The reasons I got sacked from the police were neglect of duty and 'unsuitability as a police-officer'; these were the charges against me under the Police Discipline Code, but being constantly drunk on duty would have been nearer the truth.

An Inspector and Sergeant found me sleeping it off in somebody's parked car while half the Force was out looking for me, assuming I'd landed into trouble up one of the backstreet warrens. I was three hours adrift and hadn't rung in from my hourly beat-points. Two officers took me home in a prowl-car – not out of generosity, but because they didn't want the horror of a drunk policeman reeling up the High Street with cape draped like a scarf round his neck, and helmet at an almost impossible angle.

When I got into my flat, somewhere about three in the morning, it took me a few minutes to realise that somebody was in bed with my wife. They were both asleep, and I checked and saw that the alarm clock was set for five in the morning, an hour before I was supposed to come off duty. The bloke in bed with her was Danny, a bachelor who'd got the downstairs flat and who I sometimes had a drink with. I knew for a fact that he was knocking off a Sunday school teacher's wife up the road, a little red-head. It seemed like one married woman wasn't enough for him.

They were still asleep when I set about them. She was nearest and let out a scream as I lugged her from the blankets. I threw her across the room and started on him – he was too unprepared to put up much resistance. I worked him over a bit, then hauled him to the door and tipped him down the stairs.

Then I grabbed a suitcase, piled some of my wife's things into it, chucked some clothes at her and told her to get dressed. All strong melodramatic stuff, but not so hot when I think of my own negative contribution to the marriage. While she was dressing I phoned her mam who lived twenty miles away, told the family to come and get her. The wife was crying as I locked her on the street side of the front door. I went back into the flat and started on a bottle. Inside an hour I was tanked up again, too tanked to make the stairs when her family arrived. Her brother shouted the odds and tried to kick the front door in. I opened the window and told him to bugger off. Other windows, the windows of neighbours, were wide awake and listening. 'Bloody well come down here,' the brother raged. 'Let's see how you manage with your own size.' I scooped up more of my wife's clothing and let them rain down on him. Eventually him and the rest of the family drove away.

161

I brooded over Danny. Why knock my missus off, I thought, when he's got a nice little bit of red-head down the road? I must have dozed. Voices, loud and angry, came roaring in from outside. For a minute I thought it was the wife's brother back again, with more brothers to help him. I grabbed the stave (truncheon) out of my uniform side-pocket to defend myself if they burst in. But when I got to the window it wasn't them at all. It was Danny and the Sunday school teacher from down the road – and from what I could make of it, the Sunday school feller had suspected for some time that Danny was knocking his wife off. The fellow was ranting and raving; and Danny was trying to reason with him, asking him to come inside his flat so's they could talk things over reasonably, like two sensible adults. Danny came from a top-bracket family, Very Important People, who had a mansion out in the country. He was desperately trying to keep out of publicity. The Sunday school feller finally hit Danny on the jaw. Danny let him. Time after time the feller hit him, and Danny stood there and left his hands at his sides. The Sunday school feller finally grew fed up with it and went away, and I could see Danny standing motionless for a long time. Then I saw him go inside his flat and shut the door.

I drank some more of the whisky, and in a way it sort of mellowed me, took all feelings of responsibility away from me. After a bit I decided that Danny wasn't such a bad guy after all, that it was six of one and half a dozen of the other – twice over, if you included the red-head.

'Good luck to you, Danny, mate,' I thought, and stumbled down the stairs to tell him so in person. I made my way round to the side door of his flat. I could see him in his kitchen, brooding over a writing pad. I watched. After a while he finished the letter he was writing and put it into an envelope. Then he took newspapers and folded them into strips, using the blade of a knife to wedge the strips into door and window cracks. I knew what he was about, then. But it was his business not mine. He'd fought all the way through the war as a belly-gunner in bombers, so he didn't need advice from me about rolling his personal dice.

Anyroad, I figured that he'd change his mind at the last minute and find something to live for. I went back to my own flat, dropped onto the bed, and was asleep in seconds. Some hours later I was awakened by the landlord hammering on the door.

'Gas,' he was shouting. 'I can smell gas. You left a tap on in there?' I struggled off the bed and went with him to find the leak; then I remembered Danny in the downstairs flat.

Looking through his kitchen window I saw him stretched out on the floor with his head in the gas oven. I broke the window with a yard broom, climbed inside with the landlord close behind, turned off the still hissing gas taps, and dragged Danny outside into the garden. He was still warm, and I thought he was alive. I pumped at him while the landlord telephoned for ambulance and police. But Danny was dead. The police weren't long in coming for me, neighbours gleefully telling them about the row the night before. They had the Sunday school teacher in, too.

'There were marks on his face,' the police said, 'caused by what?'

'Some came off my fists, some came off his,' I answered, pointing to the teacher, 'although I doubt if I could identify which from which.'

They took written statements from the pair of us and left us alone. The pathologist made his examination, the last letters he'd written were read, and the case was closed. Suicide while the balance of the mind was disturbed. The local paper gave him a couple of inches telling about his belly-gunner tours, and how these must have preyed on his mind, etcetera.

* * *

My wife returned for the rest of her things, armed with an escort of three brothers. She had a bruise from hair-line to chin where I'd hit her, and she had to talk without moving her jaw. I regretted having hit her, but I couldn't put the clock back, nor nurse pain with sorrow. After she'd gone I called the neighbours in and sold all the furniture, everything from the lamp fittings to the carpets; about four hundred quid's worth went for twenty-five pounds. Then I walked down to the Main Police Station to keep my appointment with the Chief Constable, carrying my uniforms and contranklements in a suitcase. In front of the Chief I tried to get my word in first, tried to resign before he could sack me. If I resigned, I could always apply to join another Force later on, but if I was sacked I'd be a marked man forever.

The Chief Constable was sharper than me – he sacked me even while my mouth was shaping words of resignation.

'Dismissed the Force,' he said. 'Unfit to be a policeman.'

' 'Shun, about turn, quick-march,' ordered the Duty Inspector; but I was an 'ex' now, so just ambled away. They could stuff their drill. I walked into the nearest pub where I steadily got drunk, but not incapable.

While I was there somebody came in and said a bank up the road had been robbed. When the second edition of the newspapers hit the street there was a detailed account of the robbery. Some feller had followed a woman into the bank, snatched a couple of hundred pounds from her, then ran like the clappers of hell before anybody could catch breath. I read the description. About five ten to six feet, slim build, light to brown unruly hair, grey suit with burgundy tie. The description fitted me and a few hundred thousand other blokes.

'What you doin' with all that brass?' a drinking acquaintance called across the bar. 'Drinks all round, is it?'

'Spend it all on yoh, and ah'll have none left,' I answered. I drank till closing time, then went to the pictures to sleep it off. When I came out it wanted half an hour to opening time, so I wandered round the streets for a bit. I was looking in a shop window – a gunsmith's, of all places – when I felt a tap on my arm. It was one of the sergeants from CID.

' 'Lo, Archie,' he said. 'Just the bloke ah'm lookin' for.'

'You found me,' I replied. 'What's your trouble? Come to give me my job back?'

'Think yoh can help us with someatt,' he said. 'Won't take long. Station's just across the road.'

Like an idiot, I went with him to the CID office.

Inside, he was no longer the friendly soul of the streets.

'Where'd you put the money?' he asked.

'What money?'

'The money yoh pinched off the woman in the bank earlier on.'

'Yoh'm round the twist,' I told him.

'That won't help you. Get it over with and we'll do what we can for you in court. Stress, strain, emotional worries. That sort of stuff.'

I tried to laugh it off, but he was in dead earnest.

'Wheer were you when the robbery took place?' he asked.

'I don't know. A pub some place. P'raps the George, p'raps the Talbot or the Railway.'

'What were you looking in the gunsmith's for?'

'That's what shop windows am for. For looking through.'

'Why a gunsmith's?'

'Why not a gunsmith's?'

'Depends on what yoh intends to do for a living.'

I stood up and made for the door.

'You know the drill as well as me,' I said. 'So put up – or shut up.'

'You'll stand an ID?' he asked. 'Yoh'll go on Identity Parade? Just to settle things?'

I considered. I was innocent. I'd got nothing to lose.

'One of the bank clerks caught a good look at the bloke,' said the sergeant, 'and so did the woman who had the money pinched.'

'I'll stand a parade,' I agreed, 'just to settle it and get you off my back.'

This became the point where I switched off from being a copper in every sense. I changed sides. I stood in line with nine men who bore no more resemblance to me than black does to white. Most of them had been pulled in off the street. A couple wore sports coats and flannels, five were in working clothes and overalls, and two were huge coppers wearing raincoats over their uniforms. A guilty man would have objected immediately at the composition of the ID. But I was innocent.

They could have put five monkeys and three pigmies in line as far as I was concerned, but Truth would out. The female bank-clerk came down the line and picked me out. I was frightened as they took her away. The other witness went up and down the line, shook her head.

'He's not in this lot,' she said.

I was taken back to the CID office for grilling, but I wouldn't wear it.

'You were positively identified,' the sergeant raged. But I was angry as well, now.

'I want to make a phone call,' I said, 'and I want a list of solicitors.'

'It's a pipe-dream, Archie,' one of the other detectives said. 'What you'm entitled to and what yoh gets is two different things.'

'Cards on table,' I answered. 'You locking me up? You going to hold me?'

The sergeant was stubborn.

'Yoh was identified,' he said. 'yoh can't get out of that.'

'I want a list of names of the fellers who stood in line,' I answered. 'Not one of them resembled me. I was the only one in line wearing a grey suit, for starters. The Parade wasn't composed as it should have been.'

'Yoh raised no objections at the time,' he snapped back and by God, he was right. 'Yoh accepted the composition without question or objection.'

'It didn't matter *then*,' I yelled at him. 'But it matters *now*. You bloody-well jury-rigged it. You set it up.'

He didn't like the feel of the case slipping away from him.

'Why bugger about,' he said. Just give us a statement, we'll bail you, and then we can shut shop.'

I dug in.

'Don't old-soldier me, Len,' I said. 'You got them bloody three stripes and a "Jacks" job through long service, not bloody common sense and intelligence.' A look of almost joy came into his face. I got my back against the wall.

'Don't come it, Len,' I warned, 'you start a beat-up and I promise you I'll put my face in the way of your fists every time. I'll *make* you leave marks.'

He was breathing heavy, and the other 'Jack' was waiting on his orders. I worked out what I'd do if they decided on a beat-up. They'd try to work on my belly, where the marks wouldn't show. But if I clenched in over my belly, got my arms and elbows to pad it, they'd have to come for my face. I'd make sure of that. With a few teeth missing, the odd black eye and a few facial bruises, there'd be some explaining to do. Especially since I had no intention of hitting back, so's they could say it was resisting arrest or self-defence.

'I lay odds of ten to one that you showed that woman a photo of me before she came down the Parade line,' I said. 'You showed her a picture of me off my police-file, so's she'd remember my face on the ID. And I'll give odds of hundred to one that she'll admit it under cross-examination.'

The sergeant scowled. 'All right,' he said at last. 'Piss off. But mark my words, chap – ah'll have you before yoh'm much older. Ah'n got no use for blokes like yoh.'

He had me, all right, but not the way he intended. A squad-car picked me up in the early hours of morning, unconscious in an alley-way; not simply drunk, but brain-exploded into coma through alcohol-poisoning. I remembered nothing for three days. When I came to I was in a clean white-sheeted bed. There were five other men in the ward with me and from time to time a nurse came in and fussed about. The moment she left the ward on some errand I grabbed my clothes from the side-locker and slipped away through the open french-window which led to the grounds. I dressed on the veranda, leaving the hospital pyjamas on the floor.

As I walked away I could hear one of the men calling for the nurse, telling her to 'come quick, 'cos the funny feller is having it away.' My legs were spongy, sorbo, and my head had little hammers beating inside, like as if all my thoughts were fighting with each other in a mad mixed up free-for-all. But after a bit the night-air took most of the muzziness away. I'd got no money so I stole a bike from outside a pub and rode to my mother's house. There was nobody in. But I knew she left the front-door key hanging from a piece of string inside the letter-box. I let myself in and went straight to the gas-meter. I used a poker to twist the lock off and emptied about four quid's worth of small silver into my pockets. I left a note inside the money drawer saying who'd done it – not for any reason of bravado or sentiment, but to rid myself of any feelings of obligation towards mam.

Spending the coins was a bit awkward. For every drink, I had to go to a different pub because in the Black Country if anybody spends more than three bob in bits of silver and pennies at one time, it's a certain bet that he's done the gas-meter. As you spend, you can never seem to change up to higher denominations. All you can do is hand over two shilling pieces and ask for a pint; when the change mounts up you pass it back with the excuse that it's dragging at your pockets, and will the gaffer please swap it for a couple of half-crown pieces. If he gives you a two shilling piece and a sixpenny bit in the change, you feel almost cheated.

I spent the last of the money on a 'bus ride back to my empty flat. The window of Danny's kitchen hadn't yet been mended, so I opened the catch and crawled inside. All his personal things had been taken away, but in the kitchen cabinet I found half a bottle of brandy. I sat supping this quietly in the dark and must have dozed off. I woke up a bit cold and I turned the gas fire on, but either I forgot to light it being three parts drunk, or the flame blew out, I don't know ...

When I woke up there was a herd of policemen tramping all over me and two ambulance men lifting me onto a stretcher. I felt as if everything except me had gone into slow-motion, and I was standing outside myself watching everything that happened. I was conscious that I'd got terrific strength in my arms, and that I was lifting the two ambulance men, one on each arm, inches clear of the floor.

'Christ,' I heard one of them say, as if from a distance. 'We can't hold the bugger,' the policemen blurred in to help. I knew my face was smiling and I tried to make the smile go away, but it was painted on and wouldn't shift. I was tossing men about as if they were dolls, and I'd got this fantastic, enormous strength, and I could hear myself laughing like a bloody mad man. They got me on the stretcher and clamped me down with leather straps. I couldn't move, and helplessness made me afraid. I was half ashamed of my tears as I pleaded with them to unstrap me.

'Shurrup, you bastard, else we'll bloody well gag you.'

Somebody stuck a needle in me; a bit after, I could hear somebody singing; before the artificial sleep hit me, I realized it was my voice singing. Next day, or the day after, I'm not too clear – I was taken from hospital to court, with a police escort. There were quite a few charges. Assault with malicious intent on my wife, robbing a gas-meter (they tried to make that one into Breaking and Entering a Dwelling house, but blood is fractionally thicker than water and my mam wouldn't wear that one) and attempted suicide. The last one shook me more than anything. The Blue-men explained how my landlord had smelled gas for the second time within a few days, how once again he'd tracked it down to Danny's kitchen and found me – spark-out and unconscious – in front of the unlit fire.

Poor sod, it seemed that his house was being turned into a lethal gas-chamber. I laughed outright as I had a mental vision of him sitting furtively and haggard on the stairs every night in case anybody felt like nipping inside his house for a bit of final solution. The laugh did me more damage than the evidence. The court packed me off to a mental institution with orders that I stay there for not less than a year, and to receive 'treatment' for chronic alcoholism. It took four of them, two policemen and two ushers, to carry me down.

So away to the long bleak corridors the memory of which will haunt to the grave, the white-coated clinical purity, the close-barred windows and the company of strange men forever staring into the cold ashes of themselves.

Chapter Fourteen

Doctor Barrabas was the psychiatrist in 'charge of my case'. He's long dead now, so it doesn't matter a damn that I tell the truth and describe him as a rotten little bastard who was more in need of a head-shrinker than anyone I ever knew. This one time he had me in his office, and he sat there at his desk peering at me over his steel-rimmed glasses, with an expression of distaste on his face like I was a dead fish somebody had left lying round for a week for the cat to play with.

A short, fat roly-poly man he was, who never missed a meal in his life. He gave me little jig-saw puzzles to play with, and a dozen ink-blot pictures. Each time I looked at one of his pictures, he asked me what I saw. I'd had these tests before, in my RAF entrance days, and Civil Police Force. I knew that Barrabas was probing for a sex-angle, so decided not to let him have one.

'What do you see there?' he asked, showing me an ink-blob picture that Picasso would have been proud of.

'Fish and chips,' I told him. He only blinked once, I will say that for him.
'This one?'
'It's an antique piss-pot used by King Alfred, and it's got his initials on.'
'This one?'
'An ink-blot.'
'Eh?'

'It's an ink-blot.'

'Yes – but what do you see?'

'I see an ink-blot. And if *you* see anything different, you'd best get another pair of bloody glasses.'

He put the ink-blots back in his drawer, observed me coldly.

'You're being difficult,' he said flatly.

'I'd say I was being bloody well impossible, meself,' I agreed.

'People like you should be in prison,' he said, 'not in our hospitals.'

'What sort of prison?' I wanted to know. 'The sort you probably worked in during the war – Belsen, and places like that?'

We hated each other's guts.

He changed tactics.

'What do you believe in?' he asked (only he said 'Vot' instead of 'what'). 'Do you believe in God?'

I decided it was steady ground to be on.

'Sometimes,' I admitted.

He pounced. 'Vot is your conception of God? Who do you think God is?'

I considered, shrugged. 'God is you, me,' I answered. 'You're God, and I'm God, God's in all of us, and we're all in God. You, me. You're God, and me.'

He completely ignored the fact that I'd included him in the deal. 'There,' he said, triumphant. 'There. Now vy should you think you are God, Mmm?' And the silly bastard wrote something on his pad. Paranoic, schizophrenic, something – that was me as far as he was concerned; something to be scribbled onto a note-pad and spiked on a file. But to give the feller his due, he'd met me under not very happy circumstances. I'd put two of his staff off duty for a couple of days, and I'd kicked him in the belly. Upon such foundations friendships are not made.

I'd tried to kill myself, that was the thing which concerned him. I'd turned on the gas, and stuck my head in the oven. The details weren't very clear in my mind (or his), they were all clouded over, as if they concerned someone else and not me. I'd put a sort of mental block up, inside my mind.

Switched-off, I called it. All I could recall were urgent wisps of memories, disjointed but vivid in parts though faded at the edges; I remember ...

* * *

... suffocating – suffocating – out – out – get it out! Get it out, can't you hear me? Hear me? It's suffocating me, what are you doing, what is it, bugger you? Take it away, leave me alone, bugger you. Smell. Smell. Gas and rubber. Taste – foul, I tell you – vomit and stench and gas and rubber – what's this buggering tube for? Why'm I being sick – in my nose, my mouth, my hair, my eyes – leave me alone, you bastards. God, God damn you ... make them leave me alone ... light my lamp, dad; take my darkness away. Go away, dad ... but take me with you, take me with you, take me with you ...

There is a window through my sickness, through my vomit. Is it morning? Is it night? Who is the man in the white coat what's he doing to me what the bloody bloody hell is the bastard doing to me ... I'm stinking in my own vomit and I can smell gas, gas. Somebody should do something about it, Mister, they've left the gas taps on you crazy bastard somebody's left the gas turned on. You fool, I'm telling you – what are you trying to do, kill me? Get it out, get it out of my stomach, go away and leave me, come back and turn the gas off. I'm being sick, I'm being crucified and I'm frightened and you are afraid ...

... peace, peace, find it in sleep. Hide deep in darkness and wear it like an amulet against trespass, and close your eyes and sleep ... sleep ... all will be well ...

Oft in the stilly night ere slumber's chain hath bound me ...

What is that echo? Where did I learn it? It was a long time ago, I learned it a long time ago in a different world in a different life when the years could have been green with childhood. I did learn it then, didn't I? Or was it someone else, someone I knew, someone who is dead?

Old Billy is God, and he will make glass ferns for me, all sparkling in white glass that looks like frost, and his last autumn rose will be reluctant to close her heart to the end of the day ...

Oft in the stilly night ere slumber's chain hath bound me, I see in a misty light other days around me ... Ahhh-h! It was me – I remember now, it was me. Billy was burning rubbish in his garden and I rescued the book with the poem in it ...

What's happening? Where'm I going? Where you taking me? Walls, a corridor, someone pushing me on a velvet-wheeled-rubber-tyred trolley and I'm covered in blankets. Am I really dead? Yes. Yes, I'm dead ... I'll see my friend Billy, I don't give a bloody damn about being dead, I don't care.

You'll put me now on a hard slab and strip me naked and the slab has a trough to it to catch the blood and liquids then you'll take up your bloody knife and slit my guts until the sides gape open and you can get to the heart and organs. What'll you expect my heart to tell you? It was only a pump, only a bloody pump, it won't pulse in your hands, it won't tell you how much it loved, will it, how much it wanted to love. And nor will it tell who I hated. So throw it back inside and close the edges of the stomach with eight regulation stitches to the regulation inch, like mail-bag sewing in a prison; now take the knife and peel back my skull, only the bloody Red Indians could do a better job than you with their scalping knives, lift the flesh and hair back like a flap over my useless eyes and pick up the saw and rasp it through bone. There it is, the lid of the skull removed like a bowler hat, like the little bit of a hat a monk wears, and there's the brain – my brain. What'll it tell you? That shadow there – that greyer shadow in the grey mess – is that anything? Was that the trouble? If I'd have cut that out while I was alive, would I have lived differently? It doesn't matter to *me* – I'm just trying to help *you*, because you know fuck-all and most of that you picked up second-hand. It's all bay-windows and French-knickers, isn't it? It all adds up to zero multiplied by zero a million zero times.

You know no more than me, mate, perhaps even less. So pour the bloody mess back into its bone cup and put the lid back on, and stitch, stitch, stitch. And then leave me alone. Because when the flesh is stricken the spirit weeps ...

Sound, rustling a long way off; meaningless ... meaningless ... meaningless? Sounds of people, of voices, and I am sliding back into the vehicle that is my body which is unscarred and un-naked, and it's a hospital bed I'm in and not on a meat-slab. And an echo is weaving in from between vague figures and vague voices, and it whispers to me alone in a green voice which is the voice of my shattered Mephistopheles, who died when Billy died ... *Oft in the stilly night ere slumber's chain hath bound me....* The mind walks long corridors of its own fashioning and sighs and remembers ... *I see in a misty light other days around me.* Where?

Where *did* I hear that, and how long ago? Why does it haunt me? Why does the echo of words disturb me now and pluck me along, and to what, and to where? Who *was* Billy, who *was* old Billy who made loveliness so touchable, so almost keepable ...?

Poetry ... it is poetry ... weaving a strange spell and spinning its web about my senses and crying to my emotions. Poetry *does* cry like that, doesn't it? Whether it be tears of laughter or sadness, it is still the language of stifled emotions.

I am twelve years old and I am writing my first poem and it is about rabbits and blue skies and love and God, all sweet-sticky words like they were written on cake with an icing-tool. But that doesn't matter, not really; it's the instinct which counts, not the words, who gives a damn if 'moon' rhymes with 'June' ... I'm sitting on a wall which overlooks a butcher's slaughter-yard and the yard is deserted and the sun is warm with me. There is green moss between the flags of the yard-paving, green moss, dark green, and it is thick and glossy like an animal's fur. The doors of the cattle sheds are old and dry, and the weathers of winters and summers have taken the paint away leaving a serene age grained into the timber. A quietness, a stillness ... and the first revelation comes. One moment only, one single moment when all senses and emotions are fused into one flash of inner radiance, a glimpse snatched from the long wide acres of Eternity when the little soul of childhood stands on tip-toe to look and listen ... then quickly as it comes, it is gone, and the emotions cry out for its return, for the deep friendship of it.

So a poem is born, an echo, a tear, a shred of laughter ... and dies at birth because there is nothing to attend it with. You strive for articulation, but do not have it; the thoughts are too strong for the words you know ...

... then suddenly the gates of the slaughter-yard are thrown open and cattle are bellowing and men are shouting, the moss is trampled under flying hooves, escaping wild hysterical hooves, and pens gape wide open like hungry jaws. The steers are roped and thrown, a man in white overalls presses a spiked pistol to an animal's head, and life is kicking and writhing in the agony of death. The man takes a knife and slits the animal's throat and the blood wells out, thick and dark. So much blood ... impossible amounts ... impossible. The steer is kicking and throbbing in its final convulsions and the man places his foot upon its stomach and treads it. The blood comes reluctantly from the animal's gashed throat as the man's foot acts as a pump. The blood is pooled upon the flags, the man's overalls are stained, the green moss is changed to red. Blood swells into the gutters of the yard and as the sun shines on it, it glistens dull and solid except for narrow riverlets of thinner and lighter blood which race along the outer edges. There is a frightening smell, sickly and sweet and acrid. It is the smell of dying life and I am afraid. Another beast is dragged down, its eyes bursting with terror, its screams of pain and final knowledge bellowing from lungs already filled with death. Death ... death ... death. The beast feels death, shrinks from it, tries to fight it. The man and his helpers do not understand, have no feelings or awareness. They are destroying, tearing at life, ripping and skinning, dismembering and stacking, and they are cold and detached. They do not understand. Their hands and arms are red with blood, their fingernails clotted with gore, their nostrils oblivious to the presence of death. The man in the white overalls turns round and I recognise him. There is something wrong with him, because his face is calm and normal, and this is wrong. His face should be twisted in pain, wet with tears, agonising to look on because of the suffering he is administering. Old Konk the poacher never did this – he never let the creatures suffer, he was always quick and clean and merciful. But this man's face is calm and reposed, and he is wiping his hands on a still-warm hide, removing the blood from his fingers. And now he is lighting a cigarette with fingers which are steady and do not tremble. And I see him and I recognise him ...

Frank, Frank – it's me! It's me, sitting on the wall watching what you are doing. Don't you remember me, Frank? You gave me a puppy, don't you remember? A little soft puppy with a damp nose and scared eyes and a pink tongue and a fat little body which was warm and squiggly. Only the puppy got run over, Frank, it got killed by a lorry, a lorry went over it and I buried it out in Moody's field. You gave me the puppy, you did, you did. You told me to look after it and to be kind to it and it would always be my friend. You took me to your house to choose my own puppy from the basketful, and your wife was there, and she was pretty and I wished my mam was half as pretty, and your eyes were kind when you gave me the puppy, and I named the puppy Frankie because *you* gave him to me.

But I hate you now, hate you, hate you! You are killing the animals and hurting them, and you didn't give me the puppy because I don't want that you should have given it to me. You told me a lie, you said to be kind and not to hurt, but you are hurting and I hate you you bastard and I hate the whole bloody stinking rotten world because you can't put your goddamned trust in anything or anybody, not even this bloody bastard roly-poly headshrinker who's got me the other side of his desk mucking about with inkblots, you can't trust anything or anybody because if you do the world will get up out of its muck and dirt and kick you in the bloody teeth ...

Run, little boy, run. Down from the wall and run, run away – get away, away from it. Away from the blood and the pain and the man who gave you the puppy, the broken promises of the world – get away from them. Cry if you like, pillow your head on Hope's tomorrow and cry, cry, cry; but don't ever let anybody see you cry, not ever or ever ... *Oft in the stilly flight ere slumber's chain hath bound me, I see in a misty light other days around me* ...

You there, funny little man who says 'vot' instead of 'what'; You finished your diagnosis yet? Or is it prognosis – I never did know the difference. That's it, little man in the white coat, Session's over, and I leave you to play with your cardboard toys, your ink-blots and case-history files. One day they might make you famous, and I'm going to do you a favour. Next time you send for me I'll invent a sex-phantasy dream for you to play with, and tell you that as a child I forgot to masturbate – and that'll tip you head over heels and you'll have to start genning up on Jung and Adler instead of Freud.

The day they'd brought me to the hospital with its locked doors and barred windows – the police brought me in a van, after the Magistrates had ordered that I receive 'hospital' treatment for a year – I'd stood in the main dormitory room looking at the men I'd got to share my life with. Some were standing, some were sitting, some were crouching, some walking up and down; all with the same expression of blankness, only their eyes mirroring helplessness and hopelessness. One man was standing in the centre of the room, talking in a loud voice with an American accent, talking to nobody who existed outside his mind.

'Why shouldn't I go to church,' he was saying, 'no one can stop me from going if I wanna. I'm a God-damned God-fearing man and a mighty worshipping one and if anybody thinks different let him step outside and take his god-damned jacket off. Trouble with the world today it's run by Communists and they've got the scientists by the balls, and I was there at Hiroshima to see the fireworks, and I'll go to hell and take the god-damned lid off if they stop me going to church. They all killed my brother but I'll get the guys, the whole god-damned German army, I'll get them. If a man owned a bus or a street-car they'd want half of it.' He rambled on, mouthing rubbish which made sense at the edges, like something from *Alice in Wonderland*. As I listened to him I grew afraid of the twelve months' 'hospitalisation' which stretched ahead of me.

A nurse had taken my arm, led me into the wash-basin recess, sat me on a wooden chair. He lathered my face with soap, started to shave me.

'Lay off,' I told him, 'I can do that for myself.'

'Not in this place, you don't,' he'd answered; and I noticed that the razor he used on me was guarded by side-shields, so that only the merest hint of blade stuck out, so nobody could really hurt themselves with it if they snatched it from him.

'I feel sore,' I said to him, 'in my belly and ribs.'

'You tried to fight the police,' he'd answered, wiping the lather from the blade. 'You didn't win,' he added.

'I'm not staying here,' I'd said, getting up from the chair, 'I'm getting out of here.' He'd grabbed me, and I'd swung at him and down he'd gone. I took the bunch of keys from his pocket, unhooked the chain by which they were clipped to his belt. I almost made it. I was heading down a corridor for a far door which led to the outside world when the male nurse recovered and yelled for assistance. I frantically tried key after key in the lock, but couldn't make one fit. I turned to meet the nurses, flung the heavy bunch of keys at the foremost; he went down like a steer to a spike-gun. Then they were on me. I got one, ripped my knuckles to shreds, trying to knock his head off his shoulders. Then they'd got me snarled up with arms up my back and legs kicked from under me. They let the base of my spine crack against the floor with every step they took. Then, when they got me back to the main dormitory, they just threw me in so that I skidded like a skittle.

'Bastards,' was all I could say, wanting the last word. I didn't know until after that Doctor Barrabas was with the nurses when they overpowered me, nor did I know that I'd kicked him in the belly, because the kick was quite accidental. From then on, though, I could needle Barrabas as easy as easy. I used to wait for him to come round our ward with a party of VIP's – I always pronounced his name after the biblical bloke, Bar-rab-ass, which he didn't like. I'd wait until he came strutting in with his crocodile of followers, wait for a hole in the conversation, then throw my penn-orth of heavy-weight in by shouting out loud – 'And the voice of the people cried out for Bar-rab-ass when they were offered Christ.' The little doctor almost climbed the wall every time, with anger and frustration. I think he tried to get his own back on me by putting me on ECT treatment (electrical-convulsive-treatment) or something. In those days you took the stuff neat – no knock-out drops to start with. You were taken into a room, placed on a padded couch with two nurses to hold you down when you convulsed so's you wouldn't break your bones; then a sort of cloth-bound bit was put between your teeth so's you wouldn't grind them into powder when the shock hit you. The doctor then placed two electrodes onto your temples, roughly one above each eye, and then the electric current hit you. You heard the power *sing* like flame through your head and body, felt your back trying to arch like a long-bow and the two nurses trying to hold you flat, then your brain was filled with pain and redness, and you literally passed out like a light as the current was switched off. When you woke up, you felt like your head was filled with little people trying to hack their ways out.

After eight jolts of ECT I told them they could stuff it, I wasn't having any more. And if they tried force, I'd smash the equipment round their necks, and I wanted to see a lawyer because I was there as an alcoholic would-be-suicide, and not a bloody madman who thought he'd blown up Hiroshima with an atom bomb, or a geriatrics case fumbling inside his own pockets and crying with self-pity because he couldn't get an erection.

But, despite moments of bull-baiting diversion, there was always the communal room, the Big Room, surrounding you like a prison. Worse than prison, really, because in prison you were at least allowed into the exercise yard for two half-hour periods a day. In the hospital I was kept locked up, with never a chance to walk in the grounds in case I absconded. I'd sit in a corner staring out through the barred windows as the slow dusk was harvested in, watching the months and the weeks go by, with Mind burning in patches as random thoughts probed and pricked among the debris of memory; and so the evening air would darken into night and only the scent of the air itself would say that a wildness of roses still lingered Outside ...

Old memories had to be fed like a drip-feed of plasma into conscious awareness, because only that way was it possible not to become One with the poor, sad madmen who rotted their small personal eternities away in glooms and half-glooms. How sad they were, those poor, poor men. I came to dread the daily ECT, which burned into my brain like flame.

Only once did I ever see Kinver Edge in anger, calling on the elements to witness its grievance. Red anger it was, red at heart, with scarlet tongues leaping and raving from ground to tree-tops. For many days that anger boiled and glowered, until exhaustion came ... but for long weeks after the Edge lay black and bleeding until strength returned with time's nursing.

But while it burned, it burned day after day, night after night, mile after mile; with fire-rangers, boy scouts, volunteers, trying to put the fire out. The sky at night was hot with reflected glow. Sometimes the fire seemed to burn itself out but when the winds whispered about, the flames came from concealment, from belly-creeping, and flared red and scarlet over gorse and ferns, until every hillside seemed to be alive with dripping fire. All the birds left it, and the rabbits, and every living thing.

I came round from the shock treatment in a half dream … remembering that it had been *me* who set fire to Kinver Edge. I was out filling the pantry with Konk and Pope Tolley, before Pope got lifted for beating the policeman. Konk had slipped into a stream, and his trousers and shoes and socks were wringing wet. He pointed to a small copse.

'Light a small fire in theer, me lover,' he'd said. 'Not too big, mind – and mek sure you lights it well away from the trees and bushes, 'cos they'm dry as tinder.'

I took the matches, gathered sticks, put dry moss under them in the stead of paper. The copse was formed like a horseshoe, with one end open, the other sides being tight-packed with bramble, gorse, heather and bushes. But when I struck the match it was like I'd lit a gun-powder trail leading to a full powder-barrel. The flames licked at the moss and the dry twigs, and suddenly riverlets of flame were pushing out in all directions, with me trying to stamp them out before they reached heavy fuel. I took my jacket off to try and stem the burning tide, but only succeeded in spreading the fire more and more. The flames reached the gorse bushes and the trees, and ate them with a hungry roar. I was scared, terrified.

A wood-pigeon, dying with feathers aflame, dropped at my feet. I tried to get back through the opening, but smoke and flames drove me back. I started to scream. Then Pope Tolley came bursting through the wall of fire, crouched low and with his jacket over his head. He grabbed me tight and lunged back through the flames. I could smell singeing hair, and found it was his and mine. Pope was white-faced, except for a livid red burn-scar one side of his face where a burning branch had struck him.

'Yoh'm all right?' Pope asked me, and I nodded, sobbing from tension and relief.

'We'd best get moving, then,' Pope said.

'What about the game?' Konk asked, pointing to the sacks of pheasants.

'Leave 'em,' Pope said tersely, 'and the gear. Half the bloody Midlands police force 'ull be here the minute they can get their trouser clips on. If we'm caught with this lot, we'm for the high jump.'

Konk fretted. It was good gear, good nets, he stood to lose.

'Ah'll never get nets like these'n again,' he complained, 'they'm too good to give up easy.'

'Gis 'em here,' Pope said, and in a couple of bounds he had reached a rock-cluster away from the spread of the fire. He found a gap in the rocks, thrust the nets and traps inside, wedged a piece of rock into the gap to complete concealment.

'We'll collect 'em another day,' he said, and we left Kinver Edge to its burning anger and went into the village where people were already gathering on their doorsteps to watch the pall of spreading smoke. From half a mile away we could hear the crackling of flames as they ate the trees. Above the smoke, cawing and croaking and crying plaintively were birds of all species, confused and bewildered. Above them, like a speck of dust in the eye, a sparrow-hawk hovered, then swooped and made his choice.

Pope grumbled at Konk.

'Yoh knew that bloody grass and stuff was bone dry,' he said, 'so why'd you give the kid the bloody matches?'

'What's done is done,' Konk said philosophically. 'It warn't his fault. It just happened. Anyroad, when Kinver Edge grows again there'll be some lush pickings, that ah do know.'

Finally, the rains came and the great fire spluttered to protesting ashes until only a haze of smoke remained. Then slowly the summer healed, and the ferns grew green again. But an experimental rubber plantation never recovered, and whoever was the experimenter packed it in and went to quieter corners. Because Kinver was our main poaching zone for pheasants, we went onto a fish diet for a bit. Konk knew where there was a

Manor House, back of Wordsley Common, and the owner kept his waters stocked with trout. We lifted the fish, but somehow we never regarded it as poaching. If it *is* poaching, then every fisherman is a poacher at heart. Fish are mostly 'placeless' (and the pun isn't really intentional); they are migratory, not resident, with but few exceptions.

I'd heard that trout could be caught by hand, but Konk scorned this as over-rated folk-lore.

'It's like gypsies and hedgehogs,' he said. 'Talk to erra body whose met a gypsy and ten to one he'll say the gypsy invited him to a meal of hedgehog baked in clay. What the hell the bloody gypsies want with hedgehogs when there's rabbits to snare and pheasants to lift, ah'm buggered if ah know.'

I suppose there are men who can 'burn the water' by shining a torch in it, then gaffing the fish as they come to investigate; but I've never met one who did it. And to spear a fish, like Tarzan at the picture-house, must have taken bloody good eyesight, because refraction in the water can cause that much confusion you'd miss the fish by a yard. In our day, polaroid glasses weren't easy come by – and that's what you need if you want to see fish in the water as and where they actually are.

Konk had two ways of catching the fish. One was for me to carry a small home-made sailing boat. When we got to the water, Konk and Pope would take the boat and hang baited hooks from its keel. Then, while I played the boat from a large ball of string, they'd go and hide in the bushes. If a keeper came along and saw me playing the boat, he'd like as not let out a yell and tell me to bugger off out of it. So I'd run off, sacrificing the boat. But if no keepers came, Konk or Pope would slip from the bushes every so often, pull the boat in, unhook the fish, rebait the hooks and set me sailing again.

I watched Pope do something one time that I'll never forget. He found a stream where the fish were plentiful, and he'd got this fourteen pound sledge-hammer with him. He waded out into the stream to a rock which stuck up in the middle. Then he started to drop feed round the rock; dead flies, maggots, bits of bread. The fish swarmed round the rock – and when they were there in plenty, Pope swung the sledgehammer high, and brought it down with all his strength against the rock he was standing on. Konk was with him in a flash, net dipping in and out and sweeping up the fish which were lying half stunned by the shock-waves set up by Pope's hammer. We had a harvest of fish that time.

But, from the window of a locked in mental hospital Pope and Konk and old Billy and Tomato Juice, and men like these, seemed a million years away. The bars at the window locked me in, and locked them out, and the men inside the dormitory with me were only half-men, were only rabbits cowering and skulking as if a ferret were cornering them in a musty bury from which they would not fight back, or even try to escape, but accepted in blind hysteria.

When Doctor Barrabas came round next time with his retinue of sightseers I tried different tactics. I stood in front of him and his crowd, with my palm outstretched.

'In Hogarth's day,' I told him, 'the people had to pay a penny to see the likes of us. So fucking well pay up.' He pursed his lips and pushed past me.

Chapter Fifteen

In the hospital I found myself in a backwater of life. I found that hate and sadness, hope and despair, gentleness and cruelty, attention and indifference were parts of the backwater. Stagnation. I found that these ingredients were not spread out as they were in the Outside World, they existed in little condensed pools, almost tangible. The ward staff changed over twice a day; I found the night-shifts not so bad, because they were in contact with us for only a couple of hours until we went to bed, and for a short while in the mornings when we got up. The Charge Nurse and his staff reflected the mood that we'd all wear for certain hours. Some of the nurses were jumped-up little bastards – the likes of which may be with us for years to come, staffing the back-wards of mental hospitals where no gleam of reasonable sanity exists to voice a protest that will be heard. Jumped-up little Hitlers who find it easy and gratifying to manipulate degrees of madness to their own whims.

I found some of the nurses were queers, homosexuals – quite a few of these find their way into nursing ranks. Yet others were decent and friendly, restoring a reasonable balance ... but few of them had time for alcoholics. I felt this attitude and it put me on the defensive. I stuck out my mental chin and dared them to take a punch at it.

I walked and I talked and I stood and I sat, and I picked a book up and stood near the window reading it. Lines of verse tumbled against my mind and I read them again and again, drank them from the pages.

> Good creatures, do you love your lives
> And have you ears for sense?
> Here is a knife like other knives,
> That cost me eighteen pence.
>
> I need but stick it in my heart
> And down will come the sky,
> And earth's foundations will depart
> And all you folk will die.

I felt the delight and laughter run through me; the starkness of it, the cruelty, the bloody marvellous logic. In eight lines of verse Housman had arrived at the single truth, the great answer, the supreme revenge. A man destroyed himself not to kill himself but to kill others; to destroy the whole bastard rotten world-pack, to wipe man's map clean. I read the verse and savoured it and liked it like Power. Then I placed the book in the open privacy of my locker for tomorrow's savouring and sat staring through the barred window as the slow dusk gathered, watching the weeks and days and months shuffle by like tired men, trying to forget the sadness and madness that lived in the same room with me.

It *was* backwater, the hospital. I just hung around and stagnated. Had I been a madman, the hospital would have served purpose. But I retained my mental faculties – the only sickness I had was a gnawing craving for drink. My mind was sane, but took bruises from the madmen around me. I went into no-man's land, a world which has no equal. There was no anchor to safely trust, my body became idle, my mind depressed. The pendulum of my emotions swung from high elation at trivial things to the darkest gloom. If you were a patient in a mental hospital because of a Court Order the hospital authorities became chary of you. Theirs was the responsibility for the body, and they found it more convenient to keep a man locked in a ward rather than risk his escape by allowing him ground parole.

I watched time go by, and there seemed no end to being locked in.

The only treatment I had was sick-pan. Every morning the charge nurse gave me apo-morphine tablets to suck; after they'd melted, about fifteen minutes later, I'd vomit. Up it would come, gushing and snorting and honking through nose and nostrils, the whole contents of my bloody belly pouring out. I'd have to catch the vomit in a pan. For half an hour every day even the madmen avoided me. My belly would heave and twist with sick-cramps – I felt as if its very lining was coming away, up through my nose and mouth. Then, after a bit, when the cramps and aches had subsided, I'd have to take the pan to the nurse for him to see. He'd nod, tell me to clean the pan. Then he'd give me a tot of brandy, whisky or gin. The idea was to set up aversion for the alcohol. But I never did. I put up with the sickness merely to get the drink. The hospital staff thought I was just being awkward.

Then one day I had a windfall. A Charge Nurse left a bottle of surgical spirits unguarded, so I won them and hid the stuff away. I briefed one of the feeble minded ones what to say. So when the nurse came looking for it, the madman mumbled that another nurse had taken it. I sat in the lavatory with the precious bottle, sipping the burning fluid, feeling my mind and body relax from tension. An hour later I was well cut and the Charge Nurse stared at me suspiciously until I croaked that the treatment had made me feel groggy. He gave me permission to go to bed and I lay there blissfully seeing the rest of the bottle away.

When morning came it was Sunday, with only the blond German nurse on duty. He came down the ward like a jackbooted SS man, ripping sheets and blankets away, leaving puddles of sick humanity shivering out at early morning. I lazed on my back, knowing that the German sod would leave me alone after I'd spared him one level look. He stopped at the next bed to mine, where a young epileptic boy lay. The nurse yanked the bedclothes back and the lad had a noticeable erection. The nurse pointed to it, roared for everyone to have a look, then flung himself on top of the boy and went through motions of having sexual intercourse with him. The boy got one hand down the side of his bed, came up with bed-bottle, tried to hit the nurse with it. Spilled urine went over both of them. The nurse lost his rag, started to punch the boy; I got out of bed, deep rage burning out from my belly. The nurse saw me coming, left the lad alone. I went into the corridor to find the Charge Nurse and report the incident. But he hadn't yet arrived. Back in the dormitory the boy started to cry out again and I saw the German dragging him away to the side-pads. I went after him, pulled the boy from him, lifted my fist. 'I'm going to mark you, you bastard,' I said. The nurse looked scared, but then somebody came at the back of me. Before I could turn two of the newly arrived staff each twisted an arm up my back.

'These two just set about me,' blustered the German; I tried to get the toe of my shoe hard into his crotch, I was that mad, but a knee or fist slammed me in the kidneys and I went down like a sack of sawdust. The epileptic was dragged into one padded cell, me another. The door was locked on me. After a while the Charge Nurse came back holding the empty surgical spirits bottle discovered in my bed.

'Balls,' I said, aware even as I said it that I wasn't being very original; the nurse went away, leaving me to contemplate the six-sided room with its quilt-padded walls and floor. Soon the doctor came, and I told him what had happened with the German nurse. He sneered his contempt.

'My staff don't do things like that,' he said. 'It's people like you who cause trouble. Prison's the place for your sort, not hospitals.'

'You cunt,' I bellowed at him. 'You're only used to dealing with fucking vegetables – you don't know sod all about *real* people.' He went out, relocked the door.

'Go and read Housman,' I shouted after him, 'and stick a knife in your fucking heart and kill the lot of us.'

I knew I was in for a week's solitary, without books or diversion. I'd got a few sleeping tablets hidden on me and I ferreted them out, collected spittle in my mouth to wash them down. But sleep didn't come. Something went wrong, my mind started to bend and warp. Perhaps it was because of the surgical spirits, or the sleeping tablets, or a combination of both added to the strain of inner tension. My eyes started to play tricks on me and there were voices and noises in my ears which I knew did not exist. I sat on the rubber bed and kept perfectly still, but the unreal tempo increased, and sound rustled from a long way off. Sounds of people, sounds of voices, and echoes of nonsense and unreality shining out from the padded walls, like an out-of-focus cinema screen. My mind walked the long corridors of its strange fashioning, sighing and weaving against distortions. I sat quite still and watched a parade of distress go by my eyes and felt the sweat staining my body....

* * *

... 'it's all a matter of perspective,' I heard a Voice say faintly, and my feet were straddling a small earth and a huge star went spinning into the black sky ...

... 'that painting is wrong,' said the Art Master, 'or rather the painting is good. It is the drawing which is wrong. You will never be an artist unless you persevere with your drawing. No amount of paint can rectify the initial distortion made by a clumsy pencil. Paint will only emphasise the faults.'

'I don't follow,' I protested loudly, from my rubber mattress.

'Simple,' he answered, 'a variety of colours only serve to pronounce the mistakes. By taking pains at the finish and not at the start you serve to set up a detrimental standard of comparison. You distort the whole for lack of perspective.'

'I still don't understand,' I called.

'You don't understand because you don't want to,' he said quietly, 'because you are afraid of the truth. You lack perspective, and everything depends upon perspective.' He walked back through the padded walls but left me paints and canvas and I dipped my brush in crimson paint and wrote P E R S P E C T I V E in even letters across the canvas. But even as I wrote the paint formed into little rivulets and trickled down the canvas until the letters grew blurred and distorted and finally meaningless ...

... my mother, my pretty beautiful kind thoughtful lovely sweet-smelling mother was reclining in a striped deckchair under a blue lilac tree with an open book on her lap. I called to her loudly as I ran to her, wanting all my friends to come and see her loveliness, but she did not raise her head.

'Mother,' I said, standing before her under the lilac tree, and she looked at me but did not see me. Her thoughts were distant and I turned away with sadness in my heart and walked towards the quiet orchard.

'Archie, where are you going?'

I turned back to her and was aghast to see that her face was blank and had no features except a toothless mouth.

'Mother, I have been wicked and I've stolen money and they will take me away from here because I have stolen it.'

'Don't be silly,' her lips said vaguely. 'You are only ten years old. You won't steal the money till seventeen more years have passed. It says so in the book.'

'But I have stolen it,' I raged, 'here it is.' And a cascade of coins and banknotes showered from my pockets around my feet, until my legs were stuck fast and I could not move.

'Look, there it is,' I said in triumph, pointing.

'It's not written here,' she said. 'I haven't read that far.' I looked over her shoulder and saw that most of the pages were blank, that the words only appeared as her invisible eyes scanned the pages.

'You fucking whore,' I screamed, 'you're cheating,' and I choked her pleasurably under the lilac tree until she was dead.

'It's all bloody lies,' I shouted, hearing my own voice bouncing back at me in the padded cell.

'It depends on which way you look at it,' my mother's sad voice was no more than a whisper coming from her melting corpse. 'You must keep things in perspective ... and everything will come right.'

'I don't understand,' I wept, weeping blood and apo-morphine. 'I don't understand.'

'You will,' said God, looking out from the padded ceiling. 'You'd better fucking understand, else your life won't be worth a chuckle.' I stood up in the padded cell and pissed hotly against the quilted wall.

'I'm going to kill myself,' I said defiantly, listening to all of them whispering and giggling inside the walls.

Then suddenly the lawn had gone, and the lilac tree, and the dark orchard had spread around me with a blackness which admitted no light; I started to run but there was no release from the darkness and there was no escape. I wanted to lay down in the stillness and wrap the darkness round me to keep the blackness away, and sleep for a million years …

… but a shadow on the wall became a crucifix, and I was pinned on it, stretched and wracked and pierced, and I could see a wraith of light in the darkness, a stumbling weeping speck which cried and miouwed, and I shouted out to the speck that was God 'Condemn them, the bastards, for they know full well what they're doing,' and the speck of light twisting out there on the writhing chaos suddenly went out because it too was afraid.…

… the confusion grew deeper and clearer. I sat still and frozen hoping that my brain and body would be rescued back to normal, but even as I sat colour and slime started to come from the walls and ceiling. They turned into mushrooms, ugly vile mushrooms which lived and moved on suckered feet, which dripped slime, which dripped down and out to merge into moving pulp on the spreading moving floor.

I watched in horror and fascination as the pools and puddles grew larger, slimy fungi springing out from nowhere, and then the ghastly mess started to drip down on me and eat me. I started to scream. I could hear my own screams thriving back at me, and the sound of my voice made the slime ooze more quickly, and it spoke with a hundred voices telling me to hush and be quiet. I moaned and hopped to the cell door, terrified to keep my feet out of the green mess. My fingernails broke clawing at the door's upholstery. Every time my fists pummelled for assistance and relief, more drops fell. Thick and green and terrifying and whispering. I stood frozen still, frightened in case I slipped down into the mess which would drown me and drink me up and clot my mouth and nostrils forever. The nurses heard my screams and came running up. They opened the spyhole to look in on me, and laughed at me and mocked me in my distress. I pleaded with them, howled and grovelled for help. They gibbered back, taunted. A desperate hysteria started to burn my mind away, and screamed more. They became worried. They fetched the Charge Nurse. He unlocked the door and I fell sobbing into his arms. I pointed back to the cell to show them the growing filth, and the two nurses started to laugh again because they couldn't see anything except my pool of piss. The Charge Nurse warned them, and sent one of them for a broom. He then swept every corner of the cell, walls and ceiling included. When I pointed out a patch that he'd missed, he patiently went back to it till I was satisfied there was no more fungi. The Charge Nurse put me back to bed as gently as friendship itself, and a needle filled with sleep pushed into my arm.

* * *

This was the first time d.t.'s had touched me. After I'd recovered I became subdued and frightened for a few days. The doctor laced into me about the surgical spirits, but there was enough defiance in me to retaliate – knowing that the doctor was more concerned about the staff nurse's carelessness than my bloody theft and drunkenness. I'd made up my mind that I wouldn't let the doctors and staff bug me; I'd not let them get through my guard. Once they got through, they'd turn you over to the welfare squads, and like as not you'd have the chaplain or padre dancing attention on all your days. Him, I could do without. They, I could do without. He, They and Them. With Them, it was all a matter of will-power. Either you had it or you didn't. They'd got it. I and Us hadn't. Will-power belonged to the welfare squads, the Social Drinkers, and the Sober World.

I found that the craving hit me hard. It was like a magnifying glass in my mind. Everything outside the magnifying glass was out of focus, irrelevant. It was alcohol I wanted, it was alcohol I must have. I'd lie for it, steal for it, cheat for it. My sober emotions were piano-wire tight. Life nibbled at my enforced sobriety. The world was too big, it would eat me up. The tension started inside me and welled into my hands and eyes and the way I moved and talked. In the hospital was only sober vacuum, with nothing to fill the hole. There was a hobgoblin in the same ward as me, a wet-brain, and I sought him out because I knew from the twitchings of the old man's face that he was near breaking point. I looked at him and knew that his days – drunk or sober – were numbered on a short list. One more winter of sleeping rough and he would fall asleep one night never to waken again. The cold would take him and leave another lump of ratmeat on the wastelands of England. I went with the old man to the kitchen to collect our daily glass of milk. The old man showed me how to do it; into the recreation room where a gas burner was fixed to the wall, allowing half an inch of naked flame for lighting cigarettes and pipes. The old man blew the flame out, let the gas run freely into each pint of milk, turning the control knob of the jet to force the gas powerfully. The milk bubbled and hissed, turned slightly dark, and the old man re-lit the jet with a contraband match. Then the pair of us sat down in a corner of the room and drank the stuff. It was vile. It stank and slurped and vomited in every molecule of itself ... it didn't seem to affect the old man very much, but after a while I began to feel hazy and to top it all I swallowed a couple of sleeping tablets and drowsed the hours till meal time. When I woke my head was muzzy and my mouth tasted like shit smells, and I wished the gas jet was big enough for me to put my head in and do a Housman. The old man nudged me towards the toilet recess; he stood on one of the lav basins, put his hand inside the cistern and came out with half a bottle of cheap wine. He drank some while still standing on the seat, then passed the bottle down to me. I gulped at it, and my mind cried that it wasn't enough. There was only enough to let the craving out of its pen, not enough to satisfy it. The vampire in me wanted its blood.

I went back to my seat by the window and looked out on the roses growing on the lawn, and I wished I were completely mad so that my mind wouldn't reason and envy ...

* * *

I sat by the window staring out at a bloom of roses, listening to a free bird singing its heart out against a falling sky where winds blew clean. I watched, from the corner of my eye, the broken-minded men sitting among the whispering shadows which tormented them eternally. Then I closed my mind and eyes and tried to plan my daydreams to lines of beauty and acceptance. But when a certain depth of dreaming was reached the plan twisted and went awry, and my thoughts came back to rest on an old unhappiness. Back to a dark bewilderment. My thoughts could drift and go with the current of memory, probe at some sadness ... it was always the living moment with impulses of authoritative urgency which pulled me back. It could be the nurse telling me to take my place for tea, or an orderly with the vitamin tablets, or a madman fumbling at my ears and person. So I'd come up from the submerged past and face the living now. I'd look at the Now and wish to God it would go away forever. A sadness of fading roses tied me to the chair. Every day I nuzzled the clock fingers with my impatience. I'd get up and walk about, sit down and get up again, pick up a book and toss it down, look at the blank stupid faces crowding me in, watch the mysterious door opening and closing as staff passed to and fro. I sat and stood and waited, the pendulum of my emotions swinging from high to low; I stood by the window looking out, swearing the filth and torment from my mind and soul to the ears of the world's indifference. I reduced God to the size of a stain on the floor and spat on him. My own misery made a giant of me, and help was a pigmy. I smoked I walked I sat. I watched madmen scrabbling with their thoughts. There was a man standing by the door picking his nose, scraping snot out with his fingers and putting it in his mouth. I wanted to go over and throttle him. There was a man, an old man, down by the lavatory recess masturbating inside his trouser pockets. The spotty-faced nurse whom I didn't like caught my eye and smiled. He was a queer. Every time he was on duty he followed me to the slash-trough and started a conversation from the next stall, his eyes peering down at what I was holding.

    I waited for the year to spend itself so that I could go out about my ways. The waiting was punctuated with pills. Into the office for the small glass of whisky and pellet-size tablets; don't hurry now, easy now, sip it, sip it, sip, roll it in the clutching mouth, sip and swallow ... and then the tablets ... and then back into the big ward with the world's nutters, waiting for the sickness to start, waiting to fill the sick-pan with stinking belly's contents.

During my months of confinement I lost weight; my head was filled with perpetual pain. It seemed to go on forever, the tantalising drink in the mornings, the tablets, the heavy tormenting sickness, the sickness and the craving, the craving and the sickness. The perpetual childbirth of one's own despair. Day after day I sat at the ward window listening to my own thoughts fumbling in the corridors of memory, tapping their child's fingers against the window of my mind. Sometimes my thoughts would skip the violence of self and seek the permanence in others, try to hold and capture. But people were circumstances quick-silver and when I closed my mental fist on them they were gone, and I was left, and my thoughts went crying down into the never-never-land of cannot-be.

Sometimes the chaplain came and tried to chat me out of it all. But I held no brief for him or his church, or narrow-gauged organised religion with fat well-fed Bishops and dignitories, or people playing bingo through so-called good works hoping for the prize of Heaven. But sometimes he almost hypnotised me into some reaction. He'd got it all so pat, so worked out, about the ways of God being mysterious but for our own good. This Creeping Jesus bloke presented dangers – perhaps not so much danger as even more disorientation; like being in a stationary train when the one alongside you starts to move, and you think feel and believe that your own train is moving and not the other. You feel a sense of shock, of outrage mixed with fear and surprise, and a bloody bagful of let-down and frustration and awful foolishness when you suddenly realise that you're standing still after all.

So I sat and thought, and thought and sat, and my own boredom was the only tangible thing belonging to me. A child's fingers in my mind would reach out with the delicacy of a butterfly's wing, a child stood at the window of my soul and puzzled at the world. A child-ghost led me back into childhood and pleaded with me to clean up the mess. I looked deep into the mess and shuddered between the then and now, and opened the match box which held my private store of amputation, and swallowed four precious sleeping pills and two boosters, and waited for the shadows to suffocate the substance of now-reality. Slowly the madmen went away and the vomit pan retreated to never-was, and the mind drowsed like a dreamer forgetting the sweet and the sour, the hope and the ruins ...

Visiting days I watched the relatives and guests of others come trooping up the driveway to the wards, watched them enter with spreading parcels and bunches of flowers, lemonade bottles and baskets of fruit. They all broke up into little groups and shut the rest of the world away from the family circle. I watched them and sometimes envied them. In the far corner would be the young schizo who never lived in the present, and hardly ever in his own body, his mind always away on strange journeys. His mother would watch over him confused anxiety and I hated the dew of compassion in her eyes. When I saw that, I had more malice in me than sperm in a randy bull-elephant. I'd move in close to her, and whisper to her, just a breath of whisper that she had to crane her ears to hear.

'You want to have him put down,' I'd whisper. 'Get the doctors to kill him. They'll do it if you ask them, it won't cost you anything, you don't have to pay. Get him killed, you'll be better off.' And the woman's face would crumble with horror, terror, silent screams. She'd look at me, and I'd make my mouth slack and limp; and conflict puzzled her mind. She read me as a mad-man, the same as her son, and held me not responsible for what I'd said. Whenever she caught my eye I'd smile at her, gentle and sweet as I could, and lift my finger to my throat and make a cutting motion.

I knew it was god-damned bestial what I was doing to the woman, but I couldn't have cared less. She was a woman, a mother who'd opened her legs to receive a squirt of inadequacy which had multiplied in bulk, instead of making her husband wear a rubber overcoat so's to leave breeding to those who could manage it better.

I looked at the boy's sister, young, pretty, embarrassed. She tried to keep her eyes off the old man who was always masturbating in his trousers pockets, but couldn't. She watched him climax, his body jerking like an old rag doll, little squeals and grunts coming from his almost toothless mouth. Her eyes were revolted, disgusted, but a little sly with curiosity. She was unmated, and probably thought of sex as a delicious act of white strong young limbs, modified by underarm talc and reasonable modesty. She probably had never before considered that old men with stick-like legs and pot bellies the colour of underside-fish and patchy greying pubic hair, had sexual fantasies. She probably thought that old men should go around with walking sticks, and not half-soft erections. She should have spent a night in our ward, and listen to the old buggers jerking themselves off, grunting, wheezing and gasping and climaxing into their fists; then fumbling, splashing and pissing into their bed bottles five minutes later, all down the row, farting and miouwing and moaning, and stinking like decay itself. God, it was enough to drive anybody to drink.

All round the room they sat, old men and young men, surrounded by wives and relatives and oranges and chocolate wrappings and biscuit tins and cigarette cartons and escape-proof windows. Propped up in a convalescent chair was the skeleton-thin man who served as the ward's complaining nuisance; the one whose reedy voice sliced razor sharp against everyone's sleep, always crying out for a nurse's attention or a bed-bottle, or the world's sympathy. There were two women to visit him, his wife and a sister. A profusion of parcels and packages was spread before him. One of the nurses came up, answered the questions put out by the wife.

'Doing well,' the nurse said. 'Looks much better, doesn't he.' The nurse leaned forwards and pinched the old man's face with heavy joviality.

'You're a rogue, aren't you?' he jollied, and the old man bubbled over with happiness and self-importance. The nurse's joviality was too prolonged, it began to sag. 'You're a bad old rogue,' he simpered, for the benefit of wife and sister, 'I don't know what we're going to do with you. But he looks well, doesn't he – I said you look well, you old rogue, you.' Wife, sister and patient were happy together. But I knew damned well that as soon as they'd gone the nurse would relegate the old man to the ranks of the world's nuisances, call him a bastard to his face, and swipe half his cigarettes and chocolate.

The Charge Nurse called my name and I looked up in surprise to see that I'd got visitors. My brother Peter and the Probation Officer who'd appeared in court, and whose report had landed me where I was. I was prepared to be agreeable to the Probation wallah if he gave me half a chance. He didn't. He got stuck into me straight away about the surgical spirits.

'The nurse told me about it,' he said indignantly, 'and he saw you with the milk and the gas jet.'

'The sod never mentioned it to me,' I answered. 'Is he getting the wind up?'

'Doing yourself no good,' the officer growled. 'Get yourself into more trouble. Can take you out of here and ask the magistrates to commit you for prison.'

'Do me a favour, prick,' I said, determined to needle him now. 'You're bloody stupid, mate. If they'd have weighed me off in the first place I'd have only drawn three months – I'd've been out by now. You stuck me in here for a full twelve months, and I've got the bloody lot to do. You go and take a running shag at yourself.'

He produced a sheaf of papers from his brief case, handed me a biro.

'Divorce papers,' he said. 'Your wife's put in for a divorce.' I blanked my face out, signed the papers, ripped my copies up and threw the bits into a bin.

'You'll end up sticky,' the Probation Officer remarked, and went away to the Charge Nurse's office to collect more malicious rumours. I sat with our Pete.

'You alright?' asked Pete. I nodded.

'You do get yourself into some funny places,' he observed, his Black Country accent sing-song as a duet, 'but I reckon you've topped everything with this bloody place.'

'I'm only doing it for a bet,' I said, keeping my end up.

'If there's anything I can do, say the word,' he said. 'You figuring on busting out?'

'It's crossed my mind,' I admitted. Then, understanding – 'No, you keep out of it. I can manage. I hear tell you're courting now. Keep out of my troubles.'

He took some banknotes from his pocket, handed them over.

'There's ten quid there,' he said, 'that's all I can manage. It'll mayhap help a bit. For, er, bus fares or someat. And this.' I could have cried. He handed me a flat bottle of whisky, golden, tawny, like pollen on the back of a bee. I stuck it in my pocket, quick.

I watched my brother walk down the hospital drive, taller than the Probation Officer, more lithe and urgent.

All the visitors departed, leaving a desolation of empty wrappings behind them. Life closed its eyes for another week. I clutched the money to me, and the bottle, and slipped from the ward and into the toilet for a good long pull.

Chapter Sixteen

I can't number the hours I sat with the madmen and tried to work things out for myself. Each hour must have been a double shift, each moment was multiplied by boredom. I sat trying to work things out in my own mind, looking for an answer but craving for a drink. Self sat on the surface of my mind and would not see beyond the now and yesterday. My man's body sat in a chair in a ward of a mental hospital, but the child's fingers in my mind went plucking and calling down the long empty years; the useless years, a child's broken toys. The traffic of life had crushed them to pieces and no one could mend them. I felt betrayed … I felt that God should be fair and take me back to childhood so that the child could come forwards and rescue the man. I felt things with startling clarity, but could not adjust to the new insight. It was like having two jigsaw puzzles mixed up in my mind, but with no way of separating them. I felt my own disharmony, I felt the strain of self pulling in two directions. I made my face seem uncaring and indifferent, but inside, my mind seethed with unhappiness and unrest. I lay between the shadow and the substance, and I longed for alcohol to reduce myself and my world to a slumbering mess which could be swept under the carpet and forgotten about … If I had drink, God would mount to heaven and put the place in order for a little while. I thought of my brothers, all iron moulders, rough and unambitious. Content with crude routines, a Sunday suit, and a girl of the same order. I used to look at them and despise them. Now, I envied them. Their very ignorance was itself a perfection.

I knew, dimly, that my character wasn't fixed; that it fluctuated according to my moods, and my moods were circumstance's playthings. I knew that my personality ebbed and flowed, tide in, tide out. I knew that I caused more suffering than I experienced. But people could get away from me, leave me, protect themselves. But I lived inside myself and could not get away, except when I had a bottle. For me, the refuge of self pity, the blundering relief from acts of aggression, the inability to face circumstances requiring mature confrontation. I blundered from degradation to degradation in search of escape. My deterioration was gradual.

As my own errors multiplied, the desire amongst others to forgive naturally palled. The whole of life became a ghastly charade. I offended people, abused them, cheated them, stole from them; and gradually their forgiveness and sympathy froze to dismay. When they showed contempt or anger I would creep away from such revelation, hide myself behind another barrier of lies and conceits. So, I thought; Up you World and life and me and you and it and they ...

I made up my mind.

I would have it away.

So I went into the toilet and took a close look at the windows. They opened up and down, not out, and each window opened for only the space of four inches. I could see that long wooded blocks had been screwed into the channels where the sashes ran; these prevented the windows from opening fully. I hunted around, stole a spoon from the kitchen. The tip of the spoon bowl fitted into the heads of the screws. Within minutes, I had all the screws out. Coats of paint held the blocks in position. I plugged each screw hole with soap, drew a line across each, so that anyone making an inspection would not notice that the windows had been tampered with. When bedtime came, I turned in with the others. I lay on my back staring up at the ceiling, letting my ears tune in at each bed, until the snores and breathing assured me that I had the wakeful night to myself. I slipped from the bed and dressed, tip-toed from the ward. Beyond the day room I could see the night nurse sitting at his desk, his back to me. I hesitated, went back to my bed and folded blankets and pillow in the shape of a phantom sleeper. When the nurse made the rounds, his torch would strike a bed shape, and his imagination would supply the sleeper.

I went into the toilets, worked the blocks loose, lifted the window gently high and climbed out into the first fresh air for eight months. Behind me, madness and sickness turned in its sleep and groped through the fitful hours. For me, the great road which led to Nowhere. I slipped past the gate keeper's cabin as silently as a ghost across a mirror, then walked down the street where quiet houses dreamed, heading for home pastures like a dog's instinct. I liked walking the night, with a high moon riding point to point across the sky's landscape. It was good to walk and breathe, and the lack of pattern held no concern for me.

At the end of the street I saw a bicycle leaning against a garden shed. I stole it, mounted it, and let the wheels croon me towards Stafford, then on to Wolverhampton. Freedom blew in my head like wine, I rode on and on into the vast night. I stopped at a transport cafe and gluttoned my way through sausages and bacon, eggs and fried bread; swilling it down with thick brown tea, as if my life depended on it. I watched and listened to the sane truck drivers, wallowed in their roughness and swearing words beauty. I was back in the land of the living. I left the cafe feeling good and wholesome, then rode the remaining miles into Wolverhampton. When I arrived, it was daybreak with a strong sun challenging its way into the sky. I left the cycle against a factory wall, then started to walk towards Stourbridge. By ten o'clock, pub-opening hours, I was in Wordsley, a stone's toss from Stourbridge, and I swung off towards Stewpony, away from the main pulse where someone might recognise me, on into the country lanes. I went into a quiet public house, and silently promised my money I would stick to beer. I liked the pub, it had a bread and cheese air, and a slowness, and wooden barrels to draw the beer from, and brow faced men with cello-drawls. Tractors throbbed from the distant fields and through the woods, far away, I could see the slopes of Kinver standing against the sky. I drank the beer and let it mellow me, the world became a pleasant place, and the men standing at the bar became my friends of a lifetime. Between us, we cured life of all its ills. But at two o'clock the towel went on, the pub closed, and the friendship of company split into ones and twos, and went different ways. I bought bottles of beer to fill my pockets, then walked the dusty sun-warmed road for a mile or two, climbed a stile and lay on my back in the hushed fields. I lay and let the sun wash over me, did not think about anything at all, just let the warmth and contentment and birds' song and whispering grass stroke at my senses until they fell asleep.

When I awoke, the sun had stepped down to evening and I opened my remaining bottle of beer before climbing back to the road again. I walked in a gathering of slow dusk, my whistle staining the air, and came onto Wordsley Hill where I stood looking down on the village. A faint touch of sadness leaned in on my mind. I had known happy days in Wordsley, happy, lost days. I shrugged the mood off and went down into the village. From pub to pub I went, looking for the ghost of something which was not there. It was never there. I went into a pub, looked round, and hoped to see something; hoped that my eyes would recognise something, hoped that the quest was ended. But it never was, and I did not know what the quest was, what I was looking for. So I drank alone at the bar, then onto the next pub, and then the next. Whatever it was I was looking for was always in the pub ahead, on the next street corner, in the eyes of a passing stranger. I drank the evening away, the money dwindled, and I could not get drunk. The amputation would not complete itself, would not take over. Gradually I left Wordsley and came into Stourbridge, keeping to back streets so that the police would not pick me up and take me back into the madhouse in Stafford. I decided to go to my sister's house, and not my mother's. I walked the streetlamp darkness to where she lived, crept up the entry and squeezed between the wall and dustbins in the backyard. My sister was alone in the kitchen, passing to and fro across the lighted uncurtained window. I started to edge towards the door when I heard a car stop in the street, and policemen came up the entry. Four of them. Two of them stood in the centre of the yard while the other two knocked at the kitchen door. I shrugged down behind the dustbins, and almost laughed aloud when I realised the policemen didn't have a torch between them. The two in the yard stood around striking matches, the light blinding their eyes rather than helping them to see. One came so close to me that I could have leaned out and lit a cigarette. One of the others pried into the brewhouse, and as he opened the door there was one hell of a clatter which woke every dog and cat in the neighbourhood. Their barks and screeches added to the din as a rusty bath and old tin cans clattered from the brewhouse where they'd been trapped. The policeman jumped back three paces. 'He's in here – I've got him.' The others went to him, saw I was not there. I wanted them to go away so's I could relieve my belly of knotted laughter. The men went away, after telling my sister to let them know if she saw me.

'Yoh're brother's a funny chap,' one said to her. 'No telling what he'll be up to next.'

My sister watched them go, arms akimbo.

'Is there a reward?' she shouted after them.

'Balls,' said a policeman.

'I didn't ask what kept your ears apart,' my sister screeched after them, 'or what you had for your bleeding breakfast.' I waited for their car to dwindle away, then went to my sister's door and knocked on it. She opened up.

'Thought yoh wouldn't be far away,' she said. 'They just missed you, then.' I slipped past her into the untidy kitchen, grateful for the cup of tea she poured me. The clock said half past nine. My sister nodded at it.

'Yoh'll atta be away afore Tom gets home,' she said. 'He'll be here at twenty past ten sharp.'

'I'll be away,' I answered, and wondered unhappily where I'd be away to. My sister fiddled about in the kitchen, came back with a newspaper parcel of sandwiches.

'Tek these,' she said. 'They'll fill a hole, mayhap.' I jammed the parcel into my pocket.

'What about money?' she enquired.

'Near enough none,' I answered.

'Me as well,' she said, 'And Tom don't get paid till Thursday.' She thought for a moment.

'There's the gas-meter,' she said.

I went to the gas-meter in its little cupboard, wrenched the lock off with a poker. I counted the money quickly, the shilling and two shilling pieces. Nine pounds seven shillings. I halved the pile, one half to her. She shook her head, no.

'Take it,' I said. 'Nobody 'ull ever know. They'll think I took the lot. I'll leave a note in the money tray, telling them as it was me.' She took a pound, no more.

'I'll be away, now,' I said. 'I'll make for London, I'll drop a line when I get fixed up.' She went ahead of me down the entry, checked the road to make sure everything was clear. I squeezed past her and melted into the night. I called at an off-licence, bought a bottle of whisky, quart bottles of cider, bottles of beer. I cut down side streets with my burden, until I reached the footbridge leading to the canal. I walked, along the towpath slowly, the sandwiches bulging one pocket, gas-meter coins the other. I carried the alcohol carefully, the night's amputation. The path I walked was flanked with hedges, the opposite bank sprawled with iron foundries and glass works, steel mills, brick-yards and coal wharfs. The canal fed them with supplies … this was the stretch of canal I'd worked with Tomato Juice and Bully Boy, and the friendly ghosts of yesteryear. Now it lay black and still, brooding under the stars. I swung off through a gap in the bushes and made my way down to the River Stour. Willow trees flanked its yellow muddied waters, and I nestled into the soft earth under the trees. I uncorked the whisky and took long, sweet, shuddering pulls. I left two inches in the bottle to greet the morning with, then pillowed my head on dead leaves and let the night hold me.

A dawn chorus of birds awakened me, and for a moment I couldn't understand where I was. My mind expected to hear the Charge Nurse's voice, men fumbling and crying, the sounds of the hospital. The morning had brought dew and my clothing was damp. I put a cigarette between my lips, but the matches would not strike. I remembered a trick from childhood;

pushed a few matches into my hair and let the heat from my scalp dry them. I collected wood and made a fire, and sat in front of it till my clothing was dry. I then drank the remains of the precious whisky. Nausea shook me, the tail-end of apo-morphine treatment received at the hospital. I waited for the sun to cross the sky towards opening time, then hand-brushed my clothes free of moss and leaves, splashed river water in my eyes, and cursed the lack of a razor. I went back along the towpath to the first public house, bought more whisky and bottles of cider. This saw the last of my money away. I went back to the osier beds and dug myself in. I broke branches and bent them to shape until I had the scaffolding of a hut, small and snug. I broke more branches and plaited them into roof and walls, then laid more branches on the floor to keep the dampness from my bones. Next I collected large stones and pebbles to make a fireplace outside the hut, and put a stock of wood fuel by. I had no plan, no fixed idea. The thing was to immediately survive, to be alone; away from the enemies outside. The one worry was lack of alcohol, once the bottles were empty. With care, I had supplies for two days. There was no food left, but food wouldn't matter for four or five days anyway. At the back of my mind was an idea that I could break into the public house one night, and steal what I could carry. I looked round me, and felt safe. The trees were tall enough to hide and disperse the smoke from my campfire, the undergrowth thick enough to prevent courting couples or children stumbling upon me. My home was in order, and I could lie in the sun on the banks of the stinking yellow River Stour. I sipped the whisky, and a three dimensional world danced over the tree tops. When I was drunk, I slept for hours; and when I awoke I didn't need a great amount to keep myself topped up. But after two days the whisky was finished, and the cider was finished, and the beer; reluctant sobriety had begun. I sweated the third day in the shivering woods as a mist of rain came through the foliage of my hut and put the fire out. My thoughts hunted across the slow hours, and the despair in my belly was very, very real. My cigarettes were finished and I moved up to the canal towpath and searched the ground for stub ends. I found a few and took them back to my hut, placed them under my armpits to dry them out, then rolled the tobacco in a piece of torn letter. I coughed bitterly as the acrid smoke bit into my lungs, and I wished I could fall asleep never to wake up. My mind and thoughts grew uncomfortable in a wet body, and went on astral wanderings into the past. On the other side of the canal stood the foundry where I used to work and sweat my dreams out. On the other side of the foundry stood the house where I used to live. The house was empty now, as all the houses in the bleak cramped street were, waiting for the bulldozers to break them into pieces, so that factories could spread across the ground they occupied. My mother and all the neighbours had been rehoused over on the New Estate. I thought of our old house, and wondered if ghosts haunted the empty rooms.

I lay shivering in the osier beds and lost count of the days; but my beard stubble suggested that perhaps three had gone. My belly rumbled with hunger, my bones and muscles protested for movement and action. My ears had told me long ago that somewhere on the other side of the fields there was a farm, I could hear the hens clucking. I waited until it grew dark then slipped slyly as a fox and screwed a couple of fat warm necks. I took them back to my hut, but had no way of cooking them. My thoughts crossed the canal and stood looking at the foundries annealing ovens. I went back up the towpath, slipped my shoes off and tied them round my neck, strapped the chickens to them with my neck tie. The water hit me cold, and I gasped my way to the other side, climbed out onto the wharf I went across to the ovens, huge cathedral archways of bricked up, locked in heat. The heat from them dried my clothing quicker than a desert sun; then I quickly and carefully plucked the hens, gutted them, chopped off their feet and heads. I bundled feathers and entrails carefully together, picked up the long furnace poker, and pushed the rubbish into the glow coals so that all evidence was destroyed. I hunted the foundry warehouse, won a knife and some salt. Also a cannister of tea and a jam jar filled with sugar. I raked some of the burning coals open, placed the chickens on roughly arranged barbecue bars. I waited for them to cook, mouth watering; I boiled water in the tin can, made a mash of tea, adding sugar. The chickens were almost raw as I ate them, ripping flesh from bloodied bones with my teeth. I washed the flesh down with scalding milkless tea, felt better for it. Before settling down I returned the things to the warehouse, left everything neat and tidy. Then I pulled a wheelbarrow forwards and sat in it in such a position that the handles touched the floor, and gave me the comfort and shape of an armchair. Comfortable and warm, I dropped off to sleep and lived through a dreaming night.

Yet all too soon the singing birds brought morning and I slammed awake, knowing I must be gone before the iron workers arrived. I replaced the wheelbarrow and went to the office foyer to look at the clock. Even as I looked, I heard a workman's tread at the tail end of the road, and I sprinted across the yard to hide in the women's lavatory. I heard the dong of the time clock as the man punched his card, and through a slit in the corrugated iron screen I watched him make his heavy way down to his work-stall. I climbed a wall, dropped into deserted gardens and made my way to our old house. It stood with its back hunched in silence, and I stepped back through ten years of time. I entered through the back door, through the kitchen, stood watching the silence floating by. The house was long empty, the window panes had been ripped out to give bonfires to small boys. I walked from room to room with old ghosts swirling around me, and trod the slow stairs to the bedrooms. Each room had a memory of distant pain; I felt the pain and misery compressed into the decaying walls. When the walls themselves were pulled down, I felt that unhappiness would still stand full and square, in the house's shape, to imprison the ghosts within. This house was a prison. I went back downstairs to the room where I had thrashed my father. The glassless windows were boarded up so that the interior was dim and vague, misty with thickening dust and creeping damp. I felt old angers and hatreds troubling my bones, the ague of hatred, the crippling passion of it. I sat down on the bare boarded floor and nursed the hatred into blackness, hoping that it would burn out of my system once and for all. But my hatred was all too familiar, of too long a standing. Perhaps it was the essential part of me, the life-force. How I hated. The rottenness of self and others, of dreams and nightmares, of world and underworld. I put on armour to keep life out, then sat inside the armour while it rusted and leaked and wearied my mind. Suddenly I felt old and tired, and deeply afraid.

I knew I couldn't stay long in the old house. I had to get away and go back to my hut near the River Stour. Children might find me, or even the police. The escape from mental hospital, the theft from my sister's gas-meter, the stolen cycle and the stolen chickens all loomed large in my mind. I felt haunted and hunted, I felt that everyone was looking for me, ready to punish and lock me away for ever. Every wood-worn creak, every gust of wind or breeze that tousled at the empty house, sent my heart racing. I knew I had to get back to my hut, and I waited for the first quiet hours of morning to wear away, and when the streets were littered with people and traffic, I went among them. I walked away smartly, like an honest man returning from night shift. When no one was looking I picked up cigarette ends, stuffed them carefully into my pocket for later.

This became my drill for nine weeks. I spent my days in the little hut, and as soon as evening came in I crossed the canal bridge, over Moody's field, through the street and empty deserted gardens, over the wall and into the iron foundry. I stole a chicken every three or four days, taking from a different run each time. The farmer never set a trap, so I decided he wasn't missing the birds, yet. Sometimes I stole eggs only; I laid wire snares, and caught rabbits twice, remembering what Konk had taught me. I stole vegetables from fields, and made rabbit stews at the foundry ovens. Cooked the lot together in a washed out bucket. Almost every night I found bits of food left over by the iron moulders, the odd sandwich or two. But one night, hunting round the foundry, I stumbled upon Heaven itself. Near the pattern-shop, I found two gallon cans – one partly filled, the other completely filled, with methylated spirits. I didn't question its presence. It was mine. I'd found it. So I took it with me back to the hut by the Stour … it tasted foul. Surgical spirits were bad enough, but meths were foul. Yet gradually my palate became accustomed to the rough sweetness, and I drew water from the canal to tone the fire of the stuff down a little. All it lacked was a lacing of cider, or beer. For several days I didn't move from the hut, even to forage. My pockets were filled with fag ends, I had newspaper to wrap the tobacco in, I had enough matches laid by. As a precaution, I split each match into two, length ways, with a safety pin.

I felt that if I were alive when the cans fell empty, it would be a miracle.

* * *

The cans fell empty one day, and I was alive. Now only sobriety danced over the tree-tops again.

I took stock of myself. I was filthy dirty – I hadn't washed for weeks – and my clothing was filled with vermin. My hair was thick and matted, head and face. I knew that I had to pull out, that I needed to clean up, that I needed to get away again. I left the osier beds as soon as it was dark, making for my sister's house. I rapped on the kitchen window and her startled face told me that she didn't recognise me.

'It's me – it's Archie,' I called urgently, and she opened the door to me, fear and pity mixed in her eyes.

'What a mess,' she moaned, swaying at the door. 'What a mess, owd man – ah thought you'd be miles out. What a mess yoh'm in.'

I stumbled past her, stood miserably blinking in the electric light. My sister avoided my eyes as I washed myself at the sink, stripped naked. I took the beard from my face with her husband's razor. My sister thrust a bundle of clothing at me.

'Some of Tom's,' she said, 'underwear an' a shirt. An old coat and trousers.' I seized them greedily, dressed quickly, bundled my discarded rags together. My sister snatched the bundle, and I heard the dustbin lid clatter as she got rid of them. She handed me an old raincoat.

'Tek it,' she said, 'it's one of Tom's. He won't miss it for a bit, an' ah shall say ah gave it to the ragman. Put it on, and get on your way.'

I buttoned the raincoat slowly, blinking the unspoken question at her. She gave me a pound note from her handbag.

'It's all ah'n got,' she said. 'Tom got paid yest'day. Tek the quid, then. If ah was you, owd man, I'd get me a skinful at the first boozer and then give meself up. It's killing you, lad.'

I turned my collar up, went back outside.

'Tek care,' my sister whispered, and I walked away. Into Stourbridge itself, into the public house I'd often used in the old days. The customers looked up, surprised to see me. The landlord came over.

'Police am lookin' for you,' he said. 'Don't you know?'

'Ar,' I said, matching his accent. 'Do they know?'

He grinned, and fetched me a drink over.

'Have that on me, me lover,' he said, and went back behind the bar. The evening slipped away, and it wanted half an hour to closing time when a plain clothes man stood at the back of me. We smiled at each other through the bar mirror.

'Have a drink?' I invited.

'Good idea,' said the policeman, and we spent a pleasant half hour talking about the weather, West Bromwich Albion, and other odds and ends. I pushed the drinking pace so's to be spent up by closing time. The policeman matched me glass for glass. Dead on closing time he looked at his watch.

'Ready?' he asked.

I nodded. The publican pushed twenty Players into my hand.

'Tek 'em, me lover,' he said. So I put them in my pocket and walked round to the police station with the detective.

Chapter Seventeen

The detective turned me over to the desk sergeant, then went away to the canteen for his supper. When he came back he brought me a plate of chips, corned beef, bread and butter and a mug of tea. I wolfed it down, then was taken upstairs to the CID office. My 'friend' Len was there, plus two other 'tecs, settled comfortably.

'How ya been living, Archie?' Len asked. 'Let's see, bin on the run quite a time now – how'n ya managed?'

'I managed.'

'Bin livin' rough?'

'Some.'

'Do any jobs?'

'None to speak of.'

'Let's speak on 'em, anyroad. What jobs ya done? Screwing, breaking-and-entering? Anything like that?'

'Nothing to interest you,' I answered, trying to keep my voice monotonous.

'Not very talkative, am ya?' he asked. 'Not very.'

'Don't have to be, with you around,' I replied, and lit a Players. He leaned across his desk and struck it from my mouth, then he settled back in his chair and spoke kindly.

211

'Don't get cheeky with me, Archie, otherwise ah shall lowk your bloody earhole.'

The one who'd brought me in looked embarrassed. 'Goo easy,' he said to the other. 'No need to treat him like that. He's no saint, but he's no bloody villain, either.' The senior man ignored him. I closed my mouth, looked at the wall, said nothing. My day was done, my bolt shot, my interest waned. I switched off.

'Breach of probation by absconding,' droned the officer, 'plus the original theft and assault charges, plus your sister's gas-meter.'

I looked my surprise.

'Your sister towd us about it tonight,' the man said. 'Her got worried about the way yoh'm carrying on. Said yoh called theer, and after yoh'd gone her found the gas-meter opened. Yoh left a note.'

I shrugged.

'Thoughtful of ya,' he said, 'wish they'd all do that, mek our jobs a lot easier. Save us no end a trouble.' I told them about the chickens, about the iron foundry; told them all the bits and pieces I'd done. The senior man looked at me thoughtfully.

'Yoh help us, we'll help yoh,' he said finally. I sat back and waited for it.

'We can speak up for you, in Court,' he said. 'Tek a few things off the book for us, and we'll pull a few strings.' I laughed at him.

'Get stuffed,' I said.

He looked at his cigarette mildly, snubbed it, lit another one, pushed the pack towards me. I ignored it.

'Bin quite a few factory break-ins,' he murmured, not looking at me, 'still cluttering our books up. Yoh knows the drill – have 'em took into consideration for us, say yoh did 'em. Clear the records – yoh knows. Then we'll goo into the box for you, pull strings, get yoh returned to the hospital – or better still, on open probation. What say?'

My arresting officer looked even more embarrassed. 'Lay off it,' he urged the other. 'What'n yoh doing to him? Tag that lot on him, and he's a dead cert for a stretch over the wall. For Christ's bloody sake, he was one of us, once.'

212

'Ar,' the chief man said, examining his cigarette. 'One of us – gets chucked off the force for being bloody drunk. Blokes like him gets the force a bad name with the public. Rogue coppers, bent coppers.'

'Ramrod straight, yourself,' I mentioned. 'Fucking paragon of virtue.'

'We'll see, in the morning,' the man said. 'Tek him down to the cells.'

Next morning I came in front of the magistrates, remanded over to Stafford Sessions, and that was my lot for a while because the Recorder put me away for three years.

'You had been a serving policeman ... you should have known better.' With good conduct, I had two years to do. So up you, sweet world and society for two god-damned years.

After trial I was taken to the local prison and placed in a large cell with several others. Heavy bars frowned at the windows, the door was kept locked under the supervision of a prison screw. This was prison reception, and this was where men ceased to exist. Back in Court, I remembered thinking 'Could this be me they are talking about?'

Could this be me, exposed and classified? *Them*, clad in pomp and ceremony, droning dogmas and formulas which left me frantic with lack of understanding? The little wrongs I did, the small simplicity of them – was that *me* standing in that place? Did I do all *that*?

Down the small cramped steps to the dungeon beneath the Court, then taken away in a blue van which is divided into little cells. My cell is so small that my hips fit its width and my knees touch the door. Behind me, a strip of reinforced glass, the glass tinted like the back window of a taxi cab so that the world outside has already lost its colour and flashes by in drab monochrome ... symbolic of that strange place which I must enter. The van swings into the prison yard, the massive iron gates clang shut.

'Sign for the bodies,' says an escorting policeman, and bodies are signed for on official forms. High walls and gaunt grey stones greet the frightened eye, and lifeless monochrome continues to unfold. We are herded along a slate causeway into this reception centre. Smell is the first thing to greet us; a mustiness and stench of lavatories hiding behind carbolic soap and floor polish, a whore's body hiding behind cheap perfume. Resident prisoners in grey flit like empty shadows, warders tower and strut in blue serge uniforms, buttons gleaming, whistle chains showing, two inches of truncheon strap hanging beneath tunic skirts. Full brothers to the policemen outside who arrested us. Long intervals of sitting and standing, shouts for silence, calling of names, stripping and searching and looking under arm-pits and up anuses for contraband; removal of civilian clothing and issue of prison drabs. Heavy, grey and patched underwear; thick socks and brutish shoes. The body loses its own identity as prison clothes are donned. Human dignity stands waiting outside the Big Gate, waiting for two years to pass. Issue of bedding, coarse blankets, knife, fork and spoon and platter mug; tooth brush and camphor chalk for scrubbing teeth. Two shirts – one to sleep in, the other to wear. Queue for the Medical Officer, queue for the Assistant Governor, queue for the Chaplain, queue for a queue that is timeless, endless, and mentally stand in that great queue which waits for the ultimate queue for freedom.

Freedom. What a word. I'd picked up the knowledge from somewhere that the Normans had brought the word with them, when they invaded Britain way back. A Norman could do what he liked with a Saxon serf, but if a Saxon defended himself or in any other way hurt the Norman, all the Saxon had got left was 'Free-doom'. The only choice he'd got was the manner of his dying, by his own hand or by a Norman's. Freedom, Freedoom; a word closely rooted to death by execution or suicide.

I kept thinking 'Can this be *me* they are talking about?' back there in Court, and in the van which brought me to prison. Could this be *me* smelled-out and sifted and sorted by the witch-doctors of the mysterious totem called Justice? Droning dogmas and formulas which left me desperate with lack of understanding – did I do all *that*? '… breaking and entering a canteen and therein stealing a quantity of food to the value of …'

'… breaking into the aforesaid gas-meter and stealing the sum of seven pounds, the property of …'

'… breaking a Probation Order previously made by a Court following an attempt at suicide …'

'... absconding from a mental hospital to which you had been confined to receive treatment for a period of not less than one year ...'

'Psychopathic ... unco-operative ... anti-social ...' droned Doctor Barrabas from the witness-stand, his German under-accent chugging along under the 'V's and 'W's.

Me there in the box thinking, you daft bastards, I didn't do all *that*, not like the way you mean. All I wanted was a bit of food to tide me over, and some alcohol to keep you away from me and me away from you.

'The prisoner should have known better. He had been a serving police officer. An example must be made ... you will go to prison for three years.'

'But I wasn't a policeman when I did it all,' I protested, 'I was sacked from the police force before it all happened ...'

'Take him down,' said God, and it's nine-steps down to the holding cell beneath the Court. Up above, pomp, dignity, the majesty of the law. Directly underneath, accumulation of dirt and litter and hard-backed benches and hob-goblins of creation. If only the people in the public gallery could unzip the floor and look at us now. They'd see past the pompous acting of wig and ermine, maybe. Up there, polished oak and no dust anywhere. Down below, a devil's brew of atmosphere, dirt, lads and men – all shut away from the searchlight of public knowledge. At midday a warder unlocked the holding cell door and two more warders came in carrying a tray loaded up with stale cobs of bread and butter, and a bucket of near-cold tea. They poured the tea into paper cups – a thin, watery brew – and the bread was tossed at us like fodder to cattle. Such was lunch; and two more hours had to pass before Judge and Barristers and Solicitors worked their ways through five-course lunches and bottles of claret at a nearby hotel.

'You got any form, son?' an old lag asked a scared youth. 'I mean, you been in trouble with the Blue-men before?'

The youngster shook his head, no.

'You'll be alright,' the lag told him, 'you'll come through.' 'That's the way on it,' said his mate, 'we all come through, son.'

Yes, I thought. We'll all come through. Murderers, rapists, robbers, child-beaters, maintenance defaulters, motor-car offenders and gas-meter bandits. We'll all come through.

After 'weigh-offs', back to the prison, each man's thoughts locked onto the time in front of him; into a conveyor-belt process of fictitious penal-rehabilitation.

Rehabilitation. To 're-invest with dignity'.

Some of the prisoners were hardly more than lads. They avidly drank up the advice given to them by older lags. A feller my own age, or maybe a bit younger, was also an alcoholic; him and me singled each other out with that inbuilt sense of recognition peculiar to alco's alone.

'I drew seven years,' a housebreaker said to me in puzzled bewilderment. 'Seven years – God Almighty, I only nicked a radio set.' I'd nothing to say to him. My emotions were cold and could not focus on the man's distress. His wife and children were mere symbols of waiting. He would be parted from them for a good many years. He had to take it and so did they. I wondered if my dad had ever given *us* a passing thought whenever he was in prison.

My name was called for reception-bath. I stripped off in front of the dead eyes of screws and trustees. My civvy clothing was taken from me to breathe camphor for two long years. A screw told me to lift my feet, he peered at each sole in turn to make sure I'd got no contraband stuck there with tape. He checked my arm-pits, told me to bend over so's he could see up my back-passage.

I was being rehabilitated. I was being re-invested with dignity. I climbed into five regulation inches of prison-issue water and scrubbed myself down with prison-issue soap which contained next to no prison-issue lather. A head popped up quickly from a bath the other side of the partition; the other alco put his thumb high as a definite sign of victory.

'I've got some tobacco,' he whispered, 'I'll split with you when we get dressed.'

'How'd you manage it?' I whispered back.

'French letter,' he said, 'I stuffed it inside a French letter, greased it with Vaseline and stuck it up my behind. Got over an ounce.'

I dropped my soap in admiration.

I climbed from the bath, dressed in prison greys, filed back to the reception centre. The alco slipped a screwed-up package into my hand. Tobacco, split matches, crumpled rice papers. I nodded thanks.

Then into a cell which measures twelve by eight, walls of unplastered brick, and iron-clad door with a Judas-hole slap in the centre for *them* to look in, but not us look out. One high barred window which overlooked the exercise yard. Iron-framed windows with two five-inch square panes that slide back and forth to admit what fresh air there is. Three of us share this little cell, occupying a space which was strictly designed to the needs of one, more than a hundred years ago. A double bunk, one over the other, and a trestle-cot which has to be folded against the wall when not in use. If anyone of us needs the toilet during the night we cannot get from the cell to the outside recess. We have to use the chamber-pots supplied and live through the stench of it till morning comes. When I belonged to a Free Society, I thought every cell was fitted with a flush toilet, like an up-to-date police station.

But they are not, not these grey English prisons which will rehabilitate us, which will re-invest us with dignity.

I ignored the other two occupants as I flopped down on the upper bed and waited for supper time. A trustee and a blue-bastard came round with a bucket of thick cocoa, a basket of bread-cobs and half-crown-size splats of margarine. The cocoa was just that. No sugar, no milk. I broke the bread into pieces, dunked it in the cocoa, and ate the lot.

I slept badly that first night, my body exhausted but my mind walking a curious tight-rope of fact, fiction and phantasy. The dreams edged into nightmare, sobbed me awake. I could hear the other two blokes snoring deep sleeps. I waited for the dawn to stare in through the barred windows, cold and sullen. A bell echoed out through the prison, loud and commanding. Locks started to rattle as the screws, the blue-bastards, went down each row of cells uncoupling the great iron tongues which kept us in, leaving each cell on hasp only. I got dressed, sat dispirited on my cot, feet dangling over the edge, in an atmosphere of stale body sweat and night-old urine from the chamber-pots. A screw finally opened up, stood to one side as trustees poured porridge into our dishes, thin tea into the mugs. The porridge had no milk in it and no sugar. We flavoured it with salt. The screw clipped the door back onto hasp as he went away, so's we couldn't get out of the cell until the official clock said so.

An hour went by, then the cells were opened up again and the silent men came trooping out, carrying their slops to the recess. Footsteps rang loud and clear, the iron tips of prison issue shoes drumming out on the slate causeways. There were four storeys of cells on each prison wing, four wings running out from the office centre like spokes from a wheel. Each tier of cells was called a landing, several officers to a landing, each in a strategic position where he could observe the prisoners allotted to his charge. A senior prison officer stood in the main centre where he in turn could observe every wing, every landing, every cell and every man. In the middle of each wing, running from ceiling to basement, was a well. The cells flanked this; stretched over the well was an iron mesh-work, like a wire-netting net, to prevent prisoners from throwing themselves or an officer to the floor below. The causeways fronting the cells were protected with iron railings. Each landing joined the one higher by way of a narrow iron staircase, so narrow that only one man at a time could use it. One officer at the top of each stairway could prevent trouble coming at him in a bunch. I slopped out with the others. I hadn't used my chamber-pot, but one of my cell mates had used his. The pots had to be emptied into a huge bosh whose running water was supposed to wash the refuse away. More often than not, the matter would not flush away, but great lumps of excretion floated there, waiting for someone to break it all into paste with a paddle. The stink was ghastly. I gagged, held my nostrils with the fingers of one hand while I lunged forwards to empty the piss from my pot. I filed back to my cell, put my prison jacket on, waited for the order for yard exercise.

I'd got the shakes. My belly was violent, my head ached unbearably; my hands shook like catkins, and a muscle in my face wouldn't let up from its twitchings. My system needed alcohol. I'd got exactly six booster tablets, passed to me by my new alco friend. I took two, just to keep the jitters away for a little while. Then I filed out with the others into the bleak yard, the gaunt grey prison walls leaning over us. It was cold, bitterly cold, and I stuck my hands inside my trouser pockets. A blue-bastard bellowed for me to take them out, and I looked round me, and did what the other prisoners did – pushed each hand up an opposite sleeve, and we all walked round like bloody Chinamen. The exercise yard was a round circle of paving slabs. Round and round we walked, the only break in the monotony being when a screw yelled for us to about face, and walk the circle in the opposite direction. The young alco brushed against me on one of the turnabouts, pushed a package at me. 'Few more pep pills,' he said. 'Surprising what you can get up your arsehole in a French letter.' I felt better. The Immediate Now could be staved off for a little while. I was almost happy. But part of my mind was latched onto the Tomorrows I had yet to serve, and I wondered how in hell I was going to get through them without any sort of hooch.

I started nightmares. Bad and black they were, eating my sleep and causing me to wake up yelling and fighting, with the cursings and ravings of my disturbed cell-mates to add reality to the nightmare itself, so that all people and conditions were caught up in the web. The prison Medical Officer put me on sedatives and sleeping pills, and also gave me a cell to myself, because I woke the others up. The single cell suited me better. Now I'd only got my own chamber-pot to bother about. Your own gut-rubbish always smells more acceptable than other people's.

I started to 'con' with the tablets. Instead of taking them, I kept them. It wasn't over-easy. Every morning I had to go to the prison centre 'sick-bay' (which was a converted cell) where a screw gave me the sedative tablets. Two of them. What I did was to take them from him, pop them into my mouth, then swallow the water he handed me. He stood over me all the time. But I learned how to 'tongue-slip' which means getting the tablets under your tongue, keeping them there while the water was being drunk, stand relaxed till the screw nodded for me to fall-out. Once outside the sick-bay I'd slip the tablets from my mouth, and keep them in my handkerchief. Same with the sleeping pills I got every evening. Then I'd go two whole days without sleeping tablets or sedatives, and on the third day take the lot at one go. This gave me the amputation I craved for, a sort of drunken condition inside my mind which relaxed and calmed me; but after six weeks, the source dried up as the Medical Officer put me back on 'fit for normal routine'. I knew I couldn't face the bulk of time lying up ahead without something – I had to have something to take the edge of self-reality away.

Then I smelled hooch on a trustee's breath, and I put it to him. He played, he knew a compulsive alco when he saw one. He'd been with the Alcoholics Anonymous crowd for several years, but finally his slip showed and brought him back into prison.

I sent a letter to the one remaining friend I'd got, in Birmingham, with a Visiting Order enclosed. He came to see me. We had reasonably open visits in a fair-sized room, facing each other across tables. Seated at desks at each end of the room were two screws, with another one pacing slowly up and down the centre of the floor. They were supposed to keep an eye on things, make sure no contraband came in or went out.

I put it to my mate, blackmailed him. Convinced him that I couldn't do my time without drink, that I'd kill myself. I'd top myself with my own belt when the depression hit me. He was worried. He coaxed a five-pound note from his wallet without any of the screws being the wiser, folded it into a little wedge, and then when I gave him the all-clear signal he flicked the wedge at me across the table. I caught it quick. While we carried on talking, I worked the note up inside my tie till it was up against the knot, nice and snug. I made arrangements for my mate to visit me again later on, and when the visit was over I was marched out with other prisoners and given a 'dry bath' on the landing. The screws made us turn our pockets out, checked us, patted us all over; but my money was safe. They never thought to check neckties. I got the money across to the trustee and he arranged the drink at half a pint a day, ten pints for the fiver. That was twenty days' ration.

All prisoners slopped out in the recess after tea, before being banged up and locked in for the night. The trustee would be waiting for me in the half-doored lavatory nearest the slopping-out bosh. As I filled my water jug I'd push the chamber-pot under the half-door of the lavatory, with my drinking mug inside. The trustee lifted the lid off the chamber-pot, tipped the ration of hooch into the mug, put the chamber-pot lid back on. I'd lift it natural-like, and carry it back to my cell.

The drink was putrid, but it was the best that life could offer. It smelled like frowzy pickled onions, and the bulk of it was made in a still at the prison farm where only trustees were allowed to go. There was yeast in it, and potato peelings which had rotted and fermented, and it was laced with surgical spirits. I never let on to my French-letter-tobacco friend that I'd got some jake, I was selfish with it. I just drank it down my own gullet in cell-privacy. There wasn't enough for halfers, for sharing.

Twenty days later the supply dried up as my money ran out. I was near desperate. I got the trustee alone and asked for credit, but he wouldn't wear it. So I proceeded to blackmail him for a daily drink, told him I'd grass to the blue-bastards if he didn't keep the stuff coming. He said he'd put the barons on to me, the tough boys who run every prison in the country. But I was past caring. I insisted. So the drink kept coming every day for a long time after, but the gang-boys and barons left me alone, never touched me. The gaff they'd got was too big to blow, they weren't risking it, and I'd already carved a name out for myself as being a bit of a nutter so they gave it best.

I saw the first eight months of my sentence through on the bare ration, but it was better than nothing. Now that my consumption of alcohol was less than on 'free-street' my body grew stronger – despite the prison menu, and not because of it – and my mind grew more alert.

I could get by.

Chapter Eighteen

In prison, in 'nick', you lie on your cot whenever you can. You lie there day-dreaming. You lie there talking to yourself in your own mind, making plans against the day of release. Only part of you stays in prison, the body part and bits of your mind. The other bits of your mind go away on long-travel journeys into the future, but more often into the past. The past is fixed, firm, established. Your mind spends most of its time there.

Before I got weighed-off I carried part of the public image of what a prison, a prisoner and a warder was. A prison was a place of correction, a place where crooked men were straightened out. Warders were dedicated men who protected Society by keeping villains locked up, men who lived in constant danger of having their lives crippled for them by stubble-chinned monsters who had raped half the children of England and murdered the other half, or were planning to.

I looked around me and was amazed at what I found. Ar, there were men doing time for murder and rape and violence – but not so many as I expected to see. Most of the blokes were the man-next-door type of thing; the feller from the next work-bench, the bloke sitting next to you on the 'bus, ordinary fellers who'd have benefited more from a kick up the arse than a lagging in prison. They – and the rest of the country – would probably have been better men in the long run if they'd been sentenced to a couple of dozen week-ends painting Old Age Pensioners' houses.

Christ Almighty, if only a bloke could describe what a prison *is*; what it *does* to you, despite what *you've* done to that Fool's Paradise called Society.

You want to know something? I found as big bastards in the ranks of the prison officers, the screws, as I did among the inmates. There was the odd exception, but such influence soon got its better side kicked out of it, it got pushed to the wall. In prison, rehabilitation is a bloody myth on crutches.

Some young kid down on the two's should never have been in nick in the first place, he should have been in an intensive-care mental-hospital. He got a razor blade from somewhere and tried to cut his penis off. I helped to clean the blood from his cell after they'd taken him away. Another prisoner was left howling and miouwing on the ones, a bottom-deck cell, a real nut-case. Every day his cell was stripped and he was left with only a bedding 'biscuit' to sit on. I was a landing cleaner, then, and I could hear him crying and howling like a bloody animal caught in a keeper's gin-trap. The warders were overworked, understaffed, and often undertrained.

For some reason I never fathomed, a tune from nowhere came into my mind and haunted me. Light and lilting in places, sad and tormented a bit in others. The tune came from my mind where it had been stored and through my lips. I kept whistling it, couldn't get it away from me, and some screw or other would shout out – 'That man there! Stop that fucking whistling.' So I'd stop whistling for a bit, and then out it would come again, almost as if it was bursting out. Screw after screw told me to 'Stop that bloody whistling', but I kept forgetting. So they got fed up with me and put me on Governor's report for failing to obey an order. I got three days loss of privileges for refusing to obey. Loss of privileges didn't mean a lot, since 'privileges' were thin on the ground, anyway. It meant I had to do without library books, no smoking, no 'free associations' period with other cons. Who cared, anyway. Not me. Yet still the tune persisted on my lips day after day, while officers screeched down the landings – 'That man. Stop whistling.'

I was still whistling it one day whilst emptying my chamber in recess; Klaus Fuchs, the atomic spy, was in the recess at the same time.

'So *you're* the man who whistles it,' he discovered.

'What's it *called*, Doc?'

'Sixth symphony,' he replied. 'The Pastoral.'

'Who wrote it?'

'Beethoven.'

A week or so later Doc sought me out.

'There's a record recital tonight,' he said, 'in the visiting room. Couple of screws for security and a prison visitor brings the record player in. Want to come? Beethoven.'

They played three symphonies from Beethoven. The Eroica, Pastoral, and the Choral. My addiction to music, especially Beethoven, was consummated that night and I wondered how I'd come through so much life without having 'met' him.

'Doc' Fuchs sat next to me, sometimes whispering an explanation, sometimes indicating a particular movement by 'conducting' with his hands. For me, Beethoven suddenly filled a vacuum. In me, he was part responsible for that mystery of evolution known as change. I felt the heart beat of the phoenix rising from the dead ashes of itself.

It seems strange to me, looking back, that one man's music could have opened a floodgate into life which I never knew existed. Stranger too that a fellow prisoner, an enemy of society, should have been the one to show me where the gateway lay. Klaus Fuchs, known affectionately as 'Doc', taking time off from his fifteen years' sentence to show me, a mental inferior, where paths of freedom lay. I only knew Doc for about a year, my discharge came before his. I received one hurried postcard from him before he disappeared into East Germany, before the world drew the curtain on his and its own misdemeanours; but he left me to carryon discovering the greatness of Beethoven, and also the wealth of Emile Coué.

Doc didn't speak about himself much there in prison; it was mostly by picking up clues from his interests that led one towards the truth about him. He loved Beethoven because, he said, the man was concerned in humanity. He liked to tell me how Beethoven had compassion for the under-dog, how he angered and raged at tyranny and oppression. In many ways I suspected that Doc had more than a love of Beethoven's music, he had an affinity with the Master which was more of a spiritual relationship.

Doc once told me that his father was a minister who had become sick and permanently horrified by the bestial slaughter of the Great War. It was from him that Doc learned the secret code that calls for personal sacrifice in striving for world peace and brotherhood; and after all, Doc received the convictions of his courage. He served ten years of the fifteen. Doc once said to me, 'There's still a chance of peace if no one has a surprise punch hidden away. You can't have peace once one country has the ultimate arsenal.' When Doc ever spoke, which was seldom, about the matters which had brought him to prison, he never showed resentment or self pity. This, I think, showed he was a big man and not a little one.

Doc didn't do prison tasks as we did. He did 'special' work, which was a closely guarded secret, although it was rumoured that he did scientific work for the Government that had put him in prison. The last I heard of Doc was that he became Director of the Atomic Research Institute at Dresden; the Reds put pressure on him until he became a lonely and bewildered man, and almost lost his fine mind in the torments of a nervous breakdown.

You learn, in nick, that the system exists for itself. Visiting magistrates have no time for your complaints, only your current misdemeanours. Seven days chokey for us, a double sherry with the Governor for them, then 'let's piss off out of here'. They'd of had a better day out by going to the zoo and watching the monkeys masturbate.

Without exception, prison rots a man; and the only thing a prisoner can do is fight like hell to see that he rots as slowly as possible. The first thing you learn is that the opinions of Home Office, screws and governors are of no consequence; the views and opinions of your fellow prisoners *do* matter, because it's with them you've got to live, it's with them and through them that you go shit-creek way, or stick your chin out from time to time and dare *them* to take a swipe at it, just to show that you're more a man than *they* are. *Them*, you can do without; but hot your fellow prisoners. Governors, creeping-Jesus-chaplains, probation officers, welfare-workers, head-shrinkers – these you can do without. But it's the man either side of your 'peter' that matters, and the blokes in the other eight hundred cells which form your manor, village, town and city. But even some of these you have to watch; the 'grass', the screws bottom-licker, is the one you've got to watch out for. The one who passes rumours or information to the authorities, in exchange for the odd cigarette and a false back-pat. This is the bloke who's the biggest danger, and once you've got a 'grass' among you you don't trust *anybody* till you find him. Then, when you've witch-smelled him out, you arrange your slop-out. You put your evidence to the barons, the 'big-boys' who really *do* run the prisons, and set your play. The barons take over from there, telling you when and where to do it. It's mostly done at recess time, when you're slopping out your rubbish. That's where the expression 'give him a slop-out' comes from – a sweet-as-a-nut expression.

The barons would arrange to have their runners placed at strategical positions, watching for screws, while you followed the 'grass' into recess – the only sections of the prison not under constant watch – and worked him over. If you took the job on, you'd got to do it right. No hiding the punches, no hitting in the belly where the marks wouldn't show. Once you'd taken the job on, you'd got to quarter-kill your man. You'd got to mark his face, you'd got to leave him dripping blood. You'd got to switch off inside as far as sympathy was concerned because you were working for the whole prison, and not just yourself. You'd got to use your fists, boots, secretly made knuckle-dusters, or any damned thing which would leave scars and blood. It was the way. The barons' runners would keep alert watch, give you the signal if it seemed a screw was coming your way; and, if your 'grass' turned out to be too big for you to take, the runners would put their weight into a minutes' worth that did almost as much damage as a truck hitting you. Once you'd slopped the 'grass' out, you'd leave him where he lay and mingle with the other prisoners for an hour's 'free-association' on the ones. If the beat-up 'grass' named you, there were a couple of hundred other prisoners to say you'd never left their sight. And if the 'grass' *did* name you, it was odds on he'd have to go on Governor's section – which meant complete isolation for his own protection. But the barons could *still* get at him, even in 'protection'. One 'grass' who had a slop-out told the Governor who'd done it. No punishments were given, because it was the 'grass's' word against a prison full. But the fact that he'd named his slop-out, the fact that he just hadn't put the hiding down to experience, marked him for further 'treatment'. The barons got a bar of prison-issue soap and wedged broken bits of razor-blades inside. It was only a matter of time before the 'grass' was screaming and yelling from his 'solitary protection', his fingers and hands cut to ribbons as he squeezed the soap to make a bit of lather.

We'd got a feller doing time with us who really should have been in a nut-house, not a nick. Outside, he'd been a milkman. And he'd been caught standing on the shafts of the milk-float doing 'an un-natural act with the mare which drew the float'. He'd got a five stretch to do, for bestiality. There was this one screw who took the piss out of him – when he was sure that the Governor or other warders weren't around. He was with us in the rag-ripping shed, keeping to himself. Our job was to cut piles of old musty clothes and stuff into cleaning rags; me, I became an expert rag-ripper. I could rip a rag with anybody. It was a toss-up which was the best job – rag-ripping or stitching GPO mailbags with eight regulation stitches to the regulation inch. I took to rag-ripping because I didn't see any prospects in the mailbag-stitching trade when I was released. But somebody might come along who wanted the odd rag ripped.

This milkman feller just kept to himself in one corner of the work shed, eyes ever downcast, ripping rags like a man in a dream. Like I said, none of the other prisoners ever interfered with him, or took the piss. They knew, instinctively, that he was a nut-house case and not jail-meat. Then one day we've got a big fat screw in charge of us, the prison-wit, the heart and soul of the warders' mess. With ponderous deliberation he went across to where the fire buckets were, lifted one up, and carried it to the milkman. He put it down in front of him, and then delivered his master-stroke. From his tunic pocket he took a fistful of grass, laid it on the milkman's lap. 'There,' said the fat screw, 'if you want to love like a stallion then you gotta eat like one.' He roared with laughter, looking at all of us, permission in his eyes for us to laugh as well. We didn't. Not one of us. We made his 'joke' fall over backwards, and carried on with our work.

After a bit I could see that the milkman was crying, he'd got his head bent down but I could see the tears dripping off him. I put my rags down and went over to him, took the water-bucket away and kicked the grass out of sight.

'Don't let the fat bugger get under your skin,' I told him out loud, 'he's a screw, and he's got a screw's mentality. Just ignore the bastard.'

I felt the shadow of the screw coming towards me, and then he was standing by me, face grim.

'Governor's,' he said, 'Governor's report for you. Outside with you.' I'd shot my bolt over half-way, so I thought I might as well let it go the whole way.

'You fat bastard,' I told him – and his hand was going down to his truncheon-pocket, and in my mind for a split second I had a glimpse of Pope Tolley out in the misty woods where we'd poached the night through with his brother Benny, and Old Konk. I could see the policeman coming up to us, and when Pope challenged him, the policeman's hand dropping towards his truncheon. And Pope saying – 'Ah wouldn't if ah was yoh, John. If ah was yoh, ah'd leave that bit of wood where it is. Otherwise ah shall bend it round yoh're bloody neck.' I looked at the fat screw.

'If you pull that, I'll bend the bloody thing round your neck,' I told him. He started for the riot-bell near his raised desk. I got in front of him. All the prisoners in the shed were silent, watching, their hands still and quiet on their laps, not working. It was my play. I'd started it, and I'd got to finish it.

'It's you on report, not me,' I told the screw. 'I'm officially requesting an interview with the Governor. I want to report the conduct of one of his officers, and to show him a bucket of water and a handful of grass. Sir.'

The screw's eyes were a pig's eyes, screwed up inside pouches of fat. The pig's eyes scanned my face with a pig's greed.

'Back to your work,' the pig said, 'and I'll bide my time and get you bang to rights yet.'

The victory went to my head a bit. I collected a gob of spit inside my mouth, and deliberately let it drop in front of the screw's boots. Then I went back to my rag-ripping. Next day, we had a different screw in charge; the fat one had requested a move to another workshop on account that the dust from the rag-ripping was affecting his chest.

The encounter with the screw stood me in good stead with the other prisoner-blokes, and one of the barons took to calling me by my first name. But I didn't want any close friendships even in prison, I just wanted everybody to keep at a distance. I'd do my porage my way, not theirs.

Sometimes I'd have a few words with Doc Fuchs about books, or maybe music. I'd started to write doggerel poetry, and tried my hand at short-stories, and Doc would read them and give his opinion and constructive criticism. But I couldn't have really deep and long conversations with Doc, he was 'way above me. From time to time he'd stop me in or around the prison and suggest that I read this or that book from the prison-library.

Before he'd finished with me I'd caught glimpses of Schiller, Jung, Nostradamus, and I'd read every bloody word of *War and Peace*. Through Doc, I read Tom Paine's *The Age of Reason* and *Rights of Man*, and in no time at all I'd put Tom Paine on the same platform as Beethoven. Great shiny beacons spearing through the darkness. Doc was such a quiet, decent and dignified bloke – even in prison drabs – that even the thickest screw treated him with respect, and you half expected the screws to call *him* 'Sir'. And the boot would have been on the right foot if they had of done. Doc belonged to some dimension way out and beyond any of them. He must have had a deeply lonely life there in the nick, with nobody his equal to talk with.

Doc was a loner amongst loners. There was an ex-ship's steward, doing life, he was a loner, too. The Law said he'd killed an actress in her cabin, and then pushed her body through the port-hole. There was a young prisoner whose partner-in-crime had been hanged, despite the fact that he was reputedly in police hands when the prisoner had fired the bullet which took a policeman's life on a warehouse roof-top in London. Loners all, reluctant to mix with others unless we had to.

I was a loner for two reasons. One, I didn't particularly want friends inside. Two, and this was a shade more important, I was an ex-copper, and if ever this bit of news slipped out I could expect trouble, and would probably have to go running for Governor's protection.

And *that* I wanted to do without.

Grasses, ex-coppers and child-molesters were what the prisoners hated most, next to the screws. We'd got a child-molester in our ranks. He was an oldish man, too old for the lads to give a hiding to, p'raps. But they made his life hell, just the same. They called him 'Treacle Cock' for starters, and the name stuck. He'd been weighed off for getting little kids, no older than three or four. He'd dip his penis into treacle or condensed milk and get the kids to lick the stuff off. The blokes inside didn't 'slop him out', but they got at him other ways. Like putting lavatory muck in his food, stealing his tobacco-tin and contents every so often, nipping into his cell while he was at the recess, tipping his cot over and shedding water from his jug all over the floor. Once, they put a dead mouse in his cocoa, and he'd drunk almost all of it before he found out.

From time to time there'd be a 'Sheila-row'. Here and there, a long-sentence man would take a Queer under his wing, and in no time at all jealousies would start, like as if it was a real marriage between man and woman. Either the Queer would accuse another Queer of 'making eyes at her husband', or even the other way round, with the long-termer accusing another bloke of trying to get off with his 'wife'. The feathers would really hit the fan.

Once a week we were each allowed three books from the prison library. The Queers, the 'Queens', would make a mad dash for any book – regardless of contents, those weren't important – that had a red cover. Back in their cells, the Queers would soak the red dye out of the book covers for lip-stick and face-rouge colouring. The screws always addressed the Queers by their 'maiden names' – Sheila, Shirley, Betty, June, etcetera.

In prison, nothing ever seemed to be absolutely 'un-natural'; everything seemed to be 'natural'. The screws and the prison authorities played no part in 'rehabilitation' – that existed on paper only, not in the attitudes of our custodians. All any Governor wanted was a 'well-run nick', which meant that all he wanted was peace and quiet and no trouble or else …

Once or twice I did a 'mad' act – whether consciously or not, I don't really know. When we left the main-block of the prison we had to be counted into the parade-yard for a start. Everywhere you went, you had to be counted. If you had cause to leave one section of the prison to go to another, the officer you left would shout out – 'One away, sir'. And the screw 'receiving' you would shout back – 'One on, sir'. You were counted into your cells, out of your cells, into the lavatory, out of it, into workshops, out of workshops. You felt like bloody sheep jumping stiles for the sake of somebody's insomnia.

This one morning old pig-eyes (the screw who had baited the milkman) was on count-off duty at the door which led to the court-yard-parade-ground-cum-exercise-yard. He'd got to count about six hundred of us through, single file. By the time I got level with him he was into the three-hundreds.

'Three hundred and ten, three hundred and eleven, three hundred and twelve,' he was counting out loud.

'Three hundred and ninety-seven,' I said, as I went past, and he picked it up from there.

'Three hundred and ninety-eight –.' And then it hit him.

'Come back,' he screamed, 'every bloody one of you. Back inside.' And back trooped the men, back inside, to be counted all over again. Second time through I kept my mouth shut, because you can have too much of a good thing and be found out.

I don't know why I rang the sacred bell. It just happened, and I did it; and probably made a bit of nick-history. In the centre of the prison was a great throbbing brass bell, like off a ship. This was the bell by which all Major Events were declared and ordered. It was this that rang out to wake you in the mornings, it was this which ordered slopping-out time, meal times and bed-times. It was a Very Important Bell. Polished like a guardsman's buttons, and only Very Important People – like screws – could touch it. I was passing close to it, from one wing to another, when the irresistible urge took me. I grabbed the pull-rope and made that clapper ring like it had never rung before. I made music. Doc Fuchs had told me that when

Beethoven wrote the opening notes of his Fifth Symphony – the 'V for Victory notes' – he'd said, 'Thus does Fate knock on my door.' I gave that bell Beethoven, and Beethoven rose to the occasion and stirred in his grave, and helped my hand on the pull-rope.

The Chief Officer stood half a dozen paces away, watching me in frozen amazement. Screws were fixed like statues on turned heel, or half stride; prisoners stood shock-still, all staring from rows of cells, row upon row.

Bom-bom-bom-booom, bom-bom-bom-booom.

Beethoven had a birthday.

Screws came running at me, and I stood to attention, shouting at the top of my voice, 'One away, sir. Two away, sir. All the fucking nick away, sir.' They handled me almost gently, led me like a little child into an observation cell, sat me down and patted me. Then took my flint and tinder and bit of tobacco away, in case I used the tinder to set fire to myself. I was to be observed.

Several times I heard a screw sneaking along the cat-walk of slate quarries, heard the click of the Judas-hole in the door as he lifted the flap to look in on me. Third time he did this I was ready. I heard him coming, and got my own eye at the inside lens of the Judas-hole as he lifted the flap and stuck his own orb there. P'raps there's nothing more scary in this world than looking through a hole only to find another unwinking eye staring into yours less than an inch away. I bet it could make even strong men shudder. I toyed with the idea of faking a suicide – ripping a blanket into shreds to make a rope, tying one end to the bars, the other round my neck, and slumping to the floor as if I'd garrotted myself. I gave the idea best after some reflection. There was no point to it, really. If I succeeded in convincing the authorities that I was a real nutter, they'd most probably have sent me to Broadmoor, where hell exists one infinite number of times multiplied by Dartmoor. They didn't *treat* madness at Broadmoor – they *created* it. So damn that for a lark.

After two or three days in 'observation' I was put in front of the Governor. In the interim, I'd devised a new technique. I'd made up my mind that I wasn't going to call anybody else 'Sir'. I made up a mental score-board in my head. So many merits for getting through an entire conversation with one of 'Them' without saying 'Sir', so many demerits if I let a 'Sir' pass my lips. The higher up the ranks, the higher the merit or demerit. I made a rough calculation that approximately a thousand merits or demerits would see my time over and done with.

The Governor asked me how I felt, I said fine, he said Good; then he asked me if I'd got any problems and I said No, and he said Good. Then he asked me if I'd like to be a red-band Trustee and work in the prison library, and I said No and he started to say 'Good', then corrected himself and asked 'Why?'

I was learning fast from Doc Fuchs.

'Bad grammar,' I told the Governor, 'you should have asked "why *not*".'

The Chief Officer, always present at Governor's interviews, snapped, 'Stand further back on the mat, lad. Stand up straight. And address the Governor as Sir.'

'I'm not talking to you,' I said to the screw-driver. 'I'm talking to the Governor.' I thought the Chief was going to have puppies, all of them on the delinquent side.

'Sir,' he bellowed, 'You say Sir, Sir. Sir, Sir – *SIR*.' I ignored him.

'I don't want a red-band,' I said to the Governor, 'because I don't want any favours.'

'I've been told that you have an interest in literature, and in philosophy.'

'You mean Doc Fuchs told you?' I asked, and the Governor inclined his head slightly.

'You can have writing books in your cell, if you want,' he said. 'And a pencil. You can write if you want to – but if you want to take what you write out with you at discharge, they'll have to go through the censor. You're forbidden to write anything about the prison, or prisoners. Or staff,' he added for good measure.

'How you going to censor my mind?' I asked, 'When I leave here? How you going to censor my memory, to stop me writing about nick when I'm free-side of the wall?' The Chief was still muttering about my lack of 'Sir's'.

'You address the Governor as Sir,' he bellowed again, 'he is entitled to respect, as is every officer in this prison.'

'Nobody's *entitled* to respect,' I retorted. 'In my book they've got to *earn* it. And as far as I'm concerned, none of your blue-bastards has earned any.' The Governor motioned the Chief to be quiet. When he spoke to me again he did so in a low voice, easy and natural and not without friendliness.

'Just go and settle down,' he told me. 'You're doing your time the hard way. It won't pass any the quicker, so you might as well relax and fit in, and cause no trouble.'

'You can lock my body up,' I argued, 'but you can't lock my mind up. And you can't make me say "Sir" to anybody I don't want to. I'll do my task-work and I'll obey all orders, but I'm through with "Sirring".' The Governor was so quiet and soothing that I knew I was marked as a borderline nut-case to watch. I knew I'd created a reasonably neutral vacuum where I'd be left alone in case I blew my top completely and had to be taken off in a strait jacket. I could see my dossier on the Governor's desk, and I knew that it contained all the information about my being sent to a mental hospital and etcetera. The Governor didn't want to be the one to 'push me over the brink', or let his men do so. When a man flipped his lid and had to be carted off, there was always an inquiry into the circumstances. All any Governor wanted was a well run nick with no troubles, no smoke, no fire.

The Chief took me back to my own cell.

'You want a bit of chokey, you do,' he said, 'down on the ones. Few days on bread and water. Straighten you out a bit. We've had tougher nuts than you to crack.'

'Governor's,' I replied, standing still so suddenly that he almost bumped into me.

'Do what?'

'Governor's interview. I want to see the Governor. About you. Pushing and bullying.' He'd unlocked my cell door.

'Get inside,' he said gruffly, 'and let's have no more of your bloody nonsense.' He locked me in and went away. I lay on my cot. After a bit I got up and pulled the communication handle. This caused a small bell to ring, and a small red 'flag' – like a traffic-indicator – to stick out. A screw could immediately see which cell was calling. If you got jittery in a cell and kept pulling the handle, the screws used to disconnect it from the outside, and ignore the occupant. I'd never had cause to use the system before, and soon a screw opened the door and asked me what I wanted.

'My tobacco and tinder,' I told him, 'I'm out of observation, now.' He mumbled something, locked me in, and went off. He came back an hour later with my tin of tobacco.

'Here's your smokes,' he said, 'but the Chief's confiscated your tinder because it's illegal to have it.' I sighed disappointment.

'I suppose I can chew it,' I said. He nodded; then, just as he was about to leave and lock me in, he suddenly took a box of Swan Vestas from a pocket, took half a dozen red-tipped matches out, and dropped them on the floor of my 'peter'. He didn't look at me, just dropped the matches sort of accidental-casual like. I gave myself a demerit.

'Thank you, sir,' I said.

Chapter Nineteen

Time goes by. You learn that Society is like a compulsive gambler; it carries its own talismans and superstitions. I've known compulsive gamblers who, when on a losing streak, draw a white chalk circle round the chair they're sitting in. The circle is supposed to keep all the evil influences out. Society does this. Draws a circle round itself – two circles. One to keep its own conventions in, the other round its prisons to keep the evil confined. But when the 'evil' gets out of its circle it is more putrid than when it went in. It's had time and opportunity to fester and multiply and 'educate' its own refinements.

I went inside as a gas-meter-bandit; I came out fully educated in matters criminal. I knew how to 'case' a dwelling-house, what to steal and what not to steal, how to 'rig' a stolen car, how and where to get false log-books, how to open Yale-type locks, how to recognise the difference between real furs and artificial, real jewellery and 'paste'. How to deal with a dog or dogs which might be guarding the premises, which area of London to visit if I ever wanted to buy or hire a shooter (a pistol) and ammunition. I learned more about crime and how-to-get-away-with-it in HMP than anything else. It was just a matter of listening, of being alert as the inmates talked to each other. The only effort I ever had to make was to distinguish the real from the exaggerated. Time to time you'd learn from so-and-so that he'd done a 'real big 'un' and had got the loot hidden away, all twenty thousand pounds worth, against the day of his release. Then you'd make discreet inquiries and find that the feller was only inside for a haircut of six months, and then you'd know for a cert that he was shooting his mouth off, and had done nothing bigger than lift a shirt off a store counter then try to get out without paying for it. The golden rule was that you never directly asked a man what he was inside for. It was up to him. He would tell you, or he wouldn't. It was his privilege. But, in an amazing way, if the barons of a prison wanted information on a man, they seemed to get it. And if a big case was being heard in the Courts, the Court's verdict seemed to be known to the prisoners before the first newspaper reports hit the streets. The prison grape-vine was complex, but nine times out of ten it was more reliable than the GPO telephone system.

They say you can get everything in prison except sex with women, if you've got the right money and contacts. But I served with one prisoner who got sex as well. He was a trustee on 'outside working party', engaged on painting and decorating the screws' married quarters. This prisoner would have his girl-friend come over to the house he was painting, and when the woman of the house, the particular screw's wife, went shopping the screw in charge of the working party would let this bloke's girl into the house so's they could knock a round off. The bloke had money on the outside, and a fair amount of it must have found itself into the screw's pocket.

Resentment beats in most prisoners' hearts, to be suppressed until the day of release, building up and feeding on its own fire, when it can erupt. Lying on my cot, in my cell, I puzzled at little things that Doc Fuchs said to me. Like – 'It's not sufficient to prove that the accused *knows* the difference between right and wrong – the important thing is *does he care*? If he *doesn't* care, then he has to be *taught* how to care. Nothing else has prior importance.'

Somewhere inside me, I knew Doc was right. I'd read somewhere that 'If the pupil hasn't learned, then the teacher hasn't taught'. I found no teachers within the system. I learned nothing from the prison system, except the finer arts of crime and self-defence. I learned how to defend

237

what I'd got, and inwardly – sometimes openly – defy authority. I learned that Society had a blank stupid face which you spat on when you had a mind to; that Society consisted of rich men, fit men, working men who had trades in their fingers better than a rag-ripper, hypocrites, people with comfortable houses and comfortable families, old ladies who smelled of camphor, magistrates, policemen, screws, and no mis-fits like myself. Society didn't want *me*, nor the several hundred other blokes packed like sardines in the prison-can.

So you lie on your cot and you think and puzzle, but the inner puzzle of self isn't complete, isn't a single unit. It's bits of many jigsaw puzzles tizzled up together, and you can't sort the pieces out. If They notice that you're a loner, don't want to mix, They invariably set the Chaplain on you, probably just to give him something to do. When he opens your peter up and comes in for a chat you hope for a moment that he'll give you a tailor-made cigarette, but he doesn't, so inside ten minutes flat you bore him out of your existence. Thank God you are an atheist, because the Chaplain goes off to try his luck elsewhere. You work up a parting shot which seems to make sense – 'The Disciple Peter wasn't a fisherman of men's souls – he was a bloody poacher' – but as soon as you've said it, you realise it has no meaning. That's how far you are from reality. Christ wanders from cell to cell looking for a chat, but none to talk with. Oh, Christ. Your poor, bleeding feet.

Prison suddenly becomes a haven, the cell is safety, is the dark womb of pre-remembrance. There's one door only, and you can lie on your back looking at it and you can see whoever it is who comes through it, you can't be taken by surprise. Your eyes can watch the door and your thoughts can slip away to unsafe rivers which move backwards and forwards at the whim of a wind, and so up the rotten, sodding world.... You lie in your cell and you think about the days that are gone, the sad, dark days with sometimes a gleam of sunlight to part the darkness; but mostly with a wall of thought cluttering at the doorway of your mind. When the cell door is shut, when you are banged up for the night, there is no world but self and silence and the backwards-forwards flowing river of thought. You stare up at the ceiling as you have done for so many days and nights, and will yet do for many days and nights to come. You wait for the days and the weeks and the months to peel themselves away from the Big Gate, you wait for that last landing-bell-peal to wave you world-wards, you wait for your last porridge. And in the meantime your thoughts stray and wander and delve into a graveyard filled with old bones, old memories, old waters of pain. Thoughts prick, probe, flinch, duck, dodge, hold, let go ... and back of them all is an unknown hatred, an old ambivalence.

In prison, you can keep niggling inside your mind with resentments and self-pity. But the self-pity is the most dangerous. Resentment keeps you alive, keeps you going, puts the iron of defiance into your fibres. But self-pity is the furnace where everything gets melted down and wasted. Self-pity is the Great Destroyer, and if you find it ranging through the private-property of your mind you've got to take it by the scruff of the neck, turn it inside out, and kick it around until it disappears. Self-pity is the major self-sin, the cheapest and shoddiest luxury. If you find it in you, you've got to burn it out, cauterise it, chuck it away. It'll drag you down else. Doc dropped a library book into my cell, and there was this strange, haunting poem in it, 'Tom O' Bedlam', I think it was. I don't know who wrote it. It goes something like this:

> And of your five sweet senses
> may you never be forsaken,
> nor wander from yourself with Tom
> abroad, to beg your bacon.
>
> With a host of furious fancies
> whereof I am Commander,
> with a horse of air and a shield of fire
> to the wilderness I wander ...

Wild, half-mad, haunting words to click with perfect precision into slots of memory that have been waiting for them. *Oft in the stilly night, ere slumber's chain hath bound me, I see in a misty light other days around me ...*'

Where are you now, old Billy? Where are you, Konk? And most of all, where are you, Pope Tolley? Many's the time you came into this prison to do your six months, or twelve, or eighteen. I often wonder if the cell I sleep in was the one you slept in. But I know it's not. If it were, I'd see your shadow on the wall, I'd hear your easy voice plucking the silence like strong fingers at coir (the coarse, straw-like substance used for filling prison mattresses; it comes in hard bales and has to be loosened into strands – which makes your fingers sore). You were never in this cell, because I'd know your presence, and your presence isn't here. The walls hold other people's, strangers' memories; not yours. Doc Fuchs dropped some more poetry in on me today, Pope. By somebody named Dylan Thomas. One of the poems fitted you like a glove ... I don't remember the exact words, only the essence of them, but they fitted you. Something about 'Do not go gently into that good night ... rage, rage against the fading of the light ...'

I had a sudden vision of you, Pope; dying. But not lying down to Death, not waiting for It flat on your back with supposed dignity. But waiting for It with your back to the wall, knowing It would win, but laughing at It, sneering at It, making It fight for Its trophy. I could almost see Death, putting Its hand down to a truncheon pocket, hear you saying' Ah'd leave that bit o' wood wheer it is if ah was yoh, me lover. Otherwise ah shall wrap the bloody thing round yoh're neck.'

Don't go gently into that good night, Pope. Fight the bastard, give it a grudge-fight, and I'll follow in your footsteps, in time. What was it you kept telling me? 'Always lick the other bugger before yoh sits down and rubs yoh're own bruises. There's nothing wrong in crying, me lover, if yoh doh let anybody see the tears. Always cry on the inside, and make yoh're self laugh on the *outside*.'

Well said, Pope. Well said.

On the night before I was due for discharge, my civvy shoes were returned to me so's I could 'get used to them'. It's a funny feeling after such a long time, looking down at your civvy shoes. They feel strange, too light. Your feet feel as if they want to make a mad dash for the Big Gate, your feet feel as if they're already free.

That last night, you keep away from the bulk of prisoners when it's 'free-association' time. On the one hand, you don't want to make other men envious, men who've still got a bulk of time to do. On the other, and this is probably the more important, you might fall foul of somebody. Somebody with ten or fifteen years to serve might let their envy turn to spite and malice, and involve you in a fight which could have you back on the Governor's mat, to lose all your remission, which could mean another year in the cell. I stood apart, watching a screw make his tour of the landings, peering into each cell, making sure no queers were having it off, no 'bandits' were grouped together making escape plans, or what have you.

The screw passes by me, walking from cell to cell, quiet, sane. His eyes glance down at my civvy shoes, then he looks me full in the face, winks, and passes on. The Chaplain beckons a prisoner who wants to see him, and the two of them go into the man's cell, and the door is closed to make a small box of privacy. And I think to myself, what if there *is* no God; what if there is no bridge from the Universe of flesh to a timeless Universe of spirit? If this be so, then everything which Man thinks he stands for is only the sad, sad song of earth. I'd written a poem for Doc, and I went along the cat-walk to his cell and gave it to him. He read it.

> Friend, I hear reveille's signal
> sound about the prison, plain,
> 'tis time to rise, and fold your blanket
> and to face the clock again.
>
> Leave off your dreams, or let them perish,
> they're insubstantial in the light;
> if you're alive, then friend, you'll find them
> wrapped in the safety of tonight.

Doc looked at it, and looked at me.

'You're going out, then?'

'Tomorrow morning.' Doc nodded, the expression in his eyes suddenly hidden by light reflecting from the lenses of his steel-rimmed spectacles.

'Remember,' he said, 'there can be no change without resistance, and no resistance without suffering.'

'It's deep,' I said, 'but I'll remember it.'

Doc got up from his seat, paced the nervous length of his cell, up and down, with me at the door. The first time I'd spoken with him he did this. Some of the more intelligent prisoners – and we weren't short of such – had spent a couple of days knitting a mathematical problem together. When it was gelled they took it to Doc. They gave Doc the problem. I was with them, more out of curiosity than contribution. Doc repeated the problem, stood still for a second or two, leaning in on his own mind, then he took a length of cell-strides up and down, stopped at the door and gave them the answer. From their silence, I knew they were awed. Me, I hadn't understood the question let alone the answer.

'What were you reading?' I asked Doc. He didn't answer, and then I could see it was a Bible. The sight of it soured me.

'Without man, God cannot exist,' I said to Doc, feeling that I was being very clever.

'Without God, man doesn't deserve to exist,' Doc said quietly. We chattered idly for a bit, and then the back-to-cells bell pealed out. I held my hand out. Doc took it.

'Good luck, Doc,' I said.

'Good luck,' he answered. I hesitated.

'There's an address where you can reach me,' I said, 'on the back of the poem. It's a mate of mine.'

He nodded, tolerant; partly amused.

'Thanks for Beethoven,' I said finally, and went back to my cell for the last night in.

I hardly slept. The tension of 'last night in' was equivalent to 'first night in'. I got my tobacco tin out, rolled the lot up into ten slim cigarettes. I placed these on the wooden chair beside my cot, put my flint and tinder-box with them. The tinder consisted of partially burnt rag inside a tin box. The flint was the normal sort used in a cigarette lighter, but in this instance 'copped' off one of the barons' runners. With a mailbag needle,

I'd dug out the lead in the top-end of my pencil, and stuck the flint in the hole. To a casual onlooker, the pencil hadn't been interfered with. For striking-steel I'd got a piece of razor blade. When I wanted a smoke all I'd got to do was open my tinder-box, strike the pencil-held flint with the piece of razor blade so that a spark jumped into the tinder-box. The half-burned rag would glow sufficiently to light a cigarette from. It was illegal to have such contraptions, but since two-thirds of the prisoners had got them, the screws seemed to turn a blind eye.

I got through six of the cigarettes before the 'Wake-up' bell pealed out, and the landing-screws came down the rows, unlocking the cells to hasp-only. I got dressed quick, washed with water from my slops pail, and waited to be let out. I grew impatient after a bit, and gave the communication-handle a pull. A screw came up to the Judas-hole, peered in.

'What's the fuss?' he wanted to know.

'I'm due out this morning,' I told him, 'I thought you'd forgot.'

'We haven't forgotten,' he said, 'we'll let you out at the proper time.' He went away, and it seemed ages before another screw opened up so's the two trustees could fill my mug with tea, and my tin plate with skilly. I ate the skilly, not wanting it, but knowing that the superstition existed about 'coming back for it'. The screw finally unlocked my cell and took me down to reception where I handed my blankets in, together with knife, fork, spoon, prison cape, shoes, spare socks and spare shirt. These were checked off the list, and I was motioned to sit down on a hard bench with about five other blokes waiting for discharge.

'Got anything you shouldn't have?' the desk screw called to all of us, 'such as smuggling letters out for anybody?' We all answered 'No'. We were given dry-bath searches, just the same.

Eventually the ritual was over, and we were herded into single cubicles to put on our civvy clothing. I could smell camphor adhering to my clothes, musty as a great, great grandmother. I stepped from the cubicle feeling strange and self-conscious and sort of 'exposed' in my now thin clothing, after the thick roughness of prison drabs. My trouser-legs felt too wide, my jacket too slack. I went with the others to the Chief Officer's desk.

'Stop the talking,' one of the screws snapped, 'else you'll be back in a peter . We can still keep you to do the rest of your sentences, you're not free men till the Big Gate shuts behind you.'

We each received five shillings in coins, a railway warrant back 'home', and an official letter to be taken to the nearest office of the National Assistance Board. We signed for everything, our private property as well.

'Don't let me see any of you again,' the chief said gruffly, and the screws – two of them – marched us across the front yard to the Big Gate. It was raining as the Duty Officer opened the inner gate for us, passed us through, then locked the gate. First hurdle over. We were now standing in a two-cell space, locked in by the inner gate and the Big Gate. We stood looking at the Big Gate. The Duty Officer went into his cubicle office, came out with a clipboard of paper, checked and double-checked us against the information listed there. Finally, he opened the inset door of the Big Gate, and waved us through.

'Good luck,' he said, but one of us – the last one through – put a bad touch to it.

'All screws are bastards,' he said loudly, the moment both of his feet were free-side.

'You'll be back,' the screw said calmly, and locked us out. I turned my mac collar high against the rain, and walked off on my own. I found the railway station, changed my warrant for a ticket to Birmingham, and huddled away freezing hours in a dreary waiting room.

The friend who'd smuggled money into prison for me had sent an official five pounds to be put into my private property against my release day. The notes hugged the inside of my jacket pocket. Eventually, two of the other discharges joined me in the waiting room, and we rode the Birmingham train together, staying in the restaurant-car where the beer was. After so long an abstinence, the alcohol got to work fast. By the time we reached Birmingham I was already half-ways drunk. I drank till closing time in the city, then went to a cinema to sleep it off. That evening, I rode a 'bus to where my mam lived. It was still raining. I knocked on the front door, wet and a bit miserable, and I heard my mam's voice call 'Who's theer?'

'It's me. It's Archie.'

My mam's words were nails, hammering the doors of the world shut.

'Yoh can bugger off from here,' she said. 'Yoh'm not wanted.'

So I turned away and walked back down the wet street, and I had more hate in me than it is sane to carry.

Chapter Twenty

So I went home, after prison. Not home the place with a front door and warm hearth, but home the location. The zone, the locality, the area. Stood hidden and staring, like a penniless kid at Christmas time with nose jammed against the window of a toy shop.

I went home and walked about till it was dark and cold, and the houses of the streets and council estates cringed away from street lights like beggars waiting for the policeman to pass so's they could skulk back into the light again. Lots of houses, many houses, all carved from one solid block with windows stuck in and doors and people. The back gardens were crammed plots of pigeon pens and dog kennels and lean-tos and rusty long-disused air raid shelters; but you couldn't see the rubbish clearly, only the mounded shapes of it. The details were there in your mind's memory only, because it was dark as a grave and as wet, and as miserable. Past the houses and the railway sheds and the gasometers were fields, and that's where the darkness thinned and thought's strange cleanliness began. The fields were there, wide and green and leading to Kinver where a man could be alone in clean silence and feel his mind grow up like a god's among gorse and heather. Where the ferns in springtime button-hole the earth with bunches of scent and the skies are a blue map ... but no, that's Kinver, a few miles away ... and this is Home, with the rain falling on bleak cramped streets. People pass against drawn blinds, sometimes a light flickers from an upstairs window, a baby cries somewhere, and a dog mourns doleful across the night …

… down at the corner of the street the door of the Red Lion opens and noise and laughter leaps out to stand in the roadway, holding its sides, then darts back into its beer-stained crowded lair as the door closes again.

The Red Lion crowded this night … there's always money for ale and drink, like there's always been. And, like always, sometimes the baker doesn't get paid, or the rent-man, or the grocer, or the bob-a-week-and-misses bloke, the tally-man who owns the lino on the kitchen floors and most of the clothes on the drinkers' backs. Sometimes the coalman or the butcher doesn't get paid, but there's always money for drink at the Red Lion. And, inside, the same people as always, the same conversations of old, like a play in perpetual rehearsal; the same words and phrases winnowing like fish trapped in a small tank.

'Here, Bert. Here's a pound. Ah missed the baker this morning, he'll atta wait till next week. Get me a drop o' port while you're up at the counter.'

Mr. Higgs is immediately a satisfied man with Tuesday night wealth.

'We can stop till closing time, now,' he says, 'an' ah'll get a couple a packets a crisps for the kids.'

Mrs. Perkins, sitting nearby, nursing a milk-stout on which she owes twopence to the landlady ('Ah left me purse at home, wench. Only got this bit of change in me pocket with me – strap us the twopence till tomorrow'), and which must last her till closing time unless somebody treats her, ingratiates herself towards the pound note in Mr. Higgs' hand.

'Yoh dun look after them kids o' your'n,' she says. 'They'n got a good dad. Ah tells everybody that.'

'They have that,' says Mrs. Higgs, mellow from two previous ports, 'but ah wishes I knew where their next pair of shoes is going to come from. Our Lenny's lets in the wet, and Bobby's got holes in his.'

'The money doh go round, does it,' sympathises Mrs. Perkins, keeping her fingers on her glass so's Mr. Higgs can't be off seeing how low the contents are. 'Yoh scrimps and saves, but the money doh go round.'

Mrs. Higgs sighs wearily with family responsibilities. 'Only bit o' pleasure we gets, comin' here for an hour,' she says.

'Ar, it is,' agrees Mrs. Perkins.

'Can't keep going on without *some* pleasure,' Mrs. Higgs says, warming up.

'It's the Government's fault,' says Mrs. Perkins. 'They should raise the Family Allowance, so's people can raise their kid's proper.'

'Ah do feel guilty sitting here like this,' sighs Mrs. Higgs, 'with our kids shoes letting in the wet and all – bring Mrs. Perkins a glass o' milk stout while you'm theer, Bert,' she adds in a shout, her voice shrill over the drone of voices and the stamp of a cheap piano.

Home is where the heart is, and my heart isn't here. Outside, on me, the rain still falls and the street is empty except for young Dilly Moore who shuffles and puddle-splashes her way to the off-licence to get her dad's Woodbines ... night is kind, it hides the glare of poverty and cheapness in this age of plenty.

I maunched about the streets, trying to warm myself on old memories; wanting to come in from the Outside, no matter what the Inside was like. I lingered at back gardens, seeing through uncurtained windows, craving welcome, craving contact. Higgs' house is like all the others, only the stenciled number on the front door is different. I listen to my own childhood being rehearsed over again. Carol, the youngest-but-one of five, stands bare-footed, bare-bottomed in the warm untidy kitchen.

'I'se hungry,' she shrills, 'I want's a piece.'

'Cut one, then,' says Jackie, eldest-but-one at eleven years of age, 'there's some jam in the pot.'

'Goo easy on the bread,' Ernie warns, fourteen and conscious of the authority such years carry, 'it's all we'n got left. The baker only left one loaf 'cos muth didn't pay him. Wheer'm yoh going?" he asks Jackie.

'Out to play,' says Jackie.

'It's gone nine o'clock,' Ernie decides, 'yoh'd best stop in. It's raining, for another thing.'

A dirge of wails floats down the stairs.

'The babby's crying, the babby's crying,' pipes Carol, mouth smeared with jam and breadcrumbs.

'Let her cry, then,' Ernie says, wise to the fact that the world's got more tears than laughter, 'or make a sugar-titty and stick it in her mouth.'

Over at Mrs. Perkins' house daughter Carmelia is lying under her boy-friend on the sofa. Carmelia is eighteen and has her knickers off, they lie in a pale blur on the rug. Hugh is twenty-two and too embarrassed to have his trousers down or off, and all the while he's conscious of the need to avoid telltale creases and stains. He murmurs to Carmelia while he performs, pretending that he isn't doing what he is doing, spinning things out so's he doesn't climax too soon. Mr. Perkins' photograph, in Home Guard uniform, smiles down at them from the mantelpiece. Mr. Perkins is on night-shift tonight.

I am a camera thirty years old, with only one piece of film emulsion at the focal-plane. On that film I have taken thousands, perhaps millions, of pictures; they are all the same, stretching from my birth to now, and only the faces are different.

And this is where the Smiths live, eight people cooped up in a three-bedroomed council house; not to mention the cat which comes and goes as it pleases, the dog chained forever in its wind-leaking kennel, the two pen-lofts filled with cooing restless pigeons, the half-starved rabbit in the wire-netted box, and the three dispirited hens gone to rest in the dampness of the Anderson air raid shelter. And this is where the Tylers live, this house where the glass is missing from the front door and cardboard nailed over to keep the draught out. I rap on the back door, but the rented TV drowns my knocking. I stand there, looking at the darkness, dimly making out the dustbins behind which I hid when the police were looking for me. I could hear one of them saying – 'Let us know if yoh sees him. Yoh're brother's a funny feller.'

'Is there a reward?' I could hear my sister calling after them.

'Balls,' says the policeman, voice tunnel-hollow as he goes down the entry.

'I didn't ask what yoh had for breakfast, or what kept your bleeding ears apart,' screeches me sister.

249

I knock the back door again, louder, with the toe of my shoe. She hears, she comes, she opens.

'It's yoh, then,' she says, 'they let you out.'

I walked past her into the grimy, filthy kitchen. I walked into full poverty, the reflection of my own childhood, and tried not to notice it. My sister's four children stared at me from the hearth, resenting the intruder who'd caused the sound to be lowered on the TV set. Their faces were peaked and dirty, their clothing inadequate. The table was piled with refuse, dirty crockery jostling with unwrapped bread, tea-slops staining the newspapers which served as table-cloth. Pope Tolley's voice from the past, cynical, undercurrents of anger towards my dad.

'Doh rip the table-cloth, ah've not read it yet.'

My heart bled for nieces and nephews and I hoped they would die before they grew into men and women, before they could breed children who in turn would breed children. I hoped they would fall asleep gently and never wake up again. My sister gave me tea in a chipped cup, and I was grateful for the hand-warmth it gave.

'We can't put yoh up,' she said, embarrassed. 'My bloke's against you. Yoh'll have to go, afore he gets home from the pub.'

'What's with him?' I wanted to know, blowing on the tea to cool it. I wished there was a big fire to dry my wetness.

'Yoh knows,' my sister said. 'Yoh being in prison and all that. He doh like it. Says it's not right for the kids, says it sets 'em a bad example.' I stared at her in astonishment, then at the neglected house and children, at her own faded youth and near-beauty, at the hell she had inherited from our own mam and dad. I wanted to laugh and swear all in the same breath.

'Look,' I said, 'I went to prison for stealing, not for attacking kids.'

'It's my bloke,' she answered. 'Yoh knows how it is.'

'Ar,' I said, putting my cup down, 'ah knows how it is.' She followed me to the door, tried to put her arms round me. I brushed her aside, a vision of our mam as she tried to embrace the school-teacher with greed and gratitude, flashing through my mind. I stepped out into the rain, walked to the town centre public houses. I went into the one where I'd been arrested two years ago, but it was a different landlord. A few old customers still lingered, but either their memories were fully misted or they just didn't want to know me. I wasn't bothered. I drank sparingly, getting used to the stuff again. Eventually the evening faded into 'Last orders, please' and I went back into Birmingham on a 'bus. I put up at a spike, a hostel for down and outs, and wished with a third of my mind that I were back in prison. In one corner of the doss-house was a feller with a bottle of cheap wine, and I got talking with him so's I could share his bottle. It was finished too soon.

Before turning in I remembered to place each of my shoes under a front leg of my dormitory bed so's they'd be safe until I got them back on my feet next morning. The few shillings I'd got left were tied inside my handkerchief, then strapped to my crotch by means of my necktie. Then I placed the rest of my clothing under the mattress for safety. They'd be creased come morning, but at least they'd still be mine.

When morning came I worked for a couple of hours in the kitchen, in payment for my bed so's to hold on to the bit of money I'd got. My trousers and jacket were badly creased when I put them on, and I knew that the creases wouldn't drop out, because it was cheap cloth. But you couldn't have everything. But when I was ready to leave and went to get my raincoat, it was gone. So had the wine-sharer of the night before. Someone else had left his raincoat on a bed, so I lifted it, folded it over my arm, and walked out of the doss-house. The owner caught me on the outside steps, started to create a scene. I gave back the coat with bad grace, and walked away from there.

I telephoned my friend, the one who'd visited me in prison, and he promised to leave an envelope at a caff near where he worked. When I opened the envelope I found ten one pound notes inside and a note wishing me good luck for a New Life in London. The money was welcome, the letter was a brush-off; a withdrawal of friendship, ten pounds worth of good-bye.

I'd still got the prison letter for the National Assistance Board. But I knew if I went there they'd only give me a pound for immediate 'necessities', and a voucher for a week's lodgings in a Salvation Army doss-house. I threw the letter away, hoping that somebody who could use it would pick it up and masquerade as me.

I made plans for the future. A train ride to London, a decent room somewhere, a decent job. I'd got ten pounds' worth of world, life and hope in my pockets.

Next morning I found myself waking up under a hedge on the Worcester Road, with four and fivepence in my pockets and a hangover in my head. So I brushed myself down as well as I could, then hitch-hiked through Worcester and on to London, the Big Deal City, arriving about lunch-time. I made my way to a Salvation Army hostel just off the Embankment, but took one look at the residents, and was away. I told myself I hadn't sunk to rock-bottom yet; I'd had enough of Spikes in Brum. I'd rather sleep out in Hyde Park, and pull the night over me for a blanket.

Even so, there was a frantic pendulum of unrest swinging inside me. Now I'd left Brum, I wanted to go back. So I hitch-hiked back, and as soon as I got there, I wanted to leave. I made connection with a Discharged Prisoners Aid Society, and they in turn got me into a small 'rehabilitation' centre – a private house, it was – which was in North London. I didn't stay there long. The warden and his wife were nice enough, but it didn't feel like home to me, although it seemed to suit the other fellers there. They used to have 'open nights' at the house, where the fellers could bring guests and friends in. I'd got no friends, so I used to go out for 'open nights'. I only stayed a week or two, then lit out on my own. I'd come back to the house this one night, 'open night' it was, and I looked in the kitchen. There was this big plate of sandwiches, and I thought they were for the guests and the visitors, so I picked the plate up, went into the lounge and started handing them round. It must have been an off-peak moment for the warden. He didn't shout and rave, but he took the plate off me and embarrassed me in front of them all by telling me more or less to mind my own business. It seemed that the sandwiches were for making up into packed-lunches for the men next day, when they went to work.

Embarrassment burns like acid.

Next night I went drinking with one of the other fellers, and when we got back to the house it was locked for the night, and we slept out on the porch. The warden's wife woke us at breakfast time when she came to the step for the milk. I left shortly afterwards, and struck out on my own. One way and another, I didn't strike very far.

Days, nights, self-promises, day-dreams, nightmares, ambition, lack of it; confusion inside your mind, confusion on your tongue, love-hate for everything and everybody in juxtaposition. Try for a job. Blank prison-issue insurance-cards, P45 Income Tax form devoid of details. The prospective employer looks at these, listens to your nervous story that you've been working abroad, or just come out of the Merchant Navy, and he doesn't believe you, you're so on edge that you're transparent. He's got a queue of people to choose from, so he doesn't choose you. So you drift and drift, and you drink and drink until there's no money coming from anywhere.

No one heralds your arrival on skid-row. And you don't elect to live there — it overtakes you by gradual stages. One homeless night merges with another and each morning you are more crumpled, more unshaven, more sour and disheartened. Skid-row isn't a place, it's a condition. You hardly notice its dirty mantle covering you, you don't really know how deep the deep-end is until you're in it and find you can't swim.

The first night of 'going rough', it seemed not un-natural for me to be standing in the doss-house queue hoping to get a bed for the night in exchange for a few hours work in the kitchen. But even so, somebody came out and hung a 'Full up' sign on the door, then banged his way back inside to warmth and chapel-holiness. The men around me creaked and grumbled then took their bones towards empty houses and bomb-site wastelands to find a private corner for their heads. Some made for Waterloo railway station, hoping to kip a few hours before the blue-men kicked them out of it. The Scouseman with me shrugged his shoulders philosophically.

'Back to the skipper,' he said, meaning an old condemned house which waited for the bulldozers. 'If you haven't got a place, you'd best come with me.' We exchanged names, me glad of the company and extended friendship.

'Got any money?' asked Scouse.

' 'Bout three bob.'

'I got about six. There's a pub over the way where you can buy scrumpy-cider, cheap. Keeps the cold out.'

The cider was raw and strong, cloudy in the glass, but it gave me that mental amputation I was always seeking. Scouse laced the cider from time to time with methylated spirits he carried in one of his pockets. A blue-purple bottle full when we started, empty when we left. Soon the stuff was pushing the blood round me body like it was a racing circuit. Scouse was a bit older than me, older by about seven years. He started telling me the story of his life, but we both got fed up with the telling of it. Once you've lived it, there's nothing new to say.

When closing time came we went back on to the street, and the cold was waiting for us. I followed Scouse down dingy back streets over to the Elephant and Castle. He kept 'shushing' me, telling me to be quiet, making a noise like a regiment of troops as he did so. We came to a piece of wasteland where half a dozen methies were, they stared into the darkness at the noise of us, the flames of the camp-fire lighting them up. I couldn't distinguish the sex of them at first, they just looked like bundles of old rags. Scouse introduced me, the new boy.

'This is a mate of mine,' he said, sitting down and nodding for me to do the same. 'He's a mate. They let him out of nick, over Brummy way. He knew Jacko the Wino.'

'Old Jacko,' one of the fellers said, 'how is he, mate?'

'He's still in Birmingham as far as I know,' I answered, 'wearing my bloody mac.'

Here I was, among the vagrant derelicts of England; the skid-row bums, the smellies, the skippers, dossers, drop-outs. Society's offal and rejects, methylated spirits drinkers who haunted the wastelands and disappearing bomb sites, who dwelt in decaying houses ... and holes in the ground from long dead cellars, and among tombstones in churchyards, park benches and the benches of the Embankment, a stone's toss from Parliament. It didn't seem to matter, very much.

I sprawled on the ground, in the warmth of the camp-fire, listening to the others; 'bluey', meths, was put into generous circulation by somebody. It was mixed with water to take the edge of flame from it, and it kept me topped-up. I had found a strata of 'living' which was more deformed and crippled than that of my boyhood home life; it was here that I learned that the world is flat and if you're not careful, you'll fall off the edge. It was here that I learned that Society has more dinner than appetites but won't share its surplus. It was here that I *learned*. This was *home*, for more than a year and a half.

... I live here, in this hole in the ground; sometimes I live alone, other times, other nights, more men and women join me. The hole in the ground is not mine alone, only a corner of it belongs to me through usage and custom. But sometimes I even lose this corner and have to burrow elsewhere. Sometimes another skipper dosses down where I lay my head, and he's too big or too drunk for me to argue with, so I lie down someplace else until he's gone away. Some nights fifteen or twenty of us shelter here in this cavern; other nights, there is only myself Sometimes I care about the loneliness, other times I don't. It's all a matter of degree, it all depends on how much the day has gnawed at me, it all depends on how much drink I've got in my belly and in my bottle. Above ground is a desolation and a wilderness, shrubs and weeds and the dustbin emptyings from nearby factories. Old tin cans and broken bottles and cold ashes, bits of broken bed-springs and water-sodden cardboard boxes, with hungry cats cleaving through like over-reached swimmers, coming up with stinking fishheads or bones carrying a musty memory of meat. The cats are fluid and fugitive, they haunt our cellars and keep the rats at bay. Sometimes the rats are brave and ignore the scuffed boots or the anger-directed stone. They look back at you and horrify you. Sometimes, in the night, a man would scream out as rats nuzzled to his sleeping warmth, and the scream would send them scurrying back into the shadows. They hope one night a man will be too drunk on bluey to hear or feel them. That's why I don't like being alone. The more we are, the less brave the rats are. There was one jake-drinker who lost part of an ear to the rats, another lost part of a finger.

These cellars, these caves, are wet and damp and miserable. But where else is there to go? No one could lie in them if sober; you have to be drunk so's you don't see the slimedripping walls, or hear the squeaking rats, or see and smell the stale pools of vomit and filth which litters the floor. Piles of newspaper or old rags to lie on, and in the centre of the cellar a pile of white ashes where a camp-fire once burned. No one could lie here sober, you have to be drunk, and when you're drunk you can accept anything. Recent time ago we had more bomb sites to sleep on, where the wind could at least blow cleanly through you, but now they're building on the bomb sites, and the open wastelands grow less and less. They are shrinking away, and we have to find dead houses to live in, or stay in the holes in the ground. But the police know about the empty houses, now; and they put the dogs in to drive the likes of us out. So far, the police haven't come to the holes in the ground. But they will come, they will come. The Health People will find out about us and they'll drive us away again because of the sickness and plagues which can start; they'll send us away and p'raps we'll re-form along the banks of the River Thames, in the small warrens which lead from the wharves, and p'raps they'll let us stay there for a bit, or in the big sewers, until we die. But where will the younger ones go, those who are not yet ready for dying? Many younger people are joining us. I was surprised when I noticed, I didn't think young people came this road any more. I didn't think there was any reason for them to come this way ... but they are coming ...

I sometimes consider myself soberly and try to work out how I came to this platform in life, but I haven't got the words to talk with my mind and find the answer. Wisps of impressions drift along my thoughts and if I go too deep there is pain I cannot stand, there is distress to run away and hide from. But it never comes out into the open, not right out into the open where I can see it. Sometimes I look at the others like me and wonder why they are like they are, and what led them into this mess, and why they cling to empty life with such tenacity. But they do, and there is no explanation which the mind can tolerate.

We are ugly to look at, we are unclean and vile and smelly, and our instincts erupt into violent anger if we are interfered with. We are no part of Society; we have no part of ourselves to give. We are in a permanent prison of self and circumstance. We are zoological specimens, the toys of the welfare agencies, prison-residue, the policeman's bread-and-butter. We are Emptiness, we are Nothing; we are the story of men who have no present and have no future; no plans, no promise of better things to come, no hearth, no home, no love, no laughter, no pity to give or take, no honour, no self-respect. All that we are and ever can be is carried in a bottle splashing in our pockets. When did we last smile the smile of a happy man? When did someone's eyes last light up at our coming? And in the end, what does it matter? The world has problems enough of its own.

There is no story to tell, only misery.

On skid-row, you live by begging, mostly. You stand in front of a woman going shopping, or a young feller with a girl on his arm, and you mumble at them with your hand outstretched, and either through fear or embarrassment they stick a coin or two into your hand and scuttle away. Sometimes a sixpence, sometimes a shilling, sometimes a half-crown piece. It all mounts up so when there's enough you can buy scrumpy-cider, or jake or bluey. Meths or surgical spirits. Sometimes you drop lucky round the market-places, and move crates for a stall-owner, and he drops you five bob.

No, nobody heralds your arrival on skid-row. Horizons are small at world's end; it was the neon and glitter which pulled you into the pubs when you still belonged to the world, the feeling that you were missing something if you stayed outside. You wanted the drink – but oh – how you wanted the company, the talking, laughing, swearing, palsy-walsy mixed-up company.

But when your skin is dark and black under unwashed days, and your clothing dank, and the hair of your head and beard matted and wild, you can't go into public houses. Only into scrumpy-cider dens. This is when you become a leper; this is when you by-pass even the lines of merely homeless dossers, hippies, and 'modern drop-outs'. This is when you lie in the gutters of darkness and despair; in derelict houses, in parks and wastelands, in squalor and sleazy atmosphere with the stench of self and degradation.

The skylight of sobriety does not exist; empty bottles, cheap wine bottles, empty meths and surge bottles, damp peeling walls, the rattle and creak of broken doors and window frames, unwashed flesh huddled together.

This is home.

In the still and the dark you listen to every sound hoping that a new and unfamiliar creak is not the police, is not the blue-men, coming for a slop-out. Invariably, the noise is one of yourselves returning from a late forage, with a bottle of jake clutched under tattered coat.

In the World Outside is the sound of motor-cars and people, of children laughing; and you are afraid of this. Afraid to be reminded of ourselves as we had been, so many misty years ago ...

... *Oft in the stilly night, ere slumber's chain hath bound me* ...

You are afraid to be reminded, to re-open new wounds; the past would lie heavily on you, would weary your minds.

You puzzle at little things on skid-row. The daily news, full of atom bombs and miracles, never touches you. You fret with the others, quarrel about whose turn it is to gather firewood, whose turn it is to find water to mix the bluey with, whose got a match.... You'd team up with a particular mate and one day he'd go away and you'd wait round for him, but when he doesn't come back you know he's dead some place or the Law has booked him on a Vagrancy or a 'suss', and he's in the Big House.

You don't eat much. You scrounge enough money each day to buy jake, and a bag of fried chips, or a hot-dog from a street stall. From time to time you hear rumours that half the women of London are scared of being raped by you, or their kids sexually molested. But it isn't so. Sex is dead, there's not an half-ounce of sex in you, there's just no inclination.

One morning I woke up and called to my mate but he didn't answer, he was lying stiff and cold and he'd been dead half the night. The cold had eaten into him, had eaten his life. His mouth was hard and twisted tight, as if he'd seen Death coming and spat at it to keep it away. His hands were clawed out stiff, his body seemed shrunk now that it had emptied its life out. I took my mate's tobacco tin from his pocket and walked away from him without looking back.

Night after night I sat before the small camp-fires with others of my kind, shielding the flames as best we could so's the blue-men wouldn't see us. That's how one of the methies broke his arm. The Law came onto the waste ground where we were and one of the blue-men knocked the methy down and he fell awkward, and he let the arm mend by itself, but it never set right. The blue-men carved a lot of us up that night, they had a proper slop-out, and we split into ones and twos and hid among the tombstones of a churchyard until they'd gone. And the feller with the broken arm squealing like a stuck pig there in the darkness somewhere. One time I woke up and smelled burning meat, and saw a Jock, a Scotsman, sprawled with part of his face in the open fire, too coma-drunk to know what was happening. The flames were blistering and roasting at his arm and face, but it was like he was on an operating slab after the gas, he didn't know or feel anything. I got up sick-sober to pull him clear. I kicked my own mate awake and told him to get to a public phone booth and dial three nines and ask the operator for an ambulance. We stayed with the Jock until we saw a police car and an ambulance coming, then we hid ourselves out of it. One of the blue-men pissed on the fire and put it out, and we'd got no matches to light it again; so the two of us huddled together for warmth, and saw the night away.

But school kids were worse than blue-men, in some ways. If they found one of us asleep, or reeling drunk, on their way from school they'd start pelting with bricks. When the bricks landed, they hurt. The kids would throw stones, and yell, and carry grown-up murder in their eyes, and if the methy ran they'd chase him with bricks. The methy would plead with them, ask to be left alone, but the cruellest thing in the world is a hobo and a boy with a stone.

You couldn't stick the bomb sites and old houses without jake. If you were sober for any length of time, you'd blow your top. You'd be too cold inside and miserable without drink, your mind couldn't take it. But once the drink was inside you, the bomb sites seemed better than the Sally Army hostels, or the common spikes. The only thing you wanted was booze to keep the night air from cringing bone, and keep the mind amputated from reality. Any womb in a storm. A flicker of camp-fire to sit round, and a sip from the bottle prevented the sip of a memory which could baffle and torment the mind with sadness. Sometimes, when there wasn't enough jake to see me into sleep I'd lie on my back and stare up at the stars. I saw the stars pulsing over me, and felt like a microbe under the size of it all. I felt time and space washing over me, and I was almost afraid; yet in the fear itself was a perverse satisfaction because I knew that everybody – not just myself – was trapped inside the whole cock-eyed scheme of things. I knew that no one was of permanent importance, that kings and queens and popes and bishops and blue-men and screws and prison governors all came to the same end, drunken men and sober men all landed up in the same place, at the ultimate end.

Weekends were the worst, living rough. Especially Sundays. If you walked the streets, you stood out and the blue-men could spot you a mile off. If the lawmen felt like it, if they wanted an hour or two in the station writing reports, they'd lift you. Or if the copper wanted a day off to go to a football match, he'd do you on a 'suss'. Arrest you for loitering with intent, or swear blind he saw you mucking about with car doors; with a bit of clerical juggling back at the station he could fix it so's he had to appear in Court on his day off, then he could get a day off in lieu to do as he wanted. Go to a football match, or take his kids to the zoo, go to a Bible-study class, if he wanted. The game was his. I'd done similar things when I was a copper.

You always tried to beg and bum enough on a Saturday to tide you over the Sunday. Then you could hide away out of it, drink and sleep, climb back into the womb. If you hadn't got the drink you entered Hell because there was nothing to stifle your mind and thoughts, and you became aware of the hard earth under you, and the sadness of everything, memories went whimpering into secret places and tore your heart into little pieces. Such times, you had neither the courage nor the tools to kill yourself, and because of this, you died a little more, inside.

Sometimes a woman joined your crew, sexless as a scarecrow. There was Lorna who had TB, and Scotch-Annie who used her fists and feet to fight like any man, asking nor giving quarter. There was Mad Ruth who used to be a chorus-girl so many frantic years ago and who carried dog-eared photographs of her own long-dead beauty, and the world's applause was shining in those eyes. Now she was quite mad, harmlessly mad, and the little voices in her head kept her company in a dying world. She wore a pair of old army boots, and pulled a tattered shawl round her shoulders as she crooned to the voices in her head. There was Big Mac, who lost an arm in the battle against Hitler. There was Jimmy-the-Crow, ex-sergeant-major. There was Alfie, ex-mate from the Merchant Navy, who rode war-time convoys Over-the-Lip to Russia.

There was Harry; kind, thoughtful Harry, basically honest, with eyes that had seen the worst in everyone, but sought the best; now living on a tight-rope of self-remorse. Many ex-servicemen amongst us. There was Squaddy, decorated for valour at the Arnhem-drop. There was Paul, ex-scholar, ex-priest … now living on bomb sites, drinking crude spirits, amputating himself from the long-ago accusations of little choir-boys.

The weeks and the months went by, winter into summer, and one day I looked at my companions and felt sober terror welling up like a burst artery inside me. I had to get away – even if it meant going back to prison, I had to get away from them. In the centre of my being a sober streak stood aghast and stared out at the dying men and women who shared my life. A whimper started deep inside my thoughts, a whimper of protest which swelled and exploded into a vast silent *'No!'*

I'd lost the thread of time, I'd forgotten how long I'd been living like this. Memory dipped its brush into the rainbow of better days, and brought only a sickness of comparison. I had to get away, I had to get away and find myself and find the world I'd come from, if it were still there.

O Christ, I hoped – let it still be there.

* * *

I needed to clean up and go back into the world, no matter how hostile; I needed a wash and a shave and to wear clean clothes. I needed a job and a place to live, I needed A Start.

I found a water tap and washed where I showed, without soap, and I'd got no razor. Even if I'd got the money, no barber would admit me. I was aware of lice on my body, the unwashed stink of flesh. Heaven would be to strip clean, climb into a scented bath, and when I'd bathed to have good clean clothing waiting for me.

But a razor and clean clothes were a million worlds away from where I stood, away from the living minute, and I wondered whether to give The Idea best; but the 'No' in me was bigger than the 'Yes'. So I hunched and shuffled my way back into the world's stream. First of all I tried a Discharged Prisoners Aid Society, but there was no help forthcoming. I went to a religion-oriented hostel, but didn't have the money for admittance. They told me to go the National Assistance Board for a voucher … and I walked away from that place sneering at the littleness of God.

I went to the National Assistance people. I sat waiting on the pew till it was my time to go up to the counter. Absolute poverty edged into that building; mothers and their snotty-nosed broods, ragged children, old men and women, people in real distress, idlers and scroungers. The Lot. But I was too much for them. They shrugged away from me, gave me clear room, pulled their carrier bags and children away from the deadly range of lice I carried. Eventually, I arrived up at the interview counter.

'When did you last work?'

'I – I forget. Three, four years ago.'

'Why don't you get a job?'

'I – I will. As soon as I get straight.'

'Where did you sleep last night? What address?'

'No address. I haven't got an address.'

'Where'd you sleep?'

'Park. In a park.'

'No Assistance. You can only have Assistance if you've got an address. Go get an address, then come back.'

'I can't get an address without money. I have to have money so's I can book a room. If you give me money, I can find a place.'

'No address, no money.'

I puzzled it all out.

'You stupid bastard,' I said.

'Get out, or I'll call the police,' Clean Contentment said, and turned away to drink his tea before the cup grew cold.

Chapter Twenty-one

I took my anger with me from the building. And then I wanted to sit down somewhere quiet and kindly and cry the tears from my system where no one could see, cry away the poison and torment of self and circumstance. I longed for alcoholic oblivion, but something deep inside the core of my protest wouldn't let me unstopper the bottle of jake I'd got in my pocket. I sat on a bench along the Embankment, watching a clean-clad world pass by. I watched members of the Bowler-hat and furled-umbrella brigade pass by, shopkeepers, officeworkers, honest workmen going to their places and niches. I looked at them as they passed, and held the hatred in me of one of those who has failed for those who have succeeded. The River Thames flowed past, dirty in patches, clean in others; oil slicks and bits of debris, water-logged cigarette packets, rubbish and muck, riding the river. The only purpose the water had was following the tide, the tide was the thing. Back in prison Doc Fuchs had once quoted some Chinese bloke to me; something about 'You can't step into the same river twice, because the river moves on'. Lots of things Doc had said to me came niggling back: 'There can be no change without resistance and no resistance without suffering.' And what was that other thing he'd told me? Doc was always too deep. You could understand the edges of what he said, but there were deep layers underneath which tantalised, and slipped away like a squeezed fistful of mercury when you closed your mental fingers.

Something Doc had said ... 'Revolt belongs to Youth, reaction to the middle-aged; acceptance of things for what they are lies only at the threshold of the grave, just one destroying step away from senility.'

And yet again ... 'Truth exists according to its interpretation. Liberty exists within an ever-shrinking circle of restriction. Humanity exists in a mood of permanent bereavement.'

Once more ... 'The mistakes of Society are not contained within a single generation, they reach out and contaminate all generations to come.'

Doc, you were deep, I will say that.

When you gave the atom-bomb secrets to the Reds, Doc, you didn't hurt *me* or any bloke I ever knew. Where you hurt *me*, Doc, was in showing me how to *think*. Think deep, I mean. You only gave me enough teaching to half-wake me up, and I'm stuck in limbo between sleep and waking, and the verge-dreams hurt like hell. Here's me, sitting on a bench, watching a river pass by which no man can step into twice, not in the same place, because a Chinese bloke said so. I'm watching Success pass by with bowler hats and furled umbrellas and very-important-looking brief-cases which probably contain sandwiches and library books. Temporary gentlemen, all.

I've suddenly learned something, Doc. It came to my mind without having to be whistled for; I think there's three sorts of 'Justice'. One's based upon Ignorance, the second on Indifference, and the third on Revenge. I think I've learned that blokes like me are sort of unpaid professional victims – always in lumber, always at the receiving end; and sort of proud of it. That's only half a step from self-pity, isn't it? I'm caught up in a sort of limbo tug-of-war, and there's exactly three ways to end it. Either side pulls t'other over the line – or some kind bugger cuts the rope.

There's something else you once told me in nick, Doc. Something written by Goethe, I think you said: 'Everybody wants to *be*; nobody wants to *grow*.' All of a sudden, that makes sense to me. It makes sudden and swift sense, it has meaning, it has purpose. There's a smell of adventure to it, a touch of the-long-journey, with a sort of reward, a trophy, at the end of it all. But there are so *many* difficulties. It's one thing to sit here on a bench and think about things, it's another matter to get up on your hind legs and *do* those things; abstinence doesn't seem attractive while you've got a spending-coin in your pocket, and on the other hand it isn't even part-ways attractive if you're broke. That's the tug-of-war, see. And nobody's around to cut the rope. That's what I mean by Limbo, see. There's a balls-up in my mind. A hint of possible 'good luck' up ahead, if you take a certain road, and a knowledge of 'bad-luck-certainty' if you stop where you are. A decision has to be made soon, Doc; my decision. A sort of blackmail decision ...

'So cross my palm with silver, or I cut your throat with steel ...' That's one bit of doggerel-poetry I never *did* finish. It started – 'My father was a funny sod, peculiar as a gypsy, he ruled the roost with iron rod, he was a most unhappy bod, whether dry or tipsy ...' I've almost stopped hating him; we stop burning our witches when we stop believing in them.

I got thinking about Creeping-Jesus, the prison Chaplain, this morning. P'raps I didn't give him a chance. P'raps he needed us, p'raps we were the fuel he fed his fires with; if none of us ever got into trouble, p'raps blokes like him would have a nervous breakdown ... p'raps we're *necessary* for blokes like him to exist. It was yourself who once told me that religion first came about not to embrace mankind, but to escape from it. I think you're right. Some men worship with their hearts, others with their hats; and blokes like me worship with their *hates*. Tell me what a man remembers, and I'll show you what he'll do. So where do I go from here? I know the things I remember, but do I have to go *that* way? And keep going *that* way?

My mam slammed the doorway of the world in my face the morning I came out of prison. This morning, the National Assistance Board did the same. Am I supposed to go down on my knees and thank Family, God and Society for the things I haven't got? Doc, God's got a fat belly and He's a snob of the worst order; if He were down here, He'd drive around the bomb sites in a chauffeur-driven bubble-car, that's the sort of snob He is. He's the bloody Oscar Wilde of the Galaxies, He's a fake and a sham, exhibitionist and all the like. Good words from His lips, but He slams the bloody door of His pantry and locks it when you get a few feet nearer to it. Well, so be it. Where I come from we're more involved in killing blow-flies than catching pretty butterflies. It's all a case of To Hell With Truth-Is The Lie Agreeable – isn't it? I think I'm going to 'bury the hatchet', Doc, but I'm going to hang on to the shovel I dig the hole with.

One day last week me and Scouse were wandering about and we got caught up with the Queen's Trooping of the Colours. Got caught up with the crowds, I mean. Thousands of people of every nationality were there. We arrived by accident, part drunk and nowhere to kip. 'Come on,' I said to Scouse. 'Let's get out of here. We've got nothing to do with this bloody rubbish.' And an American tourist gave his wife his camera to hold, and offered to knock our heads off for insulting Her Majesty ... so we stood and watched the wooden painted soldiers, the deliberate policemen, the pomp and the circumstance; around us, hundreds of people had patriotic erections.

But the horse the Queen rode was one of us. It didn't give a *damn*. It lifted its tail and let go. Plop, plop, plop. A three-gun salute of steaming shit. Plop, plop – hooray. I half expected a liveried flunkey to step forwards and spray the piles with perfume, and camera-men to concentrate upon the evidence of a Royal passing. Everybody pretended that the horse-muck wasn't there; like they pretend that the likes of *us* didn't exist ...

... and then my heart warmed towards the Lady on the Horse. She too could recognise shit when she saw it, and she edged the horse away from it, Royally uncomfortable on a side-saddle. I don't know what really tickled me, but I fell about laughing, and a foot-policeman came through the crowd and cut us away from it. He gave us both a right bollocking and told us to get on out of it, and if he saw us again he'd run the pair of us in on a 'suss'. Suspicion of mingling with a crowd 'with intent to pick-pockets'. I tried to reason with the blue-bod, claiming right of way as a taxpayer. I thought *he* was going to roll around laughing.

'What fucking tax?' he asked. 'What fucking taxes do *you* buggers pay?'

'There's tax on meths and there's tax on surge,' Scouse said, with, I thought, as much dignity as the Lady on the Horse could muster.

'Piss off out of it,' the blue-man told us, 'and get back to the Elly and Castle district, else we'll run you in.'

Scouse and me laughed our ways back to the 'Elly', pretending we were business men who'd bought the Royal horse-muck and were turning it into money-making advantage.

'We could make little moulds,' Scouse said, 'and make buttons from the horse-shit, then paint the Royal coat of arms on, and sell 'em as souvineers. We could varnish 'em for finishers.'

'We could flatten it out with a rolling pin,' I said, 'and make little plaques and platters, and flog 'em to Yankee tourists.'

'What about,' said Scouse, 'drying the horse-muck out then rubbing it into powder and putting it into egg-timers? "Time your eggs by the Royal shit-system." We could advertise in *Exchange and Mart*.' Both me and Scouse agreed that we'd given the Queen a throne to sit on, but she had to sit on her arse like the rest of us. And the same went for bishops, popes, and Jesus Christ ...

Anyroad, you've left the ghost-train, Doc. You've landed at your platform in life, blokes like me are still on it, ever moving and chugging, but we don't know where we're going, and we don't even know if we've got a bleeding valid ticket. P'raps we stay on the train because we're afraid to go through the ticket-collector's barrier. We've filched and pinched too many bits and pieces from Society that most of us are boomerang criminals, ricocheting from one experience to another. Caught up in 'cross-cultural shock', that's us.

I left the bench on the Embankment, left the timeless river to its tide, left Doc parcelled up in memories against another day's need, and went back to 'home' and reality in the vicinity of Kennington. Day had given way to darkening evening by the time I got there. Vagrants huddled around in threes and fours. Rows of houses gawped and gaped, empty, broken doors leering from strained hinges, waiting for the demolition gangs. We couldn't use the empty houses for living in, the police were onto it. Progress was stilt-striding the area in the shape of near-skyscraper office-blocks, and the police were anxious to move us on so's we wouldn't get in the way of the strides. If we kept to open ground, we could see them coming, the blue-men, and scuttle away. But if we were in the houses and they put the dogs in, some of us were bound to get hurt. In a far corner sitting round a small camp-fire, I found my own group. I stood in the shadows watching them, thinking 'who's pissed and who isn't, and pass the claret, Vicar'.

'Got any fags?' Jordy asked me, as soon as I stepped inside the fire-glow. I gave him my tobacco-tin to make a roll-up.

'Got a match?' he asked, and I didn't like it.

'Use the fire, you lazy sod,' I said. He creaked belligerence from cramped bones and matted rags.

'Fuck off,' he said, 'if you can't be civil.'

'Balls,' I answered, negative, tired, matching the existing atmosphere.

'I'll balls you, mate,' Jordy threatened, 'if I come over to you.' Harry, tall, quiet, decent Harry interfered with the mist of violence brewing up.

'Lay off,' he said to Jordy, 'the feller means no harm.'

'Get a mouthful of knuckles, he will, if he keeps it up,' Jordy muttered, sucking furiously at my cigarette.

'Lay off,' Harry cautioned.

'Who the fuck's he think he is?' Jordy persisted. 'Who the fuck is he? I don't know him, I don't want to know him . '

'Sorry, Jordy,' I murmured, not really sorry, just placating.

'Coming here pissing me about,' Jordy flared, hot in pursuit, 'trying to piss me about. Fuck off, why don't you. Come here poking your nose in, pissing me about. No fucker likes you.' I sat in silence, listening to Jordy moaning and groaning like a constipated belly. Harry took a package of crumbled sandwiches from his pocket, offered me one.

'I'll fucking well punch him,' insisted Jordy, glaring at me but talking to the others, 'coming here pissing me about. I'll fucking well glass him.' I called a halt to it.

'I'll knock your fucking head off,' I told him, 'if you don't shut up and lay off me.' He fell to muttering under his breath. Harry had got a bit of money from somewhere, he upped with a ten shillings worth of silver.

'Here, Jordy,' he said, 'ten bob. Fetch the jake.' Jordy grovelled upright with childish eagerness.

'Right, Harry, lad. I'll fetch it. Give me the money, just give me the money, Harry.'

'The shop on the corner,' Harry ordered. 'Fetch it from there.'

'Yers,' Jordy agreed excitedly. 'He knows me, there. I know the place. The gaffer knows me, he knows me, Harry. Him and me know each other.' He staggered away to the shop. Harry watched him.

'Go to the street and keep an eye on him,' he said to Alfie, 'else he might piss off with the stuff.' Alfie did as he was told, his thin skeleton-body tripping and sprawling over the littered rubbish. Big Mac looked up from his bundle of rags stretched out on the ground, and the others round the campfire seemed to stir and come awake with new interest now that a promise of booze was on its way.

'Could do with a pull of the wino,' Little Jimmy said contentedly. 'A good pull of wino keeps the night cold out.'

'He won't bring wine,' Harry said. 'Ten bob won't go very far. He'll bring the bluey or the jake.'

'Surge,' spat Little Jimmy. 'Can't stand it. Shit, that's what it is – how can the buggers drink it? Won't ever catch me sinking that low.' TB Lorna, scarecrow Lorna, ripped her harsh awakening breath like jagged scissors into the fabric of conversation.

'Bollocks. You drink it. You bloody well drink it, Jimmy.' Jimmy went out on a phantasy of indignation and denial.

'I fucking don't,' he said. 'No, I don't, you know. It's shit. That's what it is. Won't ever catch me drinking it.' Lorna marvelled at him.

'You bleeding liar,' she said, 'you bleeding whoreson liar. You drink it when there's nowt else, I've seen you. Yes you bleeding well do.' It seemed important to Little Jimmy.

'Don't you listen to her,' he pleaded. 'Just trying to make trouble, the cow is.'

'Bleeding liar,' marvelled Lorna. Little Jimmy tried to grow tall with rage.

'Don't you bleeding liar me, you old cow,' he screeched at her. 'I'll kick you in the bloody crotch, you old cow.' Lorna retaliated, a bundle of rags and wicked indignation. She picked up an empty bottle, smashed the body of it against a stone, lunged at Jimmy with the jagged neck of it. I caught her, slapped the weapon from her hand.

'The big twatt,' Lorna panted, 'the bloody whoreson twatt. I'll mark him, I will. I'll mark the bugger.'

'For Christ's sake,' I raved, 'there's the whole bloody world to fight without fighting amongst ourselves.' Jordy and Alfie loomed in from the now full-darkness, carrying bottles of methylated spirits.

'Whose turn to fetch the water?' Harry wanted to know. The tap was in one of the old houses, the water not turned off yet. Or maybe it was water still stored in the tank, I don't know.

'I fetched it last time,' Little Jimmy said, 'it's not my turn again.'

'Bleeding whoreson liar,' Lorna said, her eyes pools of spite in the firelight.

'I fetched it last time,' Little Jimmy insisted. 'It's somebody else's turn.'

'God'll strike you dead,' Lorna said. 'God'll strike you bloody dead, bloody well dead, my oath he will.'

'Don't listen to her,' Little Jimmy whined. 'The old cow's always on about something, mark my words she is …'

'Lay it off,' I half shouted, 'let's have some peace, for Christ's sake.' Big Mac interrupted angrily.

'Oh – for pox sake – gimme the cowin' milk bottles. I'll fetch the bloody water, gis the bottles here.'

Lorna huddled inside her rags, eyes like a snake, hungry for Jimmy. Mad Maud just sat there, but not there really; she was talking to the little voices in her head. Harry's face was part-softened by shadows, but they didn't conceal the deep pains and sorrows which haunted his eyes. Alfie crouched on piles of cardboard and old newspapers, permanently at bay with the world. Lorna, Maud, Big Mac, Alfie, Jordy, Harry, Little Jimmy; all welded forever in a dark-world's dungeon, with not even a gaoler to visit them. No remission for these, I thought, looking at Harry. Harry stirred himself, came back from the deeper twilit world of his own sad introspection, and took the water from Big Mac. He poured some of the water and some of the meths into the dirty milk bottles which waited like hungry mouths waiting to feed hungrier ones. Lorna looked up from hers and stabbed a glance at Little Jimmy.

'What you giving him any for?' she challenged. 'He said he don't drink the bluey.'

'Shut up,' Jimmy almost sobbed, 'shut fucking well up, you old bitch. I'll do you, you old bitch. I'll bloody well do for you.'

'Let's have some peace,' Harry bellowed, self-anger alerting him and filling him so that he overpowered the others: 'For Christ's sake, lay off one another – do you hear? You fucking miserable shower of shit. On and on and always on …'

Memory dipped and delved and winced and rubbed and frayed and fretted; I was a boy at the head of dusty dirty stairs looking down into a well of darkness, listening to my mam and dad squabble and fight, cursing and rowing and destroying, jangling violence and filths of rage against every nerve and emotion … Harry, quiet decent Harry, strong and cripple-sure as Pope Tolley – crippled inside by circumstances, and not on the outside where it would show – spoke low and easy, his own temper caught back to the reins of self-control.

'We can't fight amongst ourselves,' he said. 'If we do, we've got nothing left.' He was the accepted camp-fire leader. Few argued with him. He'd still got muscle to back himself with, if it was ever needed.

They sat and sipped their bluey and kept the world away. I sat with them, but didn't drink. There was this big 'No' inside me, bursting to get out. A world of rubbish. Maude picked at lice inside her clothing, picked at the itching lice of memories inside her mind, and spoke to long dead ghosts. I let my own thoughts pick at the perpetual lice of perpetual emptiness.

'Ginger's in the nick,' Alfie said at last. 'My mate's in the nick. Got his collar fingered on Waterloo station, did him for suss this time. Got weighed off for nine months, he did.'

'Ernie's in the nick as well,' Lorna said, 'and the Mole, and Joey.'

'Scots-Annie's in Holloway,' Jordy said, 'I was told. She's better off in there, they'll clean her up and look after her.'

'Shit,' snapped Lorna. 'Shit. They don't look after anybody in the nick, nobody's looked after in the nick.'

'There's a lot of fellers been knocked off lately,' Alfie said, 'a lot of them.'

'I thought I hadn't seen Ginger around,' I said. 'I missed him being around.'

'Probably in the nick,' Jordy murmured. 'He's in the nick, I shouldn't wonder. I bet he's in the nick.' Lorna blew her top at him.

''Course he's in the bleeding nick,' she said, 'you saft bastard – I just told you he was in the nick.' Jordy trembled his underlip at her.

'Don't listen to her,' he said. 'She's a trouble maker. Trying to cause trouble, she is. Always causing trouble.'

'Whoreson sod,' Lorna grumbled. 'Your bloody earholes must be bunged up. God'll strike you dead one of these days, on my poor mother's deathbed, he will.'

Harry prodded the fire to dancing life with the toe of his broken boot, sending flames and sparks dancing high. We huddled to the warmth, the others content in a rough, rabbit-burrow sort of way, now that the bluey was burning into their systems.

'Where's Scouse?' I suddenly asked, suddenly missing him. 'Where's Scouse got to?'

'Who, Scouse?' Lorna asked. 'He's gone to the cellars. He went to the cave-cellars. He's got a cold, he's not well.'

I was aghast.

'You've not let him go to the bloody cellars?' I implored, 'Christ, don't tell me he's living in them.' Harry nodded.

'He's got this cold,' he explained, 'heavy cold he's got. Said he might get it better if he could get a roof over him for a night.'

'He's better off down there,' Jordy said, 'he's always moaning and groaning about something. We don't want him here.'

'Leave him alone, you whoreson sod,' Lorna snarled at him, 'he's a bleeding sight better than you are.' Jordy cringed away from her snarling contempt, grovelled a better distance between the two of them.

'Don't you listen to her,' he begged. 'She's a spiteful old cow. She's an old bag, an old whore – she's fucking nothing. Nothing.' Lorna menaced him, tears of rage pouring down the leather of her cheeks.

'God help me,' she whispered, 'on my mother's deathbed, I'll do for you.' I got up.

'I'm going to fetch Scouse out of it,' I said. 'Make these buggers keep the peace, else the blue-men will come and put the fire out, and there's no place else to go.' I put my hand on Harry's shoulder, peered down at him.

'When we going to give it best?' I asked him. 'You, me and Scouse – we could get out of it. When shall we give it best?' His eyes were twin pools of misery.

'I don't know,' he whispered, 'I don't know, old fella.' I walked away from the camp-fire so's he wouldn't see the pin-pricks of self-pity washing my eyes.

I went through the back streets, decayed warrens of social inadequacy and bad black memories. It was half a mile to the cellars where Scouse was, and where me and Harry and the others had slept until the real wild-men took over. Rows and fights every night, and then we gave up and left. I climbed over a newly-built council wall which was supposed to keep the likes of us out, and stumbled along the worn foot-tracks which led to the tunnels below. Dark, damp, sick and miserable they were. Down crumbling steps into suffocating dark and gagging-gloom. Once, overhead, there had been a great big public house and dwelling places; now all that remained, until they filled them in and made a car-park over them, were the cellars and the hobgoblins who lived inside them. Years ago, when Europe had been liberated, allied troops had been filled with horror and anger at the violated humanity in concentration camps. But here, it existed in a Free World, in a country which boasted of its National Health State. By the dying embers of the fire I could see about fourteen men dossing in the shadows. Sleeping and dossing on old piles of rag and paper, or just shrugged up inside their ragged coats for the night. The floor was carpeted with an inch thickness of mud and slime, water dripped down the walls and oozed from the arched ceiling. Drifting against the ceiling itself was a foot-thick cloud of smoke, trying to get out. One man had messed himself, another had been sick and was lying in it, another moaned in drink-coma. Rats scoured the hidden corners, and sometimes their eyes flashed back like cats-eyes in a highway. I found Scouse and tried to wake him up without disturbing the others.

Come on, Scouse. Wake up, old son. Come on, come on, come on, you can't stay here. You've got to come away. Wake up, Scouse – wake up, wake up. Come on, you lazy no-good bastard. Let's get out of this bloody hole. Come on, you've got to come. Please, please, you can't stay down here, Scouse. Let's go back to Harry and the others, we can't stay here. Come on, Scouse. Come on. What's the point in staying? You can't be a stupid bastard *all* your life ... where's your guts, mate? Remember? They didn't give you them medals for screwing NAAFI bints.

Bugger you, then.

Stay here and rot.

You useless rotten no good rotten whoring bastard ... but shake your mind and arse out of it and let's get out of here.

... and then the shadows whispered and sneaked close, and rustled with menace. Piles of filth got up from the floor, scrabbled up from the floor in gropes of movement, like black obscene bats. Mutterings and dampness, and Christ Almighty that utter decay; they cut me off from my exit, they stood grotesque and shadow-tall, moving shit-piles of contradiction to a balanced world outside. I was afraid, deep down afraid. I was yellow to my backbone and beyond. Then one of them fished me, angled me, played me in.

'Watcha want, then? Watcha want, cock? Watcha fucking after us for then, you're not fucking Law, he don't look like Law, does he, Weasel?' Weasel weaseled, sniffed in at me, ferret eyes glowing by the light of the glowing camp-fire embers. Billows of smoke rolled round the arched ceiling, seeking outlet.

'He's not fucking Law,' said Weasel, 'he's not Law. He's Snoop. A Snoop, that's what he is.'

'My shoes am buggered,' the first one said, inching in on me. 'They'm fucked altogether. I can't piss about in these, can I, Weasel? I mean, they let in the wet and all.'

'He's got shoes, Shag,' Weasel said, pointing at my feet. 'He's got a pair on his feet. Not much cop but better than your'n.' He looked at me directly. 'What size shoes you wearing, mister? What fucking size shoes? Never mither, pass 'em here anyway. Take them fucking shoes off else I'll butt this fucking bottle in your face and leave you 'thout any eyes. Get me? I'm Weasel. I'll carve any fucker, any mother fucker, see, get me? Let's have them shoes, mister.'

There were four of them circling me now. They'd learned instinctively from the rats. Not one would be the first to touch me, they'd do it all together, in a rush, they'd bear me down and choke me. But not one had the guts to do it alone. They circled like rats, trying to get round back of me, meeting my half and quarter turns by spreading more and more, inching and footing, building up, closing in. I could feel sweat running down my back, in my groin. I felt as if I were going to piss myself with fear.

'Let's have his coat,' one of the bats said. 'Let's have the fucker's coat. It's better than mine.' He put a hand out, fingered my coat. 'It'll keep the cold out a bit,' he said. Weasel snarled his protest.

'It's my coat,' he said, 'mine. I saw it first.' To me: 'Give us your coat, mister.' I started to edge back to a wall, to get my rear covered.

'How about money,' one of them said. 'I bet the cunt's got money. I bet he's got money, Weasel.'

Weasel grinned at me, diabolical.

'Let's have your money,' he said.

I wet my lips. My voice came out like a girl's.

'I'm like you,' I shrilled. 'For fuck's sake, I'm one of you lot.' Weasel broke a bottle against the wall, crouched at me with the jagged end.

'Hand it over,' he whispered, 'all of it. Else I'll leave you 'thout any eyes.'

I backed off completely, but one of them was behind me. He pushed me back into the circle. I looked around in desperation, knowing I'd got to fight for my life, knowing I needed a weapon. There was a big feller just getting up from the floor, getting up from his sleeping bag of rags and newspapers. I pretended to know him, fussed a greeting across to him as thick as treacle.

'Hey, Paddy,' I called, 'Paddy, you old sod. It's me.' The man blinked at me, eyes red as a pig's, face flushed with the drink in him. He pulled his cock out and pissed fair and square where he'd been sleeping, blinking at me all the time.

'Huhh?' he said.

'I looked all over for you,' I gushed, frantic, desperate, 'all over I looked for you.'

'Uhh?'

'You know me, don't you? 'Course you bloody well know me. We were in the next peters together, remember, back in fifty (grunt) up in (grunt-grunt) nick. 'Course you fucking well remember – you had the bloody screws eating out of your hands. You 'member the big screw? The big ignorant bastard ? You had the daylights scared out of him alright, didn't you. And that baron – that tobacco baron – remember the time you slopped him out with the old one-two in the recess?' He blinked at me, half-drunk, three-quarters stupid; big, burly.

'Uhhh?'

'You remember me,' I insisted, hypnotising the bastard so I could live. '*You* remember. You even tamed the Governor and the Chief. They were all fucking scared of you. Your name's known in every nick in the country.' I got through to him. He looked pleased. Nodded his head.

'Yer. Sure. That's me. You know me. Yers.' I moved in swift as a ballet dancer.

'I looked all over for you,' I said, knocking Weasel's hand from my coat. 'The others told me you'd be down here – Scouse's down here, isn't he? He'll tell you – he's a mate of mine.' The big man lurched over to me, towered.

'Yer,' he said, 'I remember you now. That's right. I remember you.' I was relieved. I'd never seen the bastard in my life, but who wanted the

277

lifeboat to be painted before they climbed in from a rough sea? He cuffed Weasel round the ears, like a big shaggy bear slapping a cub.

'Hey – you – Weasel,' he roared, 'take your fucking hands off a mate of mine. He's a mate of mine, he is. He knows me.' Weasel spat back, bristling, the venom in him arched like a tom-cat's back.

'Get stuffed,' he said, 'I want his coat. Tell him to give me his coat and he can piss off.' The big man hit him. And the whole darkness seemed to stand on its legs and start fighting. I got hold of Scouse and dragged him away from the trampling feet, dragged him through the archway and back to the clean-clad world of starlight and fresh air. Behind me, I could hear the Big Feller bellowing and shouting.

'Him and me, we ruled the fuckin' nicks. He's a mate of mine, he is. We had the whole bloody lot shit-scared.'

Scouse was moaning and resisting, trying to stop our progress from that bloody place. I'd got half a mind to leave him where he was, and sling my hook. The noise behind us was muffled, remote, like as if it was contained in a box.

'Shut your bloody cake-hole,' I said to Scouse, shaking him hard, 'and get the lead out of your feet.' I half carried, half dragged him back to Harry and the others. Jordy raised his voice in complaint as soon as he saw us.

'They'm trouble, them two is,' he whined. 'We don't want him and Scouse here. They'm nothing but trouble.' I turned on him, anger raw, grabbed him by the throat.

'I'll rip your fucking tongue out,' I said. Lorna cackled approval.

'That's it, mate. You show him. You show the twatt. The louse-bound twatt.'

I shook Jordy into submission, threw him away from me. He went whimpering off into the shadows, pausing only to snatch up his bottle.

'Remember the day we met?' Harry asked. 'I hated your fucking guts for some reason. Your clothes was better then, they weren't like now. You reminded me of something I'd lost. I dunno what.'

'It was pissing down with rain,' I said, 'and it'll piss some more before we're through, and we'll both hate every fucker's guts who's standing in the dry.'

'You had a Scouse mate, then,' Harry said, 'it was a Scouse you were mates with, then.'

'He died,' I answered. 'He went to sleep one night and the cold got him, and he died. He was one of the lucky sods.' All the others had got the jake-signs now. Mad Ruth was crooning a sad little lullaby to herself, a snatch of melody stolen from an Outside World long ago. I sat still and silent, listening to Mad Ruth and noting how her face had softened, as if the music had purified her blood. Lorna was on a sad-happy-jag, talking with her mam and dad as if they stood there in front of her, as if they were real.

Harry started to cry, softly, faint, at first; then heavier as the pain of self came through the hooch. 'I got to get home,' he sobbed, 'I got me a missus and family some place. I got to get home to them, before it's too late. I got to go back North, I got to go back to them.'

I tried to stop his tears with common-sense. 'It's been too long,' I said, 'they'll all be grown up and married now, your kids will. And your missus, she might be dead or she might have married somebody else. It's over twenty years since you saw them.'

'I got to see them,' he sobbed, turning his face away so's I shouldn't see the tears. 'I got to get back.'

I shared his silence for a bit. I looked inside myself, looked to see if the 'No' was still there, or if the 'Yes' had taken over. The 'No' *was* there, like a huge muscle of strength I couldn't hold. There was a warning in that 'No', an urgency, a 'no waiting' sign.

I got up.

'I'm going,' I said to Harry, 'I'm off out of it.' A fragment of memory floated to the surface of my mind. I had the feeling I'd been here before, had said these words before. And then I saw a little boy, myself, standing in a drizzle of rain with his home-made bicycle, looking at the dad he hated and telling him – 'I'm away, then. I'm off out of it.'

And then the fragment sank back below the surface, and I repeated to Harry, 'I'm off. I'm off out of it.'

He might have heard me. I don't know. He was still crying.

'Tell my mate,' I called back to him, 'tell Scouse I'll get in touch when I can. Tell him that, Harry.'

I walked back to Waterloo railway station, found a corner of the car park behind some rubbish-skips where I might see the rest of the night out undetected. When early morning came, the first streaks of light, I went onto the station to the Gents toilet for a slash. I could feel my jake bottle pulling at my pocket, and on a sudden impulse I went into an open cubicle and poured the contents into the lavatory pan. I left the empty bottle in there. And when I'd emptied the bottle, I regretted it, because I'd got no amputation left. I'd got nothing to start a new day on.

Standing inside the wash-place, shaving himself in front of the wall-fixed mirror, was this feller. About as old as me. I stood staring at him. He sensed it, looked at me. After a bit, he spoke.

'Down on your luck?' he asked, and there was that Irish music in his voice. I nodded. He put his hand in a pocket, pulled out a ten shilling note. He offered it to me. I gulped.

'I'd sooner have the lend of your razor,' I blurted, 'it would give me a better start.' He nodded, swilled the lather from his face, picked up a towel from his work-bag and started to wipe himself.

'Help yourself,' he said, pointing to his shaving tackle. 'I've been down on my luck a time or two. I'm hoping that's all over now, though. I travelled over from Ireland to start a new job this morning.' I lathered up, and drew good friendly steel across the sprouting hairs of my face. When I'd finished, I could see the top part of my face grimed brown with dirt and weather; the lower half stood out white as a girl's, and just as smooth. The Irishman rummaged around in his bags, and then gave me a comb.

'Take it,' he said, 'it's a spare.' I combed and tugged the knots and ravels from my hair, the pain of it making me grimace. I saw my teeth in the mirror, yellow with neglect. I promised them a toothbrush at the first opportunity. The contrast of my face, brown-black-to-white troubled me. I furtively used the Irishman's soap to scrub at it, and at my neck, so that the contrast was lessened. I wiped off with a paper towel torn from a roll, carefully washed the shaving tackle *and* the soap I'd used, and gave them back to the Irishman. I muttered my thanks – I was full-up with gratitude – and turned away. He came after me as I was half-way up the steps, pushed the ten-shilling note into my hand.

'Good luck,' he said, 'and God bless.'

I could have cried.

I walked two or three miles to a Women's Voluntary Service centre, I knocked at the door and a woman called me to enter. Her eyes clouded over when she saw me, and I felt my face flush with shame. But she was more conscious of my needs than my misdemeanours, she fed clothing into my hands, my eager hands. I mumbled and stumbled thanks and went back onto the street, clutching the precious bundle to me. It felt like kitting-out parade of my Air Force days. I got into a Gent's toilet for a locked door's pennyworth so's I could change from the rags I was wearing. Underwear, socks, shirt, tie, shoes, suit – when I came out, I felt new-born, despite the fact that most of the clothing was too big for me. I stuffed my discarded rags into a street-bin. I walked back to the Salvation Army hostel near Westminster, and with my ten shillings booked a bed for the night. Next morning, I'd got an address for the National Assistance Board and collected a week's voucher for the hostel, and twenty-two shillings for my immediate needs.

And that was my goodbye to skid-row. Not that I finished with it, I merely stopped living there.

Epilogue

So I left skid-row and tried to get back into the world's stream. That was fourteen or so years ago. I left skid-row, but I didn't stop drinking. The only difference was that I could work and earn money, if the work-demands upon me weren't too great and complex. I could work and earn money, and rent my own little room in a dingy house in a dingy street, and I could shut the door and keep the world out whenever I wanted. The weeks spread into months, the months into nowhere. There were no visible signs of improvement in self or circumstances, only a two-dimensional world instead of a three. I drifted from job to job, from public house to public house, from National Assistance Board to Labour Exchange. There were days of elation, there were days of dark depression. There were dry sober days which left the nerve-ends raw and bleeding, there were drink-flushed days which took me to the pinnacle of life-amputation. There were frightened days and there were careless days. There were also nights. There were only frightened nights.

Time was loneliness and loneliness was time. The loneliness had some activity. Eat, sleep, drink, work a little to get the money to do these things. I worked at anything – just because I was a drinking-lush didn't mean that I was naturally lazy. I worked at anything, and worked as hard as any. But I drifted from job to job, from trade to trade. One week I'd be high up on London roofs, working for a tiler and slater. Another time I was swinging a pick and shovel with the road-menders. Then a stint as a grave-digger in a huge graveyard. Once, I found myself at an office desk with my own telephone and a load of responsibility in the 'in-tray' which I could never seem to get into the' out-tray'; but this job only lasted for two months. I couldn't sustain the ability to keep pace with it, and the drink interfered with my time-keeping and my thinking. I passed on, became a painter and decorator swinging in a cradle high up the flanks of London near-skyscrapers. For six weeks I held down a job as lavatory attendant, but my make-believe references caught up with me, and I got the sack. So into a scrap-merchant's yard, loading and unloading trucks. This was slave-labour, and I let the job go when I drew my money at the end of the week. I became crafty in the ways of employers who might insist upon receiving reasonable notice of job-quitting. I delayed handing over my P45 and Insurance Card until I'd had a chance to find out whether or not I was going to stay with the job for a bit. If I didn't like the job, I'd sub my money to the hilt and depart. I latched onto British Railways for a bit, casual work at Christmas time. But, three parts drunk, I let a platform waggon loaded with parcels fall onto the track, spilling its cargo like confetti. I didn't even wait to collect what money was due to me, I just got out of there, quick. I drifted and drifted in flat monotony. But I'd pulled clear of the 'spikes' and hostels, the land of the dossers. I'd got me a room and I'd got the key to it and privacy and no one to trouble me if the rent was there every week-end. The room was mine, every musty dusty inch of it. I kept at casual work, having a daily sub to buy enough beer to see me through – or whisky if there was a bonus attached to the job-earnings. I could sprawl in my room and drink myself to sleep, leaving a drop for next morning because I couldn't face the day without a slug of it burning in my belly. Sometimes I couldn't meet the rent, so I jollied the landlord along as well as I could, then flit-off out of it when his back was turned.

    Weeks and months went by in this fashion, living for today and letting Tomorrow take care of itself, and half the time wishing that there were no more Tomorrows to come. I got a job in a warehouse for a while. Working with me was a Junkie, a drug-addict. He showed me how to buy those little nose-inhalers from the chemists, and break the shell open to get at the substance inside. It was like cotton-wool, but seeped in some chemical. We'd extract this padding and roll it into little pills and then swallow them. Inside five minutes you'd feel good and powerful, and on top of the world. The same bloke used to supply me with purple-hearts; one tablet was enough to start with, but before long I was taking six, eight, ten at one time, just to keep the kicks coming. Then my work-mate took me to a pub near Euston. It was the only time in my life I'd ever sat in a pub without wanting a drink. We'd got a pint of beer each, but by the time I'd smoked a couple of sticks of cannabis provided by his friend, all I wanted to do was stare at my glass of beer and admire it, not drink it. Then this one lunch time, just after swallowing a large amount of purple hearts, I thought I was going to die. My heart started to beat and thump like an engine gone mad, like an engine trying to tear loose from its moorings. Sometimes it missed a few beats, and I could feel my whole body trembling and quivering, and running with sweat, and there was this thin high-pitched whistling in my ears and head. I had to sit down. I sat down on the pavement in a busy street and the people had to step round me or over me. I remember that I kept massaging my heart with my hand, trying to get it to settle down.

Then an ambulance came and took me away to a hospital. But after the doctors had seen me there, they sent me to a mental hospital in North London. The point was that they put me in there as a voluntary patient, which meant that I could walk out any time I chose; but for some reason I didn't *want* to leave. It was summer time, and the hospital grounds were wild with blossoms and flowers, and you could walk round the grounds for exercise or lie out on the grass. And it had its funny moments as well. I was wearing a grey suit very similar in appearance and cut to those that the male nurses wore. I was walking in the grounds with another patient, he was wearing clothes issued by the hospital, what we called 'institution clothing'. We came upon this group of workmen who were digging trenches to lay drain-pipes. The two of us stopped to watch them.

'Do you want to sell that hole?' I asked one of the workmen. He grinned at me, taking me for a male-nurse who'd got a patient in tow.

'You can have it for five shillings,' he said.

'Shall I collect or will you deliver?' I asked.

'You collect,' he answered, swinging back to his work. The bloke I was with and myself continued our walk. But, at the top end of the drive-road, we saw a gardener's handcart. The gardener wasn't to be seen anywhere. So on a sudden impulse I took possession of the cart, and with my mate wheeled it back to where the workmen were digging the trenches.

'I've come to collect the hole,' I said. To this day, I can still see the frozen blank astonishment on those workmen's faces.

I stayed at the hospital for some weeks, chumming up with another alco who'd tried a suicide bid, and was now a voluntary patient awaiting 'treatment'. He'd got money, and when the pair of us were allowed out on ground-parole we'd scale the hospital wall and make for the nearest pub.

This one time we were in the pub – it was night-time, and we'd got a late pass each on the pretext that we were visiting friends and relatives, which meant that we had to be back to our wards by no later than eleven o'clock.

Sitting there with a pint pot of beer and a tot of whisky in front of me, I suddenly didn't want it. I got up and walked out of the pub. My drinking partner didn't notice my going, he was busy chatting up some female.

I walked back to the hospital and it was raining, and I sat on a bench in the hospital grounds, wringing wet, and thought things over. I knew somehow that the volcano of anger which had been burning inside me for so many long years was at last burning itself out. I sat there in the rain and I felt this strange calmness of mind come into me, this strange sweet serenity. The fear of self was suddenly melted away, and for the first time in my life I realised that the ball was landed fairly and squarely in my own court. There were three choices open to me. Just three choices, and no more. I could continue in the same pattern, drinking myself back into prisons and an early grave, or I could break into the hospital pharmacy and steal enough sleeping tablets to get the job over and done with as quickly and unmessily as possible. These were two of the choices.

The third choice was that I could Start Again. Start all over, a new life with new purpose and a new destiny.

I made the choice. Alone and unaided, sitting in the dark garden of a mental hospital, with a drizzle of rain blowing down the wind, I made my choice. I looked out on the darkness, and I looked inside myself at where my own inner darkness had been. I looked back along the broken years, I weighed the hatreds whose pulses had beat burdens in my heart and brain, and I felt the rain on me and life itself in me, and I knew that I would Start Again. My empty years dropped like separate pebbles into time's ocean, they could not be salvaged and used again. But there were years ahead, there were untouched years, there was Hope's Tomorrow. Now that I stood alone, now that there was no one to lean upon I would find my own strength and win through, or I would go down and under forever. Time would tell.

They were not easy days which followed. But those days do stand out in sharp focus, they were no longer blurred and measured by public-house clocks. The days became individual. They became a bank-balance to be drawn out one at a time, to be spent wisely while the rest gathered interest. I found no overnight 'cure', no easy and quick way. I measured the enemy of self with my mind's eye, and checked the better part of me, and then knew I could fight because I stood a chance of winning. There was no flash of spiritual or religious insight; if a 'Higher Power' helped me, it did so without my being aware of it. I entered the fight on my own two feet. I felt Pope Tolley standing in my mind, saw the arrogance of his chin as the odds came at him, heard him telling me again that the crying had to come when the fight was won and over, and not till then. I felt Pope more than anybody, sitting there on the cold-wet bench. I felt his hand, heavy and kind, on my shoulder. I felt the essence and the power of him, felt his scorn of cowardice.

The hardest part of the battle was during the first three months. The drink-craving lay in wait at every turn, raving and pleading and bullying for attention. Time after time I stood at a sink drinking glass after glass of water, filling my belly with the stuff until there was not room left for even a spoonful of alcohol. I sickened myself with water, tea, coffee. I became cunning. I started to know that part of my mind was building up slow-rejection towards alcohol. I fought the battle in my own way, without the big guns of religion or psychiatry, which had failed me so often in the past. It became a personal battle. The first three months were the worst and at the end of them I was physically and emotionally exhausted, but I was triumphant. Each sober day that passed became a victory. Each victory became a stepping stone until there were enough stepping-stones stretched out along the road for me to know that I'd won. Won through the burning days and the torturing nights, with your own strength and on your own two feet, spitting defiance in the face of the odds. The desire and craving for alcohol had torn and ripped down to your very foundations, but the foundations held firm. Pope Tolley, Old Billy, Konk the Poacher, Tomato Juice – these are the men who shaped and fashioned those foundations, and that is why they held firm.

No, they were not easy days. Emotions changed and tumbled on a high trapeze, elation merged with depression and blended towards indifference. Moods blew and changed like spinning leaves before a chasing wind. I looked deep inside myself, and I began to understand. I could see the child in my mind which had never grown up, I could see the frightened child of self often cowering in darkness. I sat still often, and worked things out for myself, but there was purpose in my meditation. My mind no longer dwelled in the past of remorse or self-pity, but sought knowledge and comparisons with which to steer the future by. I knew, suddenly and clearly, that with an alcoholic the work of 'rehabilitation' didn't end when he came off the bottle – the work *started*. You didn't have a *better* man, you only had a *sober* man. And once the bottle was taken away from the alco's life a big hole was left, and that hole had to be filled quickly, and with the right things.

It is when you learn this, feel it, know it, that a 'coming of age' is very near. You have to build clear images in your mind, clear and well-defined. You have to give your mind food, spiritual vitamins, call it what you will. You must paint the right images on the canvas of your imagination. If you haven't got the images, you may be left facing a mass of life which blurs and frightens you. If you become afraid, too much energy is burned out with nursing the fear, and you start wasting your mental bank-balance. You have to learn which zones are positive, which are negative, and which are neutral. By slow stages and degrees you trace the roots of your personality problems back to childhood. That's where the warps started. And all that you have done since childhood is merely a continuation of those warps. You gradually learn that most of childhood was not an experience, but a shock. The shock became malignant, it spread and bruised until the original harm was lost under many scabs and layers. The whole was tainted, and once childhood was shrugged away there was no developed strength to produce the Man.

Time passed. I tagged on to an office-job, and held it down quite well. Then I met the girl who was to become my second wife, and we married, and at the time of writing we have a ten-year-old son. But shortly after our marriage, and before our son was born, I applied for – and got – a job with the Readers' Advice Bureau of a national Sunday newspaper. (The *People*). I poured out my entire life-story to the editor, the late Sam Campbell; and he said – 'With your experience, you're exactly the man we're looking for.' And I stayed for four years with the newspaper, advising readers upon their personal problems. Then one issue of the newspaper carried a picture of me to illustrate an article. A note came from Sam Campbell's office – 'I thought you'd like to see this most interesting letter, received from one of our readers.'

The letter said – 'I think this picture is one of my son. I haven't seen him for about fifteen years. Can you put me in touch with him?'

It was a letter from my father.

That week-end I took my wife and son (who was coming up on three years old, then) to see my father. He was living in Worcester, in a condemned house where he was a 'squatter'. He was living alone, long since divorced from my mother, I later learned. I knocked on the door, my wife and son standing slightly behind me. After a bit the door opened, and I felt the shock-wave hit me as I recognised my father. He'd grown very old, despite the fact he was only just about sixty. He seemed smaller, sunken, shrivelled. The years had wasted him away. He'd got a terrible enemy in his lungs, severe bronchitis, and every movement he made caused the breath to wheeze and whistle in his lungs. He opened the door, this poor shrunken shrivelled old man, and he looked at me, then past me. He looked at my son standing there on the pavement, and suddenly he leaned against the door-post, put his arm over his head and started to cry. And suddenly I knew that he wasn't crying for seeing my son; he was crying for me, and for the long wasted years.

On the journey home, back to London, my wife was troubled about my father. She felt that I should bring him home with us so that he could be nursed and looked after. But I couldn't do it. I knew in my heart of hearts that I couldn't do it. I had forward-looking visions of my father sitting at my hearth at home, talking with my son, influencing him and sharing him. And I could not, would not, let this happen. For my son was *my* son, and it was *my* influence I wanted him to steer by. I did not want him to come under the influence of his grandfather, I wanted the bad-seed of our family to be ended with my son. I did not want any contamination passed from my father to him.

I would keep my father supplied with the necessities of life and with what money I could spare. But I could not and would not share my son.

Two months after reunion with my father the police came to our house and told me that my dad was dying in a Worcester hospital. I drove up in a snow-blizzard, leaving London at ten-thirty in the evening and reaching the hospital at five o'clock next morning. My dad was quite rational. We talked a little, perhaps both of us knowing that it was to be our last conversation together, and that there was no time, no sand left in the hour-glass for us to get to know each other more. Yet, in the small talk between us, I was strangely moved to learn that while I'd been living down-and-out in London, and had 'put up' for a couple of nights at a dosshouse, my father was in that self-same doss-house while I was there, and was working as cook in the kitchen. We'd passed close to each other, but had no knowing of it, and like ships in the night we had each tacked off on a different course.

When daylight came creeping in at the hospital window dad suddenly started to talk quickly and staccato-like; sometimes his voice sank to a whisper and I had to bend close to hear what he was saying. At one and the same time he seemed to be living in the past and the present, but not the future because there was no future for him; there was nothing up ahead, except the end. He kept telling me what a good father he'd been to all of us, how he'd struggled and scrimped and saved through the bleak days of pre-war unemployment to give us love and happiness. He kept harping at it, with a little undercurrent of pleading in his voice. He kept telling me how he'd loved us all, but me especially, how I'd been his favourite. I fought that final battle with myself. 'Go to sleep,' I said, 'rest easy. You were the best dad in the world. Nobody could have asked for a better one.' I held his hand in those final minutes, then felt his grip soften and droop, and I bent over him and closed the lids of his dead eyes, and got into my car and drove back to London and home and family.

* * *

Going point to point round the country giving talks and showing films about the vagrancy I had lived through, I'm invariably asked two questions. The first – to what do I owe my own 'recovery'; the second – by what means do I sustain it. Although the answers and knowledge are simple in my mind, it is always a difficult task to put that knowledge into words. In trying to give reasons and why-fors, there's always the danger of over-simplification or over-complication. In answer to the first question – to what do I owe my 'recovery' – I answer that the means of 'recovery' always existed in me. They were originally put there by the men who influenced my boyhood, and whom I loved deeply – Pope Tolley, Old Billy, Konk the Poacher. They planted certain seeds within me, a certain strong-sure arrogance, an ability to take my good hidings from Fate without whining too much or too loud. Whereas my own father was consistently destroying my character-formation, the damage was offset by the attitudes and friendships of the men I have named. The seeds they planted in my mind were planted deep, and took a long time to reach up to the surface. Equally, Klaus Fuchs planted other seeds – more cultural and intellectual – but equally important. They too took a long time to break through to the surface.

The second one – how do I sustain my 'recovery' – is quite simple. I sustain it by hard work, the repetition of *positive* suggestion, the presence of good friends, the love of a good wife and a good son, and also by pride of certain possessions which I never want to lose because they mean so much to me. Car, cameras, stereo-player, a good wardrobe of clothing – material things, yes, but important to me. I don't want to lose them. Each day I have a 'music bath'; Beethoven, Mozart, Schubert, Bach – but perhaps with particular and affectionate emphasis upon Beethoven. This sort of thing – call it therapy, if you like – is personal, of course, and wouldn't suit everybody. But it suits me, gives me a degree of self-harmony which in turn I can communicate to my son; and it usually gives me a degree of physical exercise, because once the symphony-disc goes on the turntable, I like to do my own conducting. To a casual onlooker I probably appear to be imitating a tick-tack man at a racecourse.

But it works, for me.

And Emile Coué? Where does *he* fit in?

Ah, it's a good question – but he is the key which will open the door to many people's inner harmony and happiness, if they will take him seriously and not 'faddishly', like trying health foods for a week then stopping by saying they're doing you no good. The secret is, that no person can find improvement of self the *easy* way. The 'easy way' does not exist. One can ever make mistakes. One has to work hard for self-improvement, one has to unravel many inner conflicts and warps, but above all one has to have *faith* in oneself that self-improvement *is* taking place. All this may sound a bit corny on the outside, but I assure you it's not.

Listen. The secret that Klaus Fuchs let me into way back in our prison days, the secret of Emile Coué's doctrine, was contained in one of Coué's 'laws'. Coué said – 'Where the Will and the Imagination come into *open conflict, the imagination will always win.*' It took me a long, long time to understand the absolute and unshakeable truth of this 'law'. All down the line I'd been regarded as 'lacking in will-power' because I drank so much, and kept landing in trouble. Will-power, will-power, will-power – what a *dangerous* thing it is to harp upon the lack of such, once one learns to understand Coué. It took me a long time to discover that it wasn't 'lack of will-power' which led me to drink so heavily. Through Coué, I learned that the will-power in me *to* drink was as strong as the will-power in the most fervent abstainer *not* to drink. Through Coué, I learned that my imagination selected, and that the 'will' impelled. Coué had another 'law'. He said 'If one strives too consciously and with too much effort for a particular thing or effect, exactly the opposite will happen.'

Everyone has, at some time, tried to recall the name of a person only to find that they have 'forgotten' it. And the more they concentrate upon remembering, the more elusive the name becomes. Then, in a moment of neutral relaxation, the elusive name suddenly pops up in the conscious mind and is 'remembered'. Out in the Middle East when the bullets were thick around the Holy Lands a sergeant taught me a little trick when on night patrols. He told me that if I thought there was an enemy target directly ahead and kept staring at it in an effort to identify it, the 'target' would waver and blur, and go out of focus. He taught me that by looking slightly to one side of the suspected target, and not directly at it, the actual target would come into focus. Between us, we called this 'oblique identification'. Equally, in bright daylight with a hard sun beating down, a target would come more clearly into focus if one partially closed one's eyes and again looked slightly 'off target'. Coué expresses exactly this technique when dealing with one's personality problems. 'If you strive too hard for a particular thing to come about, exactly the opposite will happen.' Emile Coué died in the nineteen-twenties, incidentally, and many persons have tried to 'cash in' on his work by advertising 'self-improvement' courses under one name or the other. I know this – 'Couéism' works for *me*. And I use his 'techniques' constantly; so much so that they are part and parcel of my moral and mental fibre.

I do my prison-visiting through 'the back door'. That means that when I visit men in prison, or go into prisons to hold pre-release discussions, I do not disclose that I myself am an ex-prisoner. If I did, it is more than a fair bet to say that the Home Office or the Prison Governor concerned would 'put the block' on my visits. But I remember something that a serving prisoner said to me when I was going into Pentonville prison once a week to hold discussion meetings with what are termed as 'recurrent drunks'. (Incidentally, Alcoholics Anonymous members used to go into the same prison on the same night, to hold meetings with 'alcoholics'. Their meetings were held in a different part of the prison. They got the 'alcoholics' while I got the 'recurrent drunks'.

One of my blokes, a man near enough sixty, had spent twenty years of his life in prison with accumulated sentences for drunkenness, or for not having the money to pay the fine imposed for being drunk: I asked the prison authorities just *how* recurrent my bloke had to be in his drunkenness before they'd *promote* him to 'alcoholic' status). The prisoner said to me – 'It's alright for you. You've got a home, a car, a wife, a baby son, a good job. You've got everything.'

By his standards, he was right. I *had* got everything. I had material possessions, reasonable contentment, ambition and the ability to fulfil ambition; I'd got health and work, and unploughed years of opportunity ahead of me. I'd got more happiness and peace of mind I ever knew existed. I had come home to myself.

But nobody *gave* me these things. Nobody stood outside the Big Gate when I came out of prison, and thrust a parcel of these things into my arms. If I'd have depended on existing forms of 'rehabilitation' or on Society in general for my 'improvement', I'd still be in the gutter. I can go forwards, now, into the future. I have the ability and I have the desire. But they weren't *given* to me; I *earned* them, and I earned them the hard way. Perhaps I will puzzle at many things for a long time to come, perhaps never find the answers; sometimes, perhaps, unsolicited memory will sadden me for a while. But I can go forwards because I want to. Such anger and rage that I still have in me can be harnessed and directed into helping others, and not in destroying myself.

For those who come out of the jungle that I have lived in, no form of substitution will be good enough. Only the truth of self will be acceptable.

I watched the men file in drab lines back to their cells; I heard the doors slam heavily against them, and pen them in like chickens in a coop. The locked doors stood squarely in the walls of each cell; inside the cells were the imprisoned bodies, inside the bodies were the imprisoned minds.

Uniformed officers stood like sentinels, guarding the dual escape.

As I walked from the prison a Senior Officer stepped forwards to unlock the gate for me to pass through. I recognized him. He didn't recognise me. He was in the familiar blue uniform, I was wearing a Crombie overcoat, trilby hat, brief-case under my arm. For a long time I'd been a prisoner under this man's care. 'Yessir, nosir, three-bags-full-sir'.

He stepped aside for me to pass through, for me to go home to a clean and happy hearth and a family that was my own, and loved me for what I was and not for what I had been.

'Goodnight, sir,' the officer said.

'Goodnight,' I answered. From outside the Big Gate I looked back, could see the cell-lights burning row on row against the night's torment. Row upon row of burning lights.

'Full circle,' I said to myself.

Some examples of Archie Hill's photojournalism

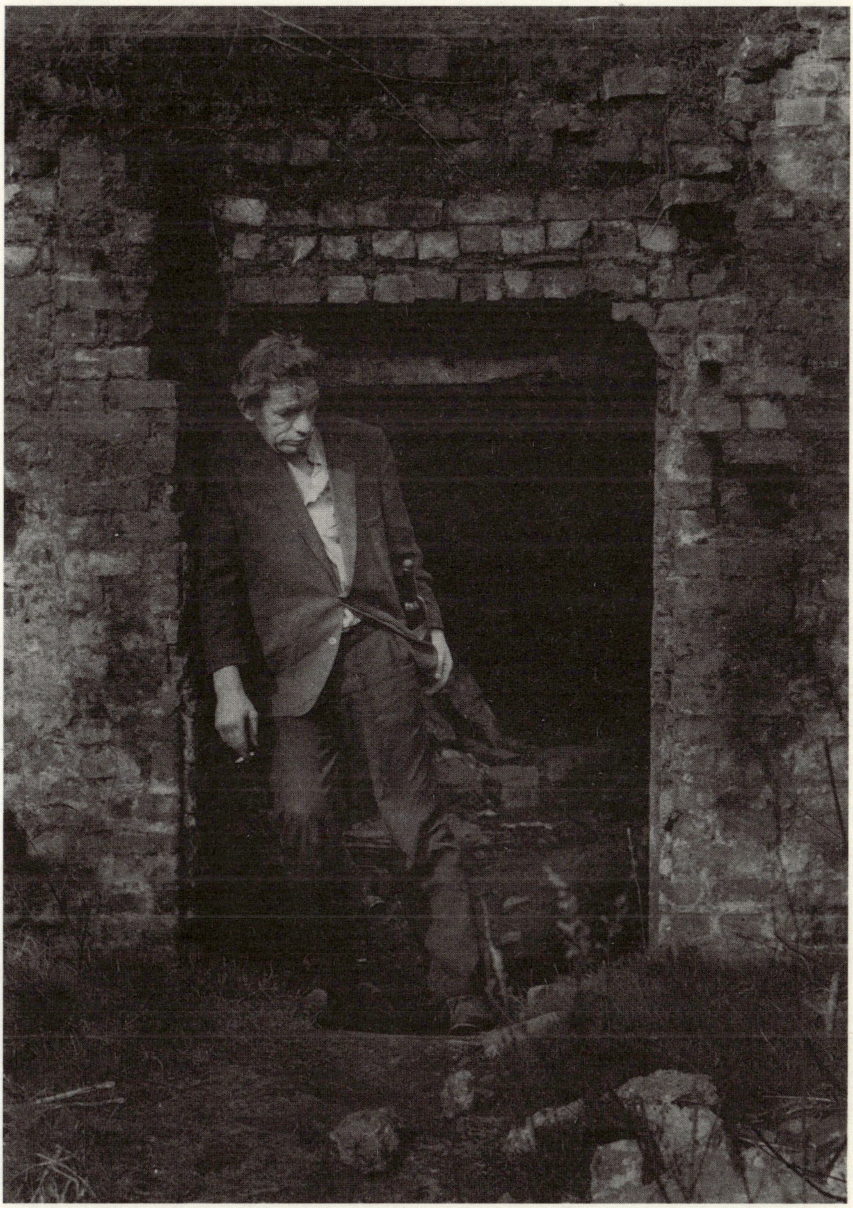

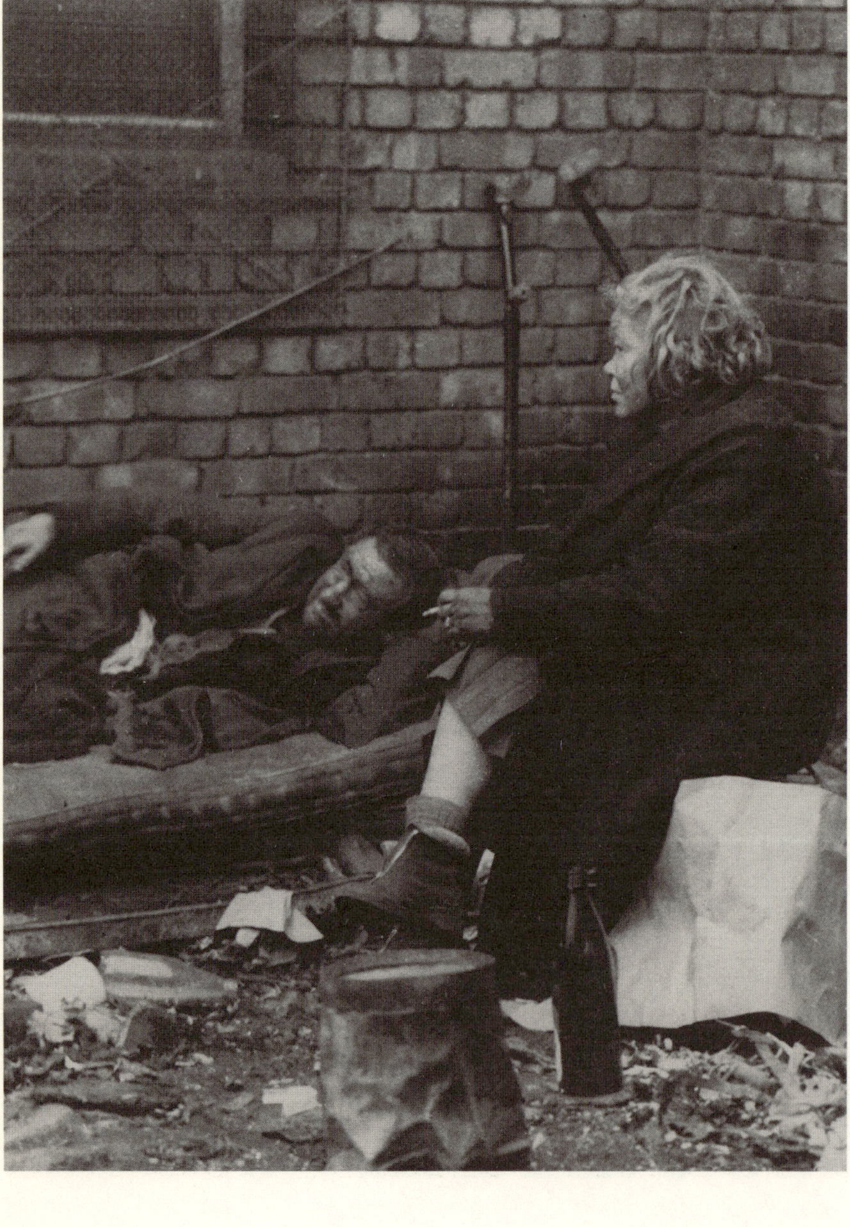

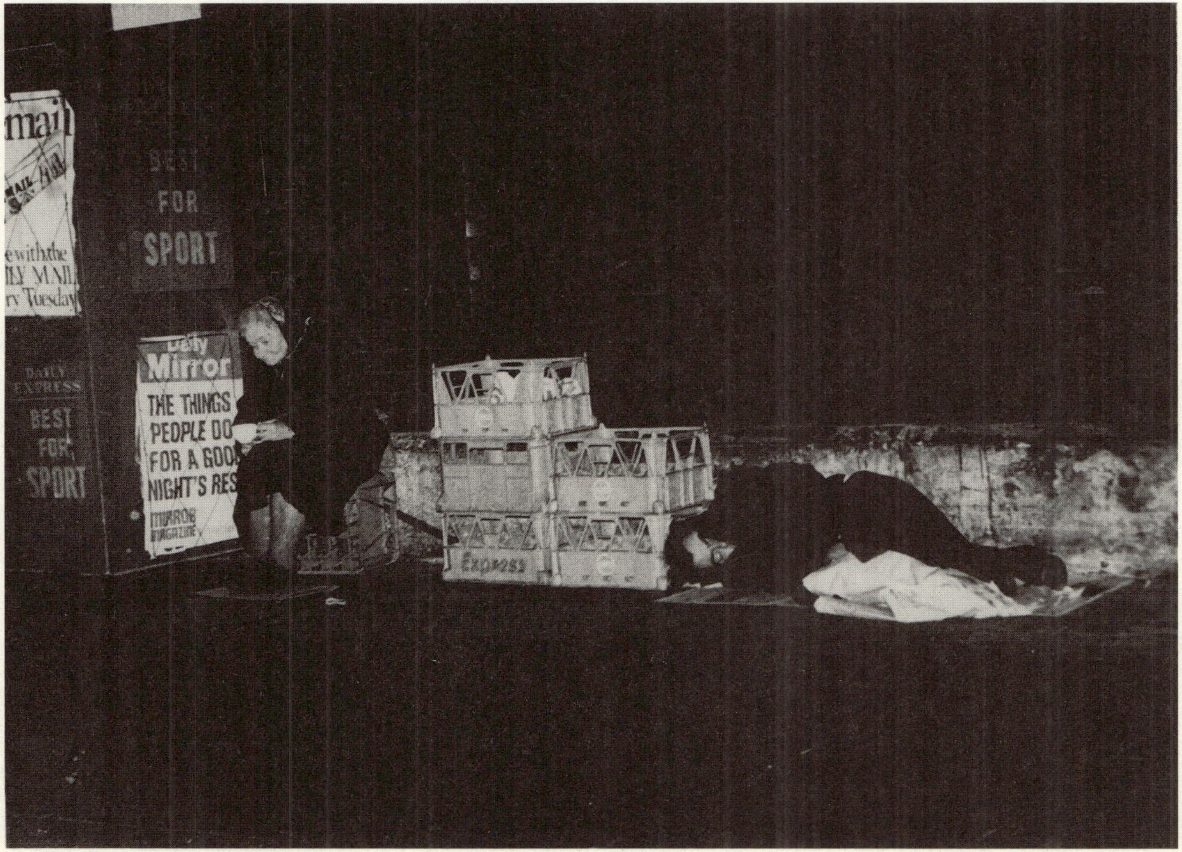
mail
BEST
FOR
SPORT
Daily Mirror
THE THINGS
PEOPLE DO
FOR A GOO
NIGHT'S RES
MIRROR MAGAZINE
DAILY EXPRESS
BEST
FOR
SPORT
Express

Born in rural Staffordshire and raised during the Depression, Archie Hill is something of an enigma. Virtually no information about him exists in public records or online. What little we do know can be gleaned from his disarmingly honest, autobiographical novels: brutal Black Country upbringing, violence, alcoholism, prison, mental hospitals, living rough on London streets and finally redemption through a love of literature. When his first book, *A Cage of Shadows*, was published in 1973, it was instantly hailed as a classic. BBC Radio 3 commissioned a spoken word serialisation later the same year. His many admirers included the British film director Joseph Losey. Buoyed up by this success and with the backing of a major publisher, novels continued to appear throughout the 1970s and into the 1980s, all to widespread critical acclaim. While he continued to work successfully as a freelance writer and broadcaster, Mr Hill was actively involved in various community projects, helping rehabilitate those who had dropped out of society, just as he had done. But after 1984's *An Empty Glass* ("The story of an alcoholic"), the books suddenly stopped coming. Perhaps because of an inability to maintain this work rate, a lifelong battle with alcoholism, or for other reasons we shall never know, Mr Hill committed suicide in 1986.

May 2017

This first edition is published
as a trade paperback; there are 126
numbered & lettered copies handbound in
boards by the Tangerine Press, Tooting, London;
lettered copies are additionally signed by
Robin Hill & contain reproductions
of the author's photojournalism.